Emerging Trends in Teaching of Physics

EMERGING TRENDS IN TEACHING OF PHYSICS

T.N. RATHO
RAVI PRAKASH

KANISHKA PUBLISHERS, DISTRIBUTORS
NEW DELHI-110 002

KANISHKA PUBLISHERS, DISTRIBUTORS
4697/5-21A, Ansari Road, Daryaganj,
New Delhi-110 002
Phones : 2327 0497, 2328 8285
Fax : 011-2328 8285
E-mail : kanishka_publishing@yahoo.co.in

Emerging Trends in Teaching of Physics

First Published 1996

Second Edition 2007

ISBN 81-7391-041-3

PRINTED IN INDIA

Published by Madan Sachdeva for Kanishka Publishers, Distributors, 4697/5-21A, Ansari Road, Daryaganj, New Delhi-110 002. Typeset by Sunshine Graphics, Delhi, and Printed at Chaudhary Offset Process, Delhi.

Preface

Science teaching has some specific purposes besides the general purposes of education which are as following:

1. An understanding of and the ability to use those fundamental concepts and relationships of science that enable the individual to interpret intelligently the conditions and happenings in the natural and the man-made environment.
2. A knowledge of and the ability to select and use scientific facts and information that help the individual to know himself and the materials and forces of the environment.
3. Skills of observation, reflective thinking and problem solving which enable an individual to face questions encountered in living and to approach answers to such questions.
4. Mental and manipulative skills which make the individual able to find success and enjoyment in using materials and forces to meet both personal and social needs.
5. Attitudes, standards and ideals relating to the materials and forces of the Universe that favour an individual's living with appreciation, poise and success in the midst of a complex environment.
6. Attitudes, standards, and ideals relating to scientists and citizens both past and present that will help to guide and guard an individual in his living with his associates and with other people. The teaching of various disciplines of science broadly correspond to the above objectives. These aims of teaching science hold good both in the developed and the developing world. The present volume is an exercise in this direction.

The present publication deals with the approaches to and contents of the teaching of physics. It is based on current syllabus and has been structured as a comprehensive aid to the teaching of physics. It covers all important topics for the physics teachers, such as, the nature, definition, from and content of physics; the course contents of physics as a secondary and college level subject; the education of science teachers; facilities for high school physics; advanced physical science; use of science and scientific methods in building a house; use of fuels to produce heat and power; making water more useful; science aids in communication and transportation; scientific facts that need to be known about textiles and quality of clothing for man; and the approach to and efficacy of the demonstration method in the teaching of physics. It is earnestly hoped that the present publication will be an indispensable aid to the teaching of physics for all teachers.

T.N. Ratho

Ravi Prakash

Contents

Contents

1

Physics

PART A—INTRODUCTION

In preparing this course of study for the physics teachers of Missouri, the physics production committee has not attempted to lay down a definite outline of work that is to be followed from day to day. It has assumed that teachers have sufficient training and initiative to adapt their daily work to the needs of their students and community as well as to the equipment, including apparatus, supplies, and library references, which is available. The committee has, however, attempted to do the following:

1. To outline the major units to be included in a high-school course in physics.
2. To suggest some techniques or methods which may be helpful in teaching high-school physics.
3. To suggest some activities and experiments that may be carried on by students.
4. To point out activities and ways that will aid in meeting the individual differences of students.
5. To list definite textbook references for each unit, and to suggest references and current magazines that will aid in teaching physics.
6. To suggest means of evaluating the work of the student and the teacher.

GENERAL OBJECTIVES

The general objectives for high-school physics as set up by the physics curriculum committee are :

1. To encourage students to gain an understanding of and an appreciation of the physical world about them.
2. To provided a knowledge of simple physical facts and principles which will lead toward good health and safe living.
3. To develop an attitude of open-mindedness, seasoned with conservatism, in dealing with scientific problems and information.
4. To develop an appreciation of the importance of accuracy in speech, in thought, in reading, and in computation insofar as the study of physics may contribute to these general qualities.
5. To lay a foundation for those students who develop an interest in physics and are capable of doing advanced work in physics or in a vocation or profession requiring a knowledge of physics.
6. To encourage students to find avocations in the field of physics for the worthy use of their spare time.

SEQUENCE OF UNITS AND TIME ALLOTMENTS

The following is a suggested outline of the units and sub-units together with a suggested time schedule. Good teaching does not demand that this outline be followed in detail, but much variance from the time schedule may cause some units to be slighted.

Evaluation sheets such as appear in the other science courses have not been included in the course of study in physics. The units are organized in a way such that the preparation of such sheets would have been quite difficult. Teachers are urged, however, to summarize their experiences in teaching all or any parts of the units and to send summaries, together with suggestions for improvement, to the State Superintendent of Public Schools.

Introductory Units. Systems and Units of Measurement (*Suggested Time : 1 week*)

Unit I. Mechanics (*Suggested time : 11-12 weeks*)

A. Gases
B. Liquids
C. Molecular and Atomic Nature of Matter
D. Force and Motion
E. Work, Energy, and Power

Unit II. Heat (*Suggested time : 5-6 weeks*)

A. Thermometry and Expansion
B. Calorimetry and Change of State
C. Heat Energy and Its Transmission
D. Heat Engines

Unit III. Sound (*Suggested time : 3-4 weeks*)

A. Wave Motion and Sound
B. Physics of Music

Unit IV. Light (*Suggested time : 4-5 weeks*)

A. Transmission and Photometry
B. Reflection
C. Refraction
D. Spectra and Colour

Unit V. Magnetism and Electricity (*Suggested time : 7-8 weeks*)

A. Magnetism
B. Electrostatics
C. Direct Currents and Their Effects
D. Alternating Currents and Their Effects

Unit VI. Modern Physics (*Suggested time : 2 weeks*)

PART B—ILLUSTRATIVE UNITS
INTRODUCTORY UNIT—SYSTEMS AND UNITS OF MEASUREMENTS

Objectives

1. To gain a knowledge of the systems and units of measurement that are most convenient to use in a study of physics.
2. To learn how to use certain measuring instruments.

Subject Matter Outline

1. Systems and units of measurement
   (*a*) English system
   (*b*) Metric system
2. Some measuring instruments of physics
   (*a*) The meter stick
   (*b*) Vernier caliper, micrometer caliper
   (*c*) The balance
   (*d*) The graduate

Teaching Procedure

The teacher should make sure that students have a knowledge of the metric system and some of the measuring instruments before beginning the regular units of the course.

Pupil Activities[1]

1. Debate on the question : The Metric system should be adopted in the United States[2].
2. Determine the number of centimeters in an inch by measuring the length of a sheet of paper both in inches and in centimeters. Then divide the length in centimeters by the length in inches.
3. To show that matter has weight and occupies space, fill a beaker with water and then try to add a rock or some other object without overflowing the beaker. What instruments of physics are needed for measurement of weight and space ?
4. Using a vernier caliper determine both the inside and outside diameters of a large test tube.
5. Using a micrometer caliper find the diameter of a hair from your head.
6. Using a platform of beam balance find the weight of several objects.
7. By using a graduate find the volume of an unknown container. Check the result by weighing the water.[3]

Provisions for Individual Differences

1. Report to the class how the entire metric system is based upon the primary unit of length.

2. Construct model liters out of cardboard.
3. List other types of measuring devices used in the laboratory.

Textbook References

Introductory Unit : Systems and Units of Measurement

Black, Newton Henry, and Davis, Harvey Nathaniel, *Elementary Practical Physics*, Macmillan, 1938, pp. 1-12.

Clark, John A., Gorton, Frederick Russel, and Sears, Francis W., *Physics of Today*, Houghton Mifflin, 1938, pp. 9-11.

Dull, Charles E., *Modern Physics*, Henry Holt, 1939, pp. 13-17.

Fletcher, Gustav L., Mosbacher, Irving, and Lehman, Sydney, *Unified Physics*. McGraw-Hill, 1936, pp. 7-9.

Fuller, Robert W., Brownlee, Raymond B., and Baker, D. Lee, *First Principles of Physics*. Allyn and Bacon, 1937, pp. 7-16.

Henderson, W. E., *The New Physics in Everyday Life*, Lyons and Carnahan, 1935, pp. 15-29.

Holly, Clifford, and Lohn, Vergil C., *Mastery Units in Physics*, Lippincott, 1939, pp. 1-14.

Millikan, Robert Andrews, Gale, H. G., and Coyle, D. C., *New Elementary Physics*, Ginn, 1936, pp. 7-19.

Stewart, Oscar M., Cushing, Burton L., and Towne, Judson R., *Physics for Secondary Schools*, Ginn, 1932, pp. 3-18.

Williard, Lester R., *Experiences in Physics*, Ginn, 1939, pp. 13-50.

UNIT I. MECHANICS

Objectives

1. To provide and understanding of the concepts of matter and energy and their importance in everyday life.
2. To develop an appreciation of the vast amount of thought and research which has led to the formulation of various theories and laws which are so important in mechanics.

3. To show how certain forces have been put to use to enable us to live comfortably, and how these same forces must be used intelligently in order that we may live safely.

4. To give the potential mechanical engineer or other pre-professional student an outline of the technical knowledge he will need and to stress to those students the fact that the principles of mechanics are applicable and indispensable in any such profession.

A. LIQUIDS

Subject Matter Outline

1. Pressure and force in liquids
   (*a*) Factors which affect the pressure in liquids.
   (*b*) Forces on sides and bottom of containers.
2. Transmission of pressure by liquids.
   (*a*) Pascal's law
   (*b*) The hydraulic press ; water systems
3. Archimedes' principle ; bouyancy.
4. Specific weight (gravity) and density.

Teaching Procedure

1. Care should be taken to distinguish between the concepts of force and pressure in liquids and between the units in which these are measured. Specific weight (gravity) should be distinguished from density.

2. Connect a glass funnel and piece of glass tubing to show that water will seek the same level. Fill a battery jar with water. Take a glass tube about 1 inch in diameter ; over lower end place a piece of cardboard or celluloid and lower vertically into water. The paper is kept in contact with the glass tube by force of the water. Pour water into tube ; paper drops off when levels inside and outside are same.
3. Demonstrate Pascal's vases.
4. Give a demonstration of a hydraulic press or a hydraulic jack.

5. Weigh a piece of metal in air and then in water. Place an overflow can full or water in one pan of a balance. Put a wooden block into can and let water displace overflow into a beaker placed to one side of the balances. The water displaced will equal the weight of the block, and the scales will remain balanced.

6. Show the use of a battery hydrometer to find the specific weight in testing a battery. Commercial hydrometers may be used to find the specific weight of several different liquids.

Pupil Activities

7. In place of the screw-plug of an ordinary hot water bottle, substitute a one-hole rubber stopper. To this connect a piece of tubing about five feet in length with a glass funnel on the end. Place two bricks on the hot water bottle and pour water into the funnel. The bricks will be raised an inch or more.

8. The pupils may do some type of experiment to show Archimedes' principle that a body immersed in a liquid loses as much weight as the volume of the displaced fluid, or to show the law of flotation.

Provision for Individual Differences

1. Report to the class upon the use of the diving bell, or the caisson.
2. Explain the operation of hydraulic automobile lifts that are used by filling stations.
3. Make and demonstrate a Cartesian diver to the class.

B. GASES

Subject Matter Outline

1. Weight, pressure, and density of air.
2. The barometer and weather : the altimeter.
3. The expansion and compression of gases ; Boyle's law.
4. Lift, force, chain pumps ; air pumps ; siphon.
5. Bouyancy.

Teaching Procedure

1. The teacher should emphasize the same important topics that were suggested under liquids.
2. Equip a gallon varnish can with one-hole rubber stopper, glass tube, and rubber tubing. Connect to filter pump and note effect of reducing air pressure. Method by condensing steam may be used instead.
3. Construct a simple mercury barometer and record the height of the column of mercury for a period of several days. Also observe weather conditions during this time.
4. Show the value of an understanding of Boyle's law in solving problems involving the pressure and volume of gases.
5. Demonstrate with aid of diagrams, or a small pump model, how water pumps work.
6. Fill a small toy balloon or soap bubble with gas to show buoyancy of air.

Pupil Activities

1. An experiment to show the relation of the volume of a gas to its pressure may be performed by students. Equipment needed includes a J-tube in which air is trapped in the closed end of the tube and then subjected to various pressures.
2. The density of air may be determined by removing the air from a spherical flask and finding the weight of the air removed. The volume of air removed may be determined by immersing the evacuated flask in water and opening the pinch cock. The volume may be determined by weighing the water or by measuring it with a graduate.

Provision for Individual Differences

1. Find out how official altitude records are made. Report to class certain devices that use air pressure for their operation.

2. Make a report on Pascal's work on the barometer and altitude. Look up the uses of an aneroid barometer in contour-map making. Study the advantages of the Aneroid barometer as compared to the mercury barometer.

3. Show why it is impossible for a person in a boat to siphon the water out of it.

C. MOLECULAR AND ATOMIC NATURE OF MATTER

Subject Matter Outline

1. General features of the kinetic molecular theory of the constitution of matter and evidence favouring it ; the molecule and the atom.
2. The three states of matter related to molecular forces.
3. Pressure in gases related to molecular motion.
4. Surface tension, capillarity, diffusion, and osmosis.
5. Elasticity.

Teaching Procedures

1. The teacher should have a clear concept himself as to the nature of the theory, and of molecular and atomic sizes and speeds. He should read recent college texts for materials and try to present the latest ideas, not necessarily those in his textbook. He should stress the fact that while this is a theory, the evidence supporting it has become almost conclusive. He should be able to point out examples of the practical uses of the molecular, atomic, and subatomic properties of matter in daily life, finding these in many places from the use lubricants to radio tubes.

2. If a microscope is available, show Brownian movements in cell of smoke or solution of bambogs in alcohol, with side illumination.

3. Adhesion of clean glass to mercury and water may be illustrated by plates suspended from beam balance and touched to liquids.

4. Surface tension may be illustrated by floating razor blades on water, rise of water in small tubes, floating

sieve, contraction of fine-haired brush when wet, soap bubbles, camphor gum on water.

5. Osmosis may be illustrated by special apparatus or by means suggested under pupil activities.
6. Diffusion may be shown by rapid spread of odor, *e.g.*, ammonia gas.
7. Elasticity may be illustrated by tests with springs, slats, and wires.

Pupil Activities

1. Adhesion and cohesion may be studied by observing uses of various adhesives, difficulty of attaching labels to tin cans, and other objects.
2. Osmosis may be shown by use of an egg with long tube carefully sealed into top, Membrane exposed at bottom, and the whole egg placed in water. A carrot or similar root with perfect skin may have a hole bored longitudinally, cavity filled with sugar, stopper and tube inserted at top and sealed in, whole placed in water. Cellophane that is not waterproof may be used as osmotic membrane. Is there osmosis in curing of salt meats ?
3. An individual experiment on Hooke's laws is recommended.

Provision for Individual Differences

1. Investigate why the outside of an oil lamp. lantern, or can persists in becoming oily after being cleaned.
2. Demonstrate how tents and umbrellas keep out water.

FORCE AND MOTION

Subject Matter Outline

1. Velocity and acceleration.
2. Uniformly accelerated motion ; rules for computing final speed and distance covered.
3. Force necessary for change of motion.
4. Parallelogram of forces.

5. Newton's laws of motion.
6. Inertia, mass, weight, momentum, impulse.
7. Centripetal and centrifugal force.

Teaching Procedure

1. The teacher should realize that this sub-unit is one of the most difficult in physics, but that it is fundamentally important. An understanding of the unit systems is essential. Strive for a clear understanding of acceleration, and of mass and weight.
2. Few experiments are available without costly equipment. Increase in speed of a ball rolling down an incline may be shown, also the increase in distance covered in successive time intervals.
3. Two loaded roller skates may be attached to opposite ends of spiral springs of different stiffnesses (*e.g.*, a door-check spring, spring from an old shade roller) and accelerations noted when springs are stretched and released.
4. Attach a small mass to a string and whirl about. Similarly, attach a mass to a spiral spring or strong rubber band and whirl about.

Pupil Activities

1. Investigate the distance necessary to stop a car moving at different speeds.
2. Estimate the possible frictional forces between tires and roads. Stop a baseball so as not to get "stung." List proper methods of blocking and tackling in football.
3. For third law, try to throw a stone when balanced on a narrow support or on roller skates. Why does a lawn sprinkler whirl ? Why does a rocket go up ? Would they work in a vacuum ?

Provision for Individual Differences

1. Examine suspended signs, poles and guy-wires, fence braces, rope rigging of various sorts.
2. Note many common uses of the property of inertia.

3. Observe car behaviour on curves, the operation of cream separators, the operation of centrifugal pumps, and playground games like "crack-the-whip."

E. WORK, ENERGY, AND POWER

Subject Matter Outline

1. The concept of work and measurements of work.
2. Energy : forms, conservation, and transformation.
3. Levers, pulleys, inclined plane, and other machines.
4. Friction, its advantages and disadvantages.
5. Efficiency.
6. Power, definition, units, and measurement.

Teaching Procedure

1. Since the entire subject of physics is closely related to energy and energy changes, this sub-unit should be stressed. The teacher should point out that energy is something we have to buy and pay for not only when we hire someone to work for us but when we pay our light, gas, or coal bill.

2. The simple procedures of lifting a weight, then pushing it over a level surface, then rolling a Hall's car over a level surface or up an incline, demonstrate work and its measurement. Emphasis should be on the fact that motion is necessary before work is done and that the force and the motion are measured parallel to each other.

3. If equipment for demonstrating acceleration is available, it may be used to show that work must be done on an object to change its speed. A pendulum show the transformation from kinetic to potential energy as does a pile-driver.

4. Levers, pulleys, and inclined planes are easily demonstrated. A 2×4 painted white, marked in feet and fourths of a foot, and suspended from a screw eye makes a satisfactory demonstration lever. It is suggest-

ed that commercial pulleys be used in demonstrations rather than small-sized laboratory units. The special rules for computing mechanical advantage should be emphasized. It is well to point out the difference between actual and theoretical mechanical advantage.

5. The reaction between friction and centrifugal force is important. Why does an automobile fail to "make a turn ?"

Pupil Activities

1. If individual laboratory work is feasible, the following experiments are suggested : the measurement of the mechanical advantages and computation of efficiency of levers, pulleys, and inclined planes.
2. Investigate friction between tires and roadway with view to minimum stopping distance of automobile at various speeds.
3. Let pupils measure their own power by measuring height of second floor and time to run upstairs. A large wheel equipped with a Prony brake may also be used to measure the power of an individual.

Provision for Individual Differences

It is recommended that individual experiments on the wheel-and-axle and measurement of coefficient of friction be assigned to only the better students.

Textbook References

Unit I. Mechanics

(*a*) Gases
(*b*) Liquids
(*c*) Molecular and Atomic Nature of Matter
(*d*) Force and Motion.
(*e*) Work, Energy, and Power.

Authors	*Topics and pages*				
	A	*B*	*C*	*D*	*E*
Black and Davis................................pp.	109—144	71—108	145—160	167—216	18—65 217—226
Clark, Gorton, Sears........................pp.	72—109	22—71	1—20	110—184	187—242
Dull...pp.	49—85	19—48	3—13 89—105	109—162	165—202
Fletcher, Mosbacher, Lehman............pp.	54—78	25—53 180—194	1—7 13—22	79—140	143—170
Fuller, Brownlee, Baker....................pp.	92—128	41—91	1—6 20—37	131—150 186—230	160—192 149—156 233—249
Henderson..pp.	77—127	33—76	128—156	157—233	219—269
Holly and Lohr.................................pp.	100—132	69—99	17—60	133—186	195—253
Millikan, Gale, Coyle........................pp.	45—73	25—44	74—84 131—146	85—130	147—187
Stewart, Cushing, Towne...................pp.	80—106	46—79	97—99 127—143	107—122 145—171	19—41 178—199
Williard...pp.	90—137	51—89	138—154	155—185	186—231

UNIT II. HEAT

Objectives

1. To develop with students an understanding and appreciation of the fact that heat is a form of energy, and that through its control much is added to our comfort and convenience.
2. To encourage the student to learn more about the properties of heat and the laws which govern it in order that our resources such as oil, gas, and coal may be conserved.
3. To provide basic training for the student who wishes to prepare for a vocation or profession in which it is necessary to have a knowledge of heat energy and its transformation into mechanical work.

A. THERMOMETRY AND EXPANSION

Subject Matter Outline

1. Measurement of temperature, thermometry, and fixed points.
   (*a*) The Fahrenheit scale.
   (*b*) The Centigrade scale.
2. Expansion and Contraction.
   (*a*) Kinetic theory.
   (*b*) Coefficients of linear and volumetric expansion.
   (*c*) Abnormal behaviour of water.
   (*d*) Changes in pressure and volume of gases ; the absolute or Kelvin scale of temperature.

Teaching Procedure

1. Demonstrate the unreliability of our sense of touch as a temperature indicator. Secure vessels of hot, lukewarm, and cold water and have a student place his hands in the lukewarm water after having had one hand in cold water and the other in hot water.
2. Make a comparison of a Centigrade and a Fahrenheit thermometer.
3. Consider various changes in physical properties of bodies which might be used for thermometers.

4. Demonstrate linear expansion of solids, and differential expansion shown by heating a compound bar.
5. Show relative expansion of a liquid and its container. Place cold water in a flask equipped with a one-hole stopper and glass tube a foot or more in length. Note the fall and then the rise of the water in the tube when the flask is heated.
6. Construct an air thermometer by inverting a small flask equipped with a stopper and glass tube in a dish of coloured water.

Pupil Activities

The following experiments are suggested, which might be performed as pupil-directed demonstrations :

1. Fixed points of a thermometer.
2. Coefficient of linear expansion.

Provision for Individual Differences

1. Investigate the construction and operation of the thermostatically controlled valves in automobile cooling systems.
2. Stretch a long iron wire between two supports and pass an electric current through it. Suspend a weight at the center and note the sag of the wire as it is heated.

B. CALORIMETRY AND CHANGE OF STATE

Subject Matter Outline

1. Measurement of quantity of heat ; calorimetry.
   (*a*) The calorie.
   (*b*) The British thermal unit (B.T.U.).
   (*c*) Specific heat ; thermal capacity.
   (*d*) Method of mixtures.
2. Change of state.
   (*a*) Melting and freezing.
      (1) Heat of fusion.
      (2) Volume change during solidification.
      (3) Effect of pressure on melting point.
   (*b*) Evaporation and condensation ; boiling.
      (1) Heat of vaporization.

(2) Effect of pressure on boiling point.
(3) Mechanical refrigeration and air conditioning.

(*c*) Moisture conditions in the atmosphere ; hygrometry.

(1) Saturated vapours.
(2) Absolute and relative humidity ; dew point.
(3) Cloud formation and precipitation.

Teaching Procedure

1. Demonstrate the fact that bodies of equal weight at the same form temperature may have different capacities. Use some form of Tyndall's heat apparatus.
2. Show expansion of water on freezing by ice bomb demonstration. A small jar with a tight fitting lid may be used as an ice bomb.
3. Show the effect of pressure on the melting point by a weighted wire cutting through a block of ice.
4. Show that evaporation is a cooling process. Use wet-and-dry bulb thermometer. Pour alcohol on one hand and water on the other. Note the cooling which accompanies evaporation.
5. Formation of clouds may be shown by using some form of cloud-forming demonstration apparatus.

Pupil Activities

1. Determine relative humidity.
2. Visit ice plant or examine an electric refrigerator. Trace the cycle through which the refrigerant is carried.

Provision for Individual Differences

1. Determine the heat of fusion of ice.
2. Plot the cooling curves of acetamide, naphthaline, or hypo.
3. Determine the heat of vaporization of water.

C. HEAT ENERGY AND ITS TRANSMISSION

Subject Matter Outline

1. Relation between heat and mechanical work.

(*a*) Joule's experiment ; mechanical equivalent of heat.
(*b*) Conservation of energy.

2. Transmission of heat.
   (*a*) Conduction
   (*b*) Convection
   (*c*) Radiation.

Teaching Procedure

1. Demonstrate transformation of mechanical work into heat, and heat produced by friction or collision.
2. Show that rods of different materials have different heat conductivities, or use some form of conductometer.
3. Convection currents may be observed in a beaker of water which is being heated.

Pupil Activities

1. Have pupils point out numerous examples of the production of heat by friction or collision.
2. Investigate house heating systems, house insulation, and a hot water heater.

D. HEAT ENGINES

Subject Matter Outline

1. External combustion engines.
   (*a*) Reciprocating steam engines.
   (*b*) Steam turbines.
2. Internal combustion engines.
   (*a*) Gas and gasoline engines.
   (*b*) Diesel engines.

Teaching Procedure

1. Explain by drawing or by a small model how a reciprocating steam engine works. A toy steam engine may also be demonstrated to the class.
2. Make a simple steam turbine by taking a circular piece of tin about five inches in diameter. Cut half-inch slits in its rim about every quarter inch and bend so as to form blades on the wheel. Support the wheel on an axle. Place the blades of the wheel in front of a piece

of glass tubing connected by a rubber stopper to a flask of boiling water. The steam from the flask will turn the wheel.

3. With a model or by drawings, show the principles of a four-cycle gas engine.

Pupil Activities

1. Visit an engine room where a steam engine is in operation.
2. To show the energy of exploding gas, punch a hole in the bottom of a coffee can. Place *two or three drops* of gasoline in the can and shake, then ignite the gas vapour by holding a match near the hole. The lid will be blown off. Emphasize need for caution.
3. Examine the parts of an old automobile carburetor.

Provisions for Individual Differences

1. Trace the development of the steam engine.
2. List some of the uses of Diesel engines.
3. Demonstrate a model airplane gasoline engine.

Unit II. Heat

A. Thermometry and Expansion
B. Calorimetry and Change of State
C. Heat Energy and Its Transmission
D. Heat Engines

Authors		*Topics and Pages*			
		A	B	C	D
Black and Davis	...pp.	232—254	269—299	255—268	300—324
Clark, Gorton, Sears	...pp.	248—275	295—326	276—294	327—342
Dull	...pp.	205—228	229—253	254—269	270—284
Fletcher, Mosbacher, Lehman	...pp.	195—212	231—263	213—223	264—278
Fuller, Brownlee, Baker	...pp.	256—294	314—316	295—313	347—367
Henderson	...pp.	270—278	278—303	303—319	319—361
Holly and Lohr	...pp.	255—283	284—320	321—332	333—354
Millikan, Gale, Coyle	...pp.	188—206	222—260	279—294	260—278
Stewart, Cushing, Towne	...pp.	207—232	256—311	233—255	312—342
Williard	...pp.	232—241 254—280	241—253 309—338	281— 08	338—365

Unit III. Sound

Objectives

1. To encourage students to gain an understanding of the nature of sound for its contribution to his knowledge and appreciation of his physical environment.
2. To provide an introduction to the physical basis of music so that the student may experience greater satisfaction in listening to music.
3. To provide fundamental training for the student who will continue his study in preparation for a vocation or profession in which a knowledge of acoustics is essential.

A. WAVE, MOTION AND SOUND

Subject Matter Outline

1. Energy transmission by wave motion
   (*a*) Water waves
   (*b*) Transverse waves
   (*c*) Longitudinal waves
2. Relationship of speed to frequency and wave length
3. Origin of sounds in vibrating bodies
4. Transmission of sound
   (*a*) Speed in various media
   (*b*) Effect of temperature on speed of sound in air
5. Reflection of sound
   (*a*) Echoes
   (*b*) Acoustics

Teaching Procedure

1. Emphasize the transmission of energy without translation of matter, the concepts of wave length, frequency, amplitude, speed, and their relationship. All sound has its origin in the vibration of matter. A material medium is necessary for the transmission of sound.
2. Waves sent along a water surface, a rope, a rubber tube, or a spiral spring can be used to demonstrate

wave motion. Wave models may be used if available.

3. Touch a prong of a vibrating fork to water or to a suspended glass bead. Touch the diaphram of a sounding auto horn.
4. Hold the stem of a tuning fork against the table, then against a meter stick held against the table or blackboard. Hold the stem of a tuning fork with a wooden disk on it in a beaker of water. Ring a bell in a vacuum, if available.
5. Place a watch at the focus of a concave reflector and show the reflection of sound.
6. Observe echoes in an empty auditorium.

Pupil Activities

1. Determine the speed of sound by the resonance tube method.
2. Measure the speed of sound directly by pistol and stop watch.
3. Make standing waves in a thread by means of an electric bell with gong removed or electric motor.

B. PHYSICS OF MUSIC

Subject Matter Outline

1. Characteristics of musical sounds
   (*a*) Pitch
   (*b*) Loudness and intensity
   (*c*) Quality or timbre
2. Resonance or sympathetic vibrations; forced vibrations
3. Interference of sound ; beats
4. Vibrating strings
5. Vibrating air columns
6. Musical scales
   (*a*) Musical intervals
   (*b*) Law of harmonious combinations

(*c*) The major scale
(*d*) The tempered scale

7. Sound recording and reproduction.

Teaching Procedure

1. Savart's wheel or siren disk may be used to demonstrate the interrelation of pitch and frequency.
2. Demonstrate resonant pendulums.
3. Beats can be demonstrated by a wax loaded tuning fork and another fork of the same frequency or slightly mistuned canary whistles.
4. Any stringed instrument can be used to make qualitative observations concerning the laws of vibrating strings.
5. Wind instruments may be used to demonstrate, qualitatively, the laws of vibrating air columns.
6. Use the piano to study the law of harmonizing combinations and the musical scales.
7. It is left to the ingenuity of the instructor to make use of phonograph and motion picture material.

Pupil Activities

Items 4, 5, and 6 under Teaching Procedure may be presented as pupil-directed activities instead of demonstrations by the teacher.

Provisions for Individual Differences

1. Students who play stringed or wind instruments may demonstrate how the instruments are operated, how the scales are produced, various registers, etc. The development of the instruments into their present forms may be reported by those interested.
2. The structure of a pipe organ may be made the subject of an interesting report.
3. The development of the present scale of equal temperament may be traced.

Textbook References

Unit III. Sound

A. Wave Motion and Sound

B. Physics of Music

Authors		*Topics and Pages* A	B
Black and Davis	...pp.	503—542	525—551
Clark, Gorton, Sears	...pp.	344—357	359—381
Dull	...pp.	287—303	304—319
Fletcher, Mosbacher, Lehman	...pp.	279—292	296—318
Fuller, Brownlee, Baker	...pp.	371—385	385—394
		398—407	408—422
Henderson	...pp.	597—632	617—619
			633—647
Holly and Lohr	. .pp.	356—384	365—366
			385—408
Millikan, Gale, Coyle	...pp.	435—457	442—445
			457—483
Stewart, Cushing, Towne	...pp.	525—543	545—576
Williard	...pp.	366—380	380—386

UNIT IV. LIGHT

Objectives

1. To gain an understanding of the nature, source, and intensity of light and how it travels through space.
2. To observe and understand how light is reflected from mirrors and how images are formed by reflected light.
3. To observe and understand how light is refracted and how images are formed by refracted light.
4. To gain an understanding of colour and of some of our common optical instruments.

A. TRANSMISSION AND PHOTOMETRY

Subject Matter Outline

1. Sources of light : self-luminous and illuminated bodies
2. Velocity of light
3. Transparency, translucency, opacity, shadows

4. Wave theory of light
5. Intensity or brightness of light; the photometer

Teaching Procedure

1. In introducing this unit the teacher may point out the necessity of light to the existence of man, and some of the uses of light to man. Point out that the nature of light is not completely understood in that some facts suggest that light is a form of wave motion while other facts seem to indicate that light is a stream of particles.
2. Hold a piece of platinum wire in a blue flame of a Bunsen burner. Observe the effect, and then hold other types of wire in the flame.
3. Observe the filament of an unfrosted electric light bulb and then show the effect of an electric current upon the wire.
4. In discussing self-luminous and illuminated bodies, point out that the sun and stars are self-luminous bodies while the moon and the planets are illuminated bodies.
5. Compare the speed of light in air to its speed in other materials such as water, glass, etc.
6. By placing a piece of glass, a paper and a book successively in front of an electric light bulb show the characteristics of transparent, translucent, and opaque objects.
7. Distinguish between umbra and penumbra by graphically showing the position of the earth, moon, and sun during an eclipse.
8. Compare light waves and sound waves.
9. Place a piece of card board, with a hole one inch square in the centre, one foot from a point source of light, then place a screen two feet from the light. Observe the area and intensity of the illumination on the screen.
10. Make a special effort to aid the pupil to understand that illumination is inversely proportional to the square of the distance from a point source of light.

Pupil Activities

1. Show that the amount of air received by a Bunsen burner affects the amount of light given off by it. Then show the effect upon the light of the flame by allowing chalk dust to enter the air supply of the Bunsen burner.
2. Assuming that light could travel in circles, compute the number of times it could travel around the earth in one second.
3. Compute the time it takes light to travel from the moon to the earth. (Distance 240,000 miles.)
4. By placing an opaque object between an extended source of light and a screen, distinguish between the umbra and penumbra. Make drawings showing this effect.
5. Visit a photographer's studio.
6. Make a pinhole camera.
7. Find out the facts that seem to support the wave theory of light and those that seem to indicate that light is a stream of tiny particles.
8. With the aid of an optical bench, standard candle or lamp and a simple photometer, measure the candle power of an electric light bulb. A simple photometer screen may be constructed by putting a drop of oil in the center of a piece of unglazed paper.

Provision for Individual Differences

1. Using reference books report to the class why light is believed to be a form of energy.
2. Report on the application of light to astronomy.
3. Compute in miles the distance light will travel in one year.
4. Report on methods of measuring the velocity of light.
5. Trace the development of the various theories of the transmission of light.

6. Locate examples of direct, semidirect, and indirect lighting in your school building or in your home.
7. Look through current literature or references to find the present recommendations for intensity of illumination (foot-candles) in classrooms, halls, offices, auditoriums, etc., in your school building.
8. Demonstrate and explain various types exposure meters.

B. REFLECTION

Subject Matter Outline

1. Diffusion
2. Reflection in plane mirrors
3. Reflection and images in concave mirrors
4. Reflection and images in convex mirrors

Teaching Procedure

1. Point out that when light falls upon an object, part of the light is reflected, the amount depending upon the object ; that is, light may be reflected from a surface just as sound is reflected from a cliff when an echo is heard.
2. In a dimly lighted room hold a plane mirror so as to receive light from a bright source. The light will be reflected in one direction. Now in place of the mirror use a sheet of paper. Is the light reflected in one direction ? Is it diffused ? Explain.
3. By illustrated drawings on the blackboard, show how to determine ths position of an image in a plane mirror.
4. To determine the nature of an image in a concave or convex mirror only two lines need to be drawn. Make sure that students are able to locate an image by drawing these two lines.

Pupil Activities

1. Report on the uses of mirrors in the home ; in business and industry.

2. Devise or work an experiment to show how light is reflected from a plane mirror; that is, prove that the angle of incidence is equal to the angle of reflection.
3. Work an experiment to show how to locate the image formed by a plane mirror.
4. Report to class concerning the new 200-inch telescope.
5. Compute the focal length of a concave mirror by using an optical bench with lamp house and a screen.
6. By experiment, determine the nature of images formed by concave mirrors. State whether they are real or virtual, erect or inverted, larger or smaller than the object.
7. In a similar manner determine the type of images formed by convex mirrors.

Provisions for Individual Differences

1. Make a periscope and demonstrate it before the class.
2. Make a reflecting telescope.
3. Draw a diagram of the new 200-inch telescope.
4. Make a list of the various uses of convex mirrors.

C. REFRACTION

Subject Matter Outline

1. Bending of light
   Index of refraction
2. Images and convex lenses
   Spherical aberration
3. Images and concave lenses
4. Optical instruments

Teaching Procedure

1. Point out that refraction is the bending of a ray of light out of its course as it passes from one medium into another of different optical density.
2. Place a meter stick at about a 60 degree angle in a large beaker of water. Does it appear to bend ? How is its apparent length affected ?

3. Place a coin in the bottom of a dish. Stand back so that the coin is just out of sight, then have an assistant fill the dish with water. Can you se: the coin ?
4. Make sure that the student understands and can apply the lens formula in finding : the distance to an image, distance to an object, and the focal length ; also how to determine the size of an image when the size of an object and the distances to an object and an image are known.
5. Demonstrate available optical instruments to the class—kodaks, movie cameras, movie projectors, lantern slides, opera glasses, prism binoculars, etc.

Pupil Activities

1. Determine the index of refraction of glass by using a piece of glass about three inches square having polished edges. Pins and a drawing board are needed.
2. Determine the path of light as it passes through a flat, triangular glass prism. Pins and a ruler are needed.
3. Determine the focal length of a convex lens by using an optical bench and source of light, lens holder, and screen.
4. Use the necessary materials to determine the nature of images formed by both convex and concave lenses.
5. Make a simple microscope.
6. Make a refracting telescope using lenses in the laboratory.
7. Find the magnifying power of a small telescope.

Provision for Individual Differences

1. Demonstrate some optical illusions.
2. Compute the velocity of light in a diamond, in crown glass, and in water.
3. Determine the critical angle in glass.
4. Determine the focal length of a reading glass. See if it will burn paper.
5. Report to the class concerning the use of convex and concave lenses in fitting spectacles.
6. Devise a method for making a simple proiection lantern.

7. Using books in the library, find out how lenses in opera glasses, movie projectors, etc., are constructed.

D. SPECTRA AND COLOUR

Subject Matter Outline

1. The spectrum ; the spectroscope
2. Colours and the mixing of colours ; colour printing
3. Polarized light
4. Interference of light

Teaching Procedure

1. If a spectroscope is available, demonstrate and explain a continuous spectrum, bright line spectra, and a dark line spectrum. A 60 degree prism may be used to show a continuous spectrum.
2. Point out the primary colours and show that the other colours may be obtained by mixing the primary pigments.
3. If a polaroid kit is available, demonstrate varicus polarisation phenomena.
4. Explain by use of a diagram what causes interference of light. A diagram showing that two reflected light waves a half wave length apart neutralize each other will help the student to understand interference of light.

Pupil Activities

1. Make an artificial rainbow by placing a glass of water on the edge of a table which is in the sunlight. A resemblance of a rainbow will be seen on the floor.
2. Show by a diagram the path of light from the sun when primary and secondary rainbows are seen. How are the colours in each arranged ?
3. Visit a print shop where colour printing is done.
4. Mix two primary pigments and observe the colours formed.
5. Look up the meaning of complementary colours. List the complementary colours.
6. Take the lenses out of a pair of polaroid sun glasses. Place one upon the other and slowly turn one lens. Explain what happens.

7. Place two pieces of plate glass one on top of the other, with a piece of paper between them at one end. Observe the black interference bands formed when the image of a sodium flame is viewed by reflection.

Provisions for Individual Differences

1. Make a simple spectroscope out of available prism and lenses.
2. Tell how spectrum analysis is important to science.
3. Illuminate your face by a sodium flame in a dark room. Explain your strange appearance.
4. Report upon the use of a polaroid material for car windshields and head lights. List other uses of polaroid materials.
5. Blow a soap bubble and observe the colours, or with a heated piece of glass blow a thin glass bubble and observe the colours. Explain.

Textbook References

Unit IV. Light

A. Transmission and Photometry
B. Reflection
C. Refraction
D. Spectra and Colour

Authors		*Topics and Pages* A	B	C	D
Black and Davis	...pp-	555—565	565—578	579—618	619—636
Clark, Gorton, Sears	...pp.	383—398	390—414	414—443	447—459
Dull	...pp.	323—336	337—349	350—385	386—400
Fletcher, Mosbacher, Lehman	...pp.	497—519	520—537	538—578	579—603
Fuller, Brownlee, Baker,	...pp.	423—437 509—568	438—455	456—496	497—508
Henderson	...pp.	662—674 682—687	674—675 691—701	676—682 701—720	729—744
Holly and Lohr	...pp.	414—428	430—446	448—478	482—499
Millikan, Gale, Coyle	...pp.	487—504	521—526	504—518 527—538	541—556
Stewart, Cushing, Towne	...pp.	580—597	601—609	612—638	643—666
Williard	...pp.	395—414	415—431	432—458	459—470

UNIT V. MAGNETISM AND ELECTRICITY

Objectives

1. To teach that the energy laws and principles developed in previous unit apply also in explaining the behaviour of electricity.
2. To teach the fundamentals of magnetism and electricity that everyone should know and to correct some common erroneous beliefs.
3. To encourage the interested and capable student to pursue further the study of magnetism and electricity.

A. MAGNETISM

Subject Matter Outline

1. Magnets, natural and artificial.
2. Magnetic poles and their interaction.
3. Magnetic fields, magnetic transparency, and permeability.
4. Theory or magnetism.
5. Terrestrial magnetism
   (*a*) Magnetic compass, magnetic declination.
   (*b*) Magnetic inclination.

Teaching Procedure

1. Probably most high-school students have had some experiences and fun with magnets. There is some mystery about magnetism which makes it an interesting study. This unit should clear up some of the mysteries for students, but it should be pointed out that there are still many things unknown about magnetism. There is good reason for studying the known facts and present theories.
2. Suspend pieces of limestone, granite, quartz, and lodestone from a support by threads. Sprinkle iron fillings over these stones to see if they are natural magnets.
3. Magnetize a nail, by stroking with a pole of a permanent magnet.

4. Suspend a bar magnet from a support by a thread so that it will act as a compass. Bring other bar magnets near it to show attraction and repulsion of poles:

5. Show the effect of heating and hammering on magnets.

6. Demonstrate that a magnet exerts attraction through glass, paper, wood, rubber, etc., but not through a sheet of iron.

7. Magnetic fields surrounding magnets may be demonstrated by sprinkling iron fillings upon a sheet of paper or a piece of glass which rests on one or more magnets. Small magnets may be made from pieces of old hack-saw blades for this purpose.

8. Explain the theory of magnetism as discussed in recent texts and, with the aid of diagrams, show the arrangement of particles in an unmagnetized bar, in one partially magnetized, and in one fully magnetized.

9. Holding a piece of iron pipe or an iron bar in line with the magnetic lines of the earth, magnetize it by hitting it several times on the end with a hammer.

10. Using a magnetic compass, test for magnetism vertical pipes, east and west pipes, north and south pipes, radiators, iron seat supports.

11. Using a dipping needle, measure the magnetic inclination or angle of dip for your locality.

Pupil Activities

1. Each student may carry out for himself section 3 under Teaching Procedure. Several magnets and pieces of iron are needed and should be arranged in several ways for plotting lines of force.

2. By use of maps in textbooks showing isogonic lines, estimate the direction in which a compass needle will point in your locality. Compare the compass indication with the direction of the north star.

Provision for Individual Differences

1. Make a report on William Gilbert's work on magnetism.
2. Report to the class why it is impossible to make permanent magnet from soft iron.
3. Tell how magnetism is of aid in navigation.
4. Make and demonstrate a dipping needle to the class.

B. ELECTROSTATICS

Subject Matter Outline

1. Historical development of electrostatics:—Thales, 600 B. C. ; Gilbert, 1600 ; Otto von Guericke, 1672 ; Benjamin Franklin, 1752.
2. Types of electric charges ; the electron theory.
3. Production and transmission of electrostatic charges ; the electroscope.
4. Electrostatic induction.
5. Effect of the shape of electrostatic conductors.
6. Comparison of magnetism and electrostatics.

Teaching Procedure

1. Some of the students' previous experiences in electrostatics will include : rubbing a cat's fur and obtaining sparks, attraction of a comb for the hair, electrical storms and their effects on radio.
2. To aid in the understanding of electrostatics, it will be necessary to introduce and explain the fundamentals of the electron theory. Recent texts should be consulted for the latest developments.
3. Consult references as to the historical development of knowledge of static electricity.
4. Suspend two toy balloons or two ping-pong balls by threads so they are free to swing near each other. Charge a hard-rubber or sealing-wax rod and touch to them and note the repulsion. Pieces of elder pith covered with aluminium paint may be used instead. Repeat using a positively charged glass rod. Show the

effect of charging one ball negatively and one positively.

5. Demonstrate the use of an electroscope in detecting and identifying charges.
6. Charge an electroscope by conduction and induction from the same source. Point out the difference.
7. To the positive terminal of an electrostatic machine connect a sharp nail or needle and hold the flame of a lighted candle in front of the point. Note the repulsion of the flame. It may even be blown out.
8. The effect of lightning rods may be demonstrated by connecting the terminals of a static machine to two parallel metal plates several inches in diameter and about three inches apart. Upon the lower plate set a metal ball upon a suitable support so that the distance between the ball and the upper plate is less than an inch. The upper plate represents a cloud and the ball a building. Sparks will jump between the ball and the upper plate. If a pointed metal rod is placed beside the ball, it will stop the sparking.
9. Demonstrate the electric whirl.
10. Compare magnetism and static electricity as to polarity and sign, attraction and repulsion, materials in which the phenomena appear, conduction of the effects, and variance of force with distance.

Pupil Activities

A study of the electroscope and its use in detecting and identifying electrostatic charges both by conduction and induction may be carried out by each pupil.

Provision for Individual Differences

1. Reports on the work of Thales, Gilbert, Otto von Guericke, and Benjamin Franklin may be made.
2. Reports may be made on the fluid theories and the electron theory.
3. Make and demonstrate an electroscope; a small Leyden jar.
4. A report on the Van de Graaf apparatus may be made.

C. DIRECT CURRENTS AND THEIR EFFECTS

Subject Matter Outline

1. Cells, curtent, and voltage.
2. Resistance and Ohm's law.
3. Circuits : series and parallel.
4. Electromagnetic effects ; the telegraph and telephone.
5. Electrolysis, electroplating, and storage batteries.
6. Heating and lighting by electricity.
7. Electrical energy and power, direct-current motors.

Teaching Procedure

1. In this sub-unit the teacher should try to "get across" the difference between current and voltage, and to eliminate the idea that current gets weaker the farther it goes.
2. If much demonstration is to be done, a good, large lecture-table galvanometer is almost indispensable. An instrument with proper shunts and resistors so that it can be used either as a voltmeter or ammeter is desirable.
3. With an instrument such as described above, the teacher can demonstrate quickly the voltages of various galvanic cells. It is well to emphasize at this point the necessity for a complete circuit, voltage drops across various parts of the circuit, and that the current is the same in all parts of a series circuit.
4. Ohm's law can be quickly-verified on the lecture table.
5. A piece of iron wire wrapped about an asbestos core and connected in series with an ammeter and dry cells may be heated by a burner or by the current itself. The decrease of current shows the increase of resistance with temperature.
6. Several boards, each 1 inch by 1 inch by 42 inches, each with one meter of wire stretched upon it, of different sizes and materials, are convenient for demonstrating laws of resistance. A number of flexible wires with small battery clips attached to each end are useful for making connections.

7. The apparatus of 2 and 3 above will be useful for demonstrating the laws of series and parallel circuits.
8. A large electromagnet may be demonstrated.
9. Most texts describe experiments demonstrating electrolysis. A cell of copper sulfate solution with a copper anode and a cathode made from the carbon pole of an old dry cell is useful for showing copper plating.
10. Heating effects are easily shown. See Unit II, Heat, A-2, Provision for Individual Differences.
11. A watt-meter is useful but not essential. If direct current is used, power may be computed as current times voltage. With alternating current, this will hold for straight-wire conductors and approximately for lamps but not for motors.
12. The St. Louis motor may be demonstrated.

Pupil Activities

1. A committee experiment on measurement of current and voltage in different parts of a circuit is suggested.
2. Individual experiments to show (*a*) the voltmeter-ammeter method of measuring resistance, and (*b*) that the voltage drop across a conductor is directly proportional to the resistance of the conductor, are recommended.
3. The laws of resistances in series and parallel may be verified by the above method. Students should work individually.
4. Study and work with telegraphs and telephones.
6. Investigate various types of heating appliances. Note properties of materials used and the large currents used. If a 60-watt lamp and a 100-watt lamp are connected in series across a 115-volt line, which produces more heat ? Which, if they are connected in parallel ?

Provision for Individual Differences

1. Investigate the Wheatstone-bridge method of measuring resistances singly and in combination.

2. Set up two-way telegraph and telephone systems, using relays with the telegraphs.
3. Verify Joule's law and determine the mechanical equivalent of heat by the electrical method.
4. Investigate the efficiency of an electric hot-plate heating water in a kettle on the plate.

D. ALTERNATING CURRENTS AND THEIR EFFECTS

Subject Matter Outline

1. Induced currents :
   (*a*) Lenz's law ; self induction
   (*b*) The alternating-current generator and the direct-current generator
   (*c*) The induction coil and its applications
   (*d*) The transformer
   (*e*) Long-distance transmission systems.
2. The alternating-current motor :
   (*a*) The synchronous motor and the electric clock
   (*b*) The induction motor
   (*c*) The universal motor.
3. Characteristic features of alternating-current circuits :
   (*a*) Meaning of volt and ampere in alternating current
   (*b*) Impedance compared with resistance
   (*c*) Three-phase systems
   (*d*) Power factor
4. Rectification of alternating current.

Teaching Procedure

1. At the high-school level, mathematical treatment of this subject should not be attempted. Try to make clear the essential nature of alternating current and the important differences between direct-current and alternating-current principles.
2. With coils, magnets, and a galvanometer the fundamental principles of current induction may be demonstrated and the rules for current direction made clear. Lenz's law should be pointed out as a necessary consequence of the conservation of energy.

3. It should be emphasized that the "natural" e.m.f. generated in a coil rotating in a magnetic field is alternating. This may be shown by connecting a large coil to a galvanometer and slowly rotating the coil in the earth's field. The same may be shown by the use of an old telephone magneto or a hand dynamo.
4. Use a spark coil to show the lighting of gas, explosion of a gas-air mixture, or of powder.
5. Toy train transformers or demonstration transformers may be used. If voltmeters are available, show voltage relations. Emphasize the fact that the transformer is a voltage changer and not a rectifier.
6. Point out the special features of each type of motor, *e.g.*, radio interference by most brush motors, but none from induction motors, and the reasons for this.
7. Indicate why special definitions are necessary for the volt and ampere in the alternating-current case, and what these definitions are.
8. Call attention to cases where alternating current cannot be used and hence why rectification is necessary; battery charging from alternating-current lines.

Pupil Activities

There are not many experiments with alternating currents that can be recommended for high-school laboratory work. Visits to power plants or transformer stations may be feasible. Study of various household motors may be of value. A study of battery charging systems can be made.

Provision for Individual Differences

The slower members of a class may be expected to learn the essential difference between direct and alternating currents, that most power systems transmit the latter type, what is meant by 60-cycle current, and that it sometimes is necessary to specify the type of current available when ordering household electrical equipment.

The better students may be interested in finding out why a shock from alternating-current line at 115 volts is more severe than one from direct current line at the same rated voltage, why alternating-current generators are rated in KVA instead of in kilowatts, what a three-phase system is, and why such systems are so commonly used.

Textbook References

Unit V. Magnetism and Electricity

A. Magnetism
B. Electrostatics
C. Direct Currents and Their Effects
D. Alternating Currents and Their Effects

Authors		*Topics and Pages* A	B	C	D
Black and Davis	...pp.	329—343	346—366	368—447	448—499
Clark, Gorton, Sears	...pp.	473—480 489—494	463—470 538—550	497—537 480—489	552—508
Dull	...pp.	403—414	415—430	433—495	496—528
Fletcher, Mosbacher, Lehman	...pp.	347—369	310—346	370—442 546—570	443—496
Fuller, Brownlee, Baker	...pp.	522—545	571—588	589—602 609—679	680—718
Henderson	...pp.	365—381	385—410	414—496	497—570
Holly and Lohr	...pp.	503—517	521—540	542—575 611—644	575—595 601—610
Millikan, Gale, Coyle	...pp.	297—309	312—333	334—390	391—432
Stewart, Cushing, Towne	...pp.	345—362	365—387	391—449	450—522
Williard	...pp.	481—507	508—521	524—594	595—620

UNIT VI. MODERN PHYSICS

Objectives

1. To impart some information about the recent epoch-making discoveries in physics and the applications of these discoveries.

2. To dispel, to some extent, the contempt many people have for the study of things too small to be seen and to them impractical.

3. To give the capable student an introduction to the atomic and subatomic world and to the field or radiation.

Subject Matter Outline

1. Phenomena of the discharge of electricity through gases
   (*a*) The electron and its properties
   (*b*) Positive particles and their properties
   (*c*) Practical uses of the discharge of electricity through gases
2. X-rays ; how produced, their properties.
3. Radio-active substances and the rays they emit.
4. The atom ; structure, constituents, transmutation of elements.
5. Cosmic rays.
6. Radio, vacuum tubes, electrical waves.

Teaching Procedure

In most high schools there can be little demonstration in this unit, except under sub-heading 1, where the Geissler tube may be demonstrated, and under sub-heading 6. The teacher should endeavor to keep up to date and to present the most recent ideas, regardless of what the textbook may say, especially if old editions are in use.

Pupil Activities

1. Visit a neon sign maker. Find how different colours are obtained.
2. Visit the office of a physician or dentist who has X-ray equipment and has the time and willingness to demonstrate it.
3. If there is a short-wave operator in the class or in town, visit his station.
4. Demonstrate some of the uses of a photo-electric cell.

Provision for Individual Differences

1. List some of the uses of X-rays.
2. Look up the contributions of Arthur N. Compton in connection with X-rays and cosmic rays.

3. What was the contribution of Madame Curie relative to radioactive substances? Report your findings to the class.

4. Make a collection of old radios and show them to the class. Point out improvements made from year to year.

Textbook References

Unit VI. Modern Physics

Authors			*Pages*
Black and Davis	..	..	646—690
Clark, Gorton, Sears	...	...	599—630
Dull	..	...	531—564
Fletcher, Mosbacher, Lehman	...	..	604—644
Fuller, Brownlee, Baker	...	...	719—754
Henderson	..	..	571—596
			753—769
Holly and Lohr	..	...	647—677
Millikan, Gale, Coyle	...	..	564—626
Stewart, Cushing, Towne	...	..	671—722
Williard	..	...	621—640

References

1. The numbers in parentheses following each suggestion refer to the topics in the subject matter outline. They are used in all units under these topics : teaching procedure, pupil activities, and provisions for individuals differences.
2. Page references from each of the above ten textbooks in physics are given with each unit of the course of study. In later units these texts will be designated by authors only.
3. Refers back to both 1 and 2 in the subject matter outline.

2

Facilities for High School Physics

Beacause physics is concerned with energy and matter and their interrelationships, it should be an integral part of the education of all youth, Through the experiences that can be provided in physics, young people can appreciate the majesty of the forces within the nucleus of the atom and determine the size of a fuse for an electrical circuit. High school physics can provide for present appreciations and understandings of our universe and for the future development of advanced competencies of scientific and technological nature.

A Look of Physics Teaching

The details of the teaching of physics in the Blue Creek High School were quite clear to Eldon Carpenter, the state high school supervisor, as he reflected upon his recent inspection trip. Blue Creek High was a small, rural school in a rugged area—a region not too favored with economic resources. Charles Morris taught the general science, biology, chemistry, physics, and mathematics and also served as the physical education teacher and bus driver. His load was not quite so formidable as the array of duties suggests; the chemistry and physics were offered in alternate years, and the classes in each subject were rather small.

The school consisted of a collection of frame buildings on the edge of a patch of woods. The "science room" was a separate building which resembled hundreds of one-room school houses scattered over many sections of the country. The room, of course, lacked running water or gas. There were no standardized cabinets, laboratory desks or tables, tackboards, or other visual education facilities. The furniture was crude—mostly ordinary kitchen tables, stools, and chairs of an ancient and dubious history. Storage provisions were sparse and primitive. The closest resemblance to a work room, or place for teacher and students to carry out projects, was a small shop used by another teacher for the vocational agriculture work. The supervisor had wandered around behind the science room and noticed with regret the proximity of a small junk pile—it resembled an automobile "grave yard"—to a building used daily by school children. At first he wondered why such debris had not been removed in the annual clean-up campaigns common to many schools.

Despite the wretchedness of the scene, and the apparent paucity of equipment, supplies, and accommodations for teaching and learning, it had been clear that an excellent course in physics was being offered at that very spot. One of the keys to the excellence of the course was the junk pile nearby.

Charles Morris—with vision, imagination and hard work—was turning the apparent shortcomings of his situation into stepping stones and resources which enabled him to offer one of the best physics courses in his state. He was teaching his physics course so well that Mr. Carpenter was taking steps to provide financial aid for Mr. Morris to continue his education, and to increase the annual appropriations for science in this particular school.

The physics of the automobile furnished the nucleus of the course. An old Model T Ford and a 1929 Chevrolet, as well as a collection of cast-off parts from other automobiles, household appliances, and salvaged items from a hundred neighbourhood junk piles furnished the equipment and supplies for curricular experiences in physics.

Students used the farm shop to disassemble and rebuild, as well as to improvise needed equipment. Some of the activities connected with salvaging and improvising were done as projects. Demonstrations and laboratory experiences were provided often in the old cars rather than in a laboratory—which, after all, did not exist in the formal sense.

As for course content, the electrical system of the old automobiles furnished material for topics in electricity ; the cooling system was the source of experiences in heat ; the gears, transmission, springs, and levers, as well as a hundred other parts on the cars, led the students through many aspects of mechanics. Important principles of physics were uncovered, demonstrated, and applied by the students in this course. The high degree of interest among students, the development of appreciations of accuracy, precision and good workmanship, and the functional understandings which arose in this course built on a junk pile attested the value of the course.

Now, as Mr. Carpenter thought over the teaching of science in the various schools in the state, his thoughts turned to the teaching of physics at the Community City High School, Community City was a well-to-do community with considerable local industry and it had the good fortune to be located in the center of a good agricultural region. The citizens provided well for their schools and were quite proud of them.

Robert Perry taught the physics as well as the chemistry at Community City High School. He, too, was doing splendid teaching. Because of the circumstances, he had a wide range of physical resources. The rooms were quite ample and they had good furniture of conventional design. There were cabinets and shelves well-stocked with much of the conventional teaching equipment. In addition, Mr. Perry had a modest budget upon which he could draw for some replenishment and additions each year, as well as to provide for operating expenses.

In spite of such resources, Mr. Perry was not content to stop with what could have been a traditional situation. On a recent visit Mr. Carpenter had observed at greater length than usual in the science department. He had been quite intrigued with some of the work that he saw going on. The details came back to him quite clearly. Following a physics class that he had observed, he had inquired of Mr. Perry what the basis was for the report that he had heard two students give.

"Those boys obtained some surplus electronic equipment from one of the dealers here in Community City. It so happens that they have been working with this equipment for several months. Yesterday as the class was discussing the theory of electromagnetic waves, it occurred to me that some work that the boys had been doing in the field could make a significant contribution to today's work. When we had some free time I asked them if they could tell the class what they had been doing and the reports today are what you heard."

Following the reports there had been some discussion which led to a proposal that the class should visit a local radio station to study the transmitter there. There was also planning for an invitation to a television repairman to come to the school and talk with the students about some aspects of television receivers.

The discussion led on to Mr. Perry's elaboration of the many resources that he had for this particular kind of work. On his shelves were not only conventional pieces of equipment designed for the study of radio, but there were in addition a demonstration radio transmitter and a demonstration receiver. He had obtained from one of the companies that produce electronic equipment some charts which show the structure and operation of radio tubes. There were filmstrips that he could use and there was a motion picture on electromagnetic waves that a committee from the class was planning to preview to determine whether it would be appropriate for their use. The supervisor had noted also several books placed on the reading table, as well as some materials from various companies that would interest the students in radio.

Before Mr. Carpenter left, Robert Perry showed him some of the materials that had been used in previous years in their study of radio. These materials included work-sheets and tests that indicated that the expected achievement might be of rather conventional character. However, Mr. Carpenter had noted in an announcement just a few days ago that the students in physics from Community City High School had received high ratings in the judging of the projects on exhibit at the state science day.

Here too, Mr. Carpenter reflected, was good teaching of physics and he could not help but meditate upon the difference in resources that stood in such contrast with the singularity of purpose shown in the two schools. In both instances the teachers were using the resources that they had available to the very best advantage ; in both instances boys and girls were learning ; and in both instances they were obviously happy and enthusiastic. A further task for him, he decided, was that of exploration of the idea of helping each of these two physics teachers and the many others like them to extend their range of resources even further. Surely, this too is one of the functions of a state supervisor, he reflected.

Such are two examples of the many different types of physics courses and methods of teaching which are suitable for secondary schools. Within these examples are found evidence of the principles of organization of physics courses as they have been formulated by the Committee on Science Education in American Schools :

(*a*) (There should be) unification about a central theme.
(*b*) Social implication of the material (should be stressed).
(*c*) Material should be of immediate personal interest and value to students.
(*d*) The number of topics or units taught during the year must be reduced.

(*e*) The course should be organized largely or entirely about problems.
(*f*) Students should have a considerable share in setting the goals of class instruction.
(*g*) Physics teaching at the high-school level should largely reject the preparatory function and stress the contributions of physics to the general education of American youth.

The interpretation of these principles leads to a concept of method characteristic of a desirable high school physics course. The course should be taught in such a way as to provide as much experience as possible in the laboratory and field. It is through such experience that the student gains the basis for scientific argument and tests of hypotheses. These experiences need not be elaborate. They may be simple exercises with homemade materials or observations of everyday phenomena. Efforts should be directed toward developing appreciation for and skill in using precise measurements and calculations. The course work should show the relation of physics to the solution of human problems. Definite attemps should be made to adapt work to the interests and abilities of all students, yet extend beyound the student's immediate environment and experience. The techniques of presentation should include all possible media which may enrich experience, such experimentation, motion pictures, exhibits, demonstrations, and field trips.

An Analysis of Activities

In view of the preceding principles and characteristics of good physics courses for secondary schools, physics teaching may be analyzed with respect to activities required or expected of students and teachers during the learning process. The physics course taught at Blue Creek High School may be profitably re-examined as a cass in point.

In this instance the physics of the automobile furnished the broad organizing theme. More generally speaking, the fundamental concept underlying the course was *all physical phenomena are based upon energy transformations.* The automobile was the medium through which application was made of important generalizations and principles bearing upon this concept.

The gasoline engine of the automobile was treated as a device for converting the stored chemical energy of the gasoline into heat, and the heat into mechanical energy for turning wheels, fans, pumps, generator, and other devices. The generator was studied as a device for converting the mechanical energy into electrical energy, which in turn could be stored in the battery as chemical energy to be released later as electrical energy when needed. The headlights were considered as devices for converting electricity into heat and light, while the horn transformed the electricity into magnetism, and then produced sound.

The discussion of friction in the automobile, the necessity for lubrication, the cooling system, and the heat developed in the moving parts built up the understandings of the generalization that energy may be transformed into forms which are not desirable and provisions must be made to allow for this possibility. Besides these understandings, others of importance were developed.

With respect to method, the students worked individually and in groups on projects, demonstrations, and experiments which included such activities as : collecting parts ; salvaging usable materials ; learning to drive, repair, and maintain a car ; building and improvising homemade equipment as substitutes for commercial items ; and testing and figuring alternative solutions to sm ll problems created by the lack of ready supplies and equipment. One group assembled a homemade automobile as part of the physics course. The experience in measuring, fitting, planning, improvising, making and testing hypotheses, as well as sharing in labou and expenses were numerous.

From the brief description it can be seen that the course possessed a large number of the desirable characteristics of good physics teaching. It was based on a broad unifying theme. It contained a iew broard topics for a year's work. The materials were of immediate personal interest to students and they could immediately realize some practical values. The problems approach was paramount, with the students having opportunity to use imagination, skills, and individual initiative on problems that were of real concern to them, while being socially significant. Because of these qualities this course was rated excellent by the majority of those who knew it well.

An analysis of the activities in the physics class at Community City High School would reveal a correspondingly broad range of activities, similarly directed toward the achievement of commonly accepted objectives. Such analyses define the need for specific provisions within the school. Provisions which serve the minimum needs of activities and reflect present trends in science teaching are :

(1) A class and demonstration area.
(2) Individual and group work areas.
(3) Library resources.
(4) Storage facilities for individual and group use.
(5) Facilities for project development and special interest work.
(6) Exhibit space and tackboards.
(7) Audio-visual facilities.
(8) Workshop facilities.
(9) Darkroom provisions.

In addition to such facilities which are used for the usual instructional procedures, provisions should be made for :

(1) Instructor's office.
(2) Preparation or workroom.
(3) Sources of current electricity, running water, and gas.
(4) Apparatus and supply storage.

Those persons who are planning physics rooms should take into consideration the fact that in many schools the same room is used for physics and chemistry. Aside from possible space and cost economies there are other advantages of curricular nature in using one room for both courses. The necessary modifications in design are few ; they provide needed flexibility in room use. Initial consideration to this combined use was given. There is further development of such plans in the following pages.

PLANNING FACILITIES FOR HIGH SCHOOL PHYSICS

The provision of physics facilities must be constructively approached and may not be left to chance or expediency. There is no single arrangement of facilities that can meet most effectively the needs of all types of learning situations. Each combination of desirable facilities must be adapted to local needs and must represent careful planning on the part of architects, administrators, and science teachers.

This planning process must revolve around such considerations as activity requirements, elements of safety, attractiveness, and flexibility of use, necessary new installations or additions, and renovation of existing facilities to meet new or expanded functions.

Activity Requirements of the Program

One of the first problems to be decided in the planning stage concerns the type of physics program which will be offered in the school. Questions such as the following should be answered at this time :

Will much student time be devoted to projects and the building of equipment ?

Will emphasis be placed upon individual laboratory experimentation ?

Will experiences in radio and electronics be offered and to what extent ?

Will both physics and chemistry be taught in the room ?

To what extent will photography, meteorology, and astronomy be included in the physics offerings ?

Will physics be interrelated with other courses in the curriculum ?

A closely related problem is the estimation of the number of students which the program must serve at present and in the near future.

Safety Provisions

An early consideration in planning rooms to be used for physics or for physics and chemistry is careful attention to safety hazards. In addition to those provisions of more general nature, the following precautions should be observed :

(1) Any electrical circuit with a potential of more than 25-v., a. c., should be grounded.
(2) Motors, generators, and switchboards should be so arranged that students are protected.
(3) Approved guards should be used on any power tools in the workshop or preparation room.
(4) Colour codes should be used wherever safety hazards exist :

   (*a*) Red : for exit signs, fire protection, and fire-fighting equipment.
   (*b*) Yellow : for caution, on or around working parts of power tools and switch boxes.
   (*c*) Green : for safety, on first-aid kits and deluge showers.

CLASSROOM AND LABORATORY FACILITIES FOR HIGH SCHOOL PHYSICS

The first necessary provision for physics teaching is that of classroom and laboratory facilities. These facilities include rooms and their equipment, utilities and services, and equipment and supplies.

Room Orientation and Location

The location of physics rooms with reference to floors depends upon local requirements. For schools which have several floors, some arguments have been advanced for placing the physics rooms on the upper floors, while others have been presented for placement of these rooms on the first floor, not including the basement. Adherents of the upper-floor position point out the advantage of storing delicate, easily corroded equipment as high as possible in a damp climate. The proponents of the ground-floor location point out advantages of their position as : proximity to crafts and homemaking areas, accessibility to the out-of-doors for projects requiring such access, and the case with which heavy equipment such as motors may be brought into the physics classroom.

Space Requirements

The pertinent literature indicates a unanimity of opinion on the provision of an auxiliary room adjacent to the regular physics and physics-chemistry classroom-laboratory, although there are some minor differences in details of the several proposals. Engelhard suggests the sharing of storage rooms by several classrooms, and the use of locked cupboards for delicate instruments and dangerous chemicals; provision of a special darkroom for photography; and perhaps additional space for a planetarium, an observatory, and a weather station. The proposal of the American Association of School Administrators recommends a minimum of 125 sq. ft. of floor area for storage. It further suggests that chemicals be stored separately from the storage space used for apparatus and other supplies. In small high schools this special chemical storeroom, if equipped with a sink, may also serve as a photographic darkroom. The National Council on School-house Construction concurs with these recommendations, suggesting in addition that where a storeroom serves two laboratories, 150 sq. ft. should be provided.

Furniture

In rooms where physics is to be the only subject taught, the furniture may well consist of movable tables of the 2-student type. This 2-student table makes possible the seating of all students facing the demonstration desk. The plans utilize this type of furniture. Where three rows of tables are to be used in a classroom of average size a smaller table is suggested ; one-student desks are sometimes used. Tables can be modified by the installation of electrical outlets for a.c. and d.c. which can be connected to floor boxes in sub-floor channels by flexible cables and by the provision of Formica tops of Linenized finish, or wood finished in a light colour rather than the usual black.

Movable tables for the central portion of the room require that work space provided with water, gas, and electricity be arranged around the perimeter of the room. Wall tables can be provided for this purpose. The tables are equipped with running water ; gas and electrical outlets are placed in the splashboard. These tables should include cabinets of shelves and drawers for the storage of the pieces of apparatus and the supplies that are commonly used.

Other Special Instructional Facilities

Other facilities that are of considerable value in making teaching and learning more effective are the following :

(1) *Room Library or Reading Center*. Laboratory work and reading go hand in hand. One way to provide for this is the isolation of a corner of the room as a study area. Bookshelves and filling cabinets for pamphlets may be arranged for an L-shaped or U-shaped area enclosed by temporary partitions.

(2) *Darkroom*. A photographic darkroom is a convenient adjunct to the physics laboratory. Not only is it needed for ordinary photographic work but may be used for optical experiments and demonstrations. For a large school where photography is offered to large groups, it may be advisable to fit out a special photographic classroom.

(3) *Workshop*. The physics course requires tools, materials, and space for making and repairing things. Student projects, handmade devices, mock-ups, cutaways, demonstration panels, and repair and maintenance of equipment require saws, screwdrivers, nuts, bolts, screws, wood, paint, solder, tin, and other materials and tools. A workbench, drill press, power saw, and lathe are necessary if much of this kind of activity is attempted. These facilities should be provided in a workroom that is adjacent to the physics classroom. In many schools, the industrial arts shop facilities are available to the physics teacher, but even in these cases, a small shop in the physics storeroom pays dividends by its being accessible at all times.

(4) *Miscellaneous Facilities.* Certain miscellaneous items are necessary or desirable. A wall clock with second hand is valuable for timing experiments, as well as for telling time. Where locked drawers or storage cupboards are provided for individual students, a key cabinet is needed. This should be located in a place that is accessible to all students—possibly near the entrance to the room.

Waste jars of earthenware, or metal, should be placed at convenient spots in the classroom, storeroom, work room, and darkroom.

UTILITIES AND SERVICES

In the planning and equipping of modern secondary school physics and chemistry rooms, careful choice and proper location of adequate service facilities will repay in convenience, utility, and working efficiency. The following discussion does not present an exhaustive listing of service facilities but does suggest those facilities which experience has shown to be most frequently needed in the physics classroom.

Service facilities required in a physics laboratory are :

(1) Running water at various outlets
(2) Sinks and other means of drainage
(3) Gas
(4) Electricity, a.c. and d.c. at various voltages.

Running Water

An adequate number of hot and cold running water outlets should be available in each classroom. All faucets should be of the slow-compression type, with working parts of metal resistant to corrosion and abrasion. Chromium finish is often used for such parts. Some of these faucets should be fitted with serrated hose connectors. Stone sinks of suitable sizes and shapes are recommended for both physics and chemistry laboratories.

Air Compressors and Vacuum Pumps

Compressed air for small laboratories may be provided by a portable air compressor unit which usually consists of a small tank, a compressor unit, and an electric motor mounted on a suitable platform. A portable commercial pump can be used for both pressure and vacuum. For larger science units, vacuum pumps and compressors may be installed to activate compressed air and vacuum lines in the laboratory including an outlet on the demonstration desk.

Electricity

The electrical services needed in the physics room are many and varied. Provisions should be made for alternating current and direct current outlets at all anticipated work areas, for switchboard and controls, for outlets for projection devices, and outlets for radio antennae.

In general, three types of alternating current circuit may be provided within the room :

(1) General purpose outlets for 110-v., 15 ampere circuits for lighting and other general use.

(2) Appliance outlets for 110-v., 30 ampere circuits for elecltric heaters, motors on lathes, drills, and other power tools.

(3) Individual outlets for 110 to 220-v. circuits for motor-generators and other special devices.

Where movable tables are used, several covered floor boxes should be provided. These floor boxes must be placed in sub-floor channels which are free from flooding by water. If the tables are fitted with flexible extension cords as suggested in the discussion of the floor plan, electricity is readily available wherever the tables are moved.

A source of direct current is necessary in physics classes. This need may be met by several arrangements. In the larger schools, a motor generator set is a worth-while installation. Where the demand for direct current is lower, or infrequent, a tungar rectifier unit may be satisfactory. If not more than six volts at three amperes is required, several low voltage sub-stations may be used. These portable devices operate from standard 110-volt, 60 cycle a.c. circuits; the usual output range is 0-6.5 v., d.c. and 0-11 v., a.c.

Ample d.c. outlets should be provided near the major work areas. Some of these outlets should be polarized, some fitted for jacks, and others fitted with binding posts. They may be of the flush type or pedestal type as the need requires. Whatever the type, they should be fitted with the proper extension cords for polarized plugs, jacks, or binding post clips.

To control the distribution of current to the several work stations, a switchboard should be provided. Switchboard panels may be secured from laboratory equipment designers and suppliers, as well as from electrical products manufacturers. These penels may be fitted in the knee space of demonstration desks, installed in glass-enclosed cabinets, or mounted as wall panels in the workroom.

Projection equipment requires additional circuits.

Radio and television are becoming part of the equipment used in physics courses. For use of these devices special antennae should be provided outside the building. Both types of antennae will require special conduits to bring the coaxial cable and antenna wire into the classroom.

A laboratory water still is a valuable addition to the work of the course.

EQUIPMENT AND SUPPLIES

Experimental and Demonstration Apparatus

The array of apparatus to be used in the teaching of physics is extensive, as the list in Appendix II indicates. In addition to the commonly used apparatus of commercial production there is a wealth of resources from the environment, many of them showing applications of principles of physics. Such devices as automobile jacks, tire pumps, light switches, light bulbs, neon and fluorescent tubes and fixtures, circuit breakers, radiator thermostats, and toys showing principles of science are a few of the many that are obtainable in most communities.

The selection of apparatus and supplies to be used in physics teaching is directly related to the curriculum and to the method of teaching. The achievement expected of the students expressed as principles, facts, skills, attitudes, interests, and appreciations must enter into the decision. The breadth of experience provided depends upon the range of physical resources. The amount of demonstration equipment and the number of duplicate pieces of apparatus depend in part upon the method used. Thus the decisions as to the range of apparatus, the accuracy required, the amount of demonstration equipment, and the extent of duplicate pieces should be made in each school or school system

The selection of the kind and amount of supplies used in physics teaching requires attention commensurate with that given to apparatus. In addition to copper wire, rubber dam, cotton string, rubber tubing, and matches, many less conventional supplies are required by the curriculum that provides for individual needs and interests in the field of physics. Among the latter are such things as cellophane, plastic, glue, sheet metal, wood, nails, screws, and nuts and bolts. The building, improvising and repair of apparatus have many educational values.

Locally-Made Apparatus

To a limited extent the resources of apparatus can be extended through local effort. Certain pieces can be produced in the school ; with care in construction they can be as valuable as factory-made equipment. In other instances the use of only machine-produced apparatus is satisfactory. The values derived by the students who design and make the apparatus must be taken into consideration in planning the curriculum and in making decisions as to the selection of apparatus.

Auditory and Visual Equipment

The use of auditory and visual materials has been steadily increasing in modern teaching. Physics is no exception. A discussion of the general aspects of audio-visual facilities is found.

The need for a generous amount of exhibit space for physics, particularly, should be stressed. The nature of the field is such that the number and variety of specific materials to be exhibited require extensive space. Many of the materials are rather large and, in some instances, heavy. Consequently the tables and shelves planned for such use should be sturdy.

There is a potentially extensive use of mock-ups and working models in the teaching of physics. In many instances these can be mounted upon plywood panels. The study of electrical devices and circuits lends itself particularly well to this approach. Such circuits as those for the door bell, radio transmitter and receiver, audio amplifier, and the telegraph may be used, the actual devices being attached to circuits drawn on a board. In other instances, the panels may be used for the display of such devices as switches and fuses, and industrial processes and products such as those of a chemical nature.

The teaching of physics can take advantage of the wealth of illustrative materials that appear in scientific and popular magazines, as well as an extensive array of charts. The minimum dimensions of tackboard for the display of such materials are 12 ft. by 3 ft. 6 in.

FACILITIES FOR STORAGE AND PREPARATION

Adequate storage is essential in the physics room. Well-planned storage is important for convenience and efficiency in class work as well as showing a concrete example of the scientific necessities of orderliness and neatness. Flexibility should characterize all storage facilities in order to give students an opportunity to plan for organizing materials to be stored. Such flexibility may be secured by the use of adjustable shelving, movable partitions, drawers, racks, and cupboards.

In the physics room, and in rooms used for physics and chemistry, the storage problem centers around the following functions :

(1) Segregation and protection of chemicals. This includes protection of students from acids and other injurious substances.

(2) Storage of delicate and costly as well as less expensive equipment.

(3) Storage of supplies needed in current physics experiences.

(4) Storage of audio-visual materials of instruction.

(5) Storage of books and notebooks.

(6) Storage lockers built into equipment for student use.

Several types of storage arrangements provide for these functions. They include : (1) a separate storeroom, (2) built-in

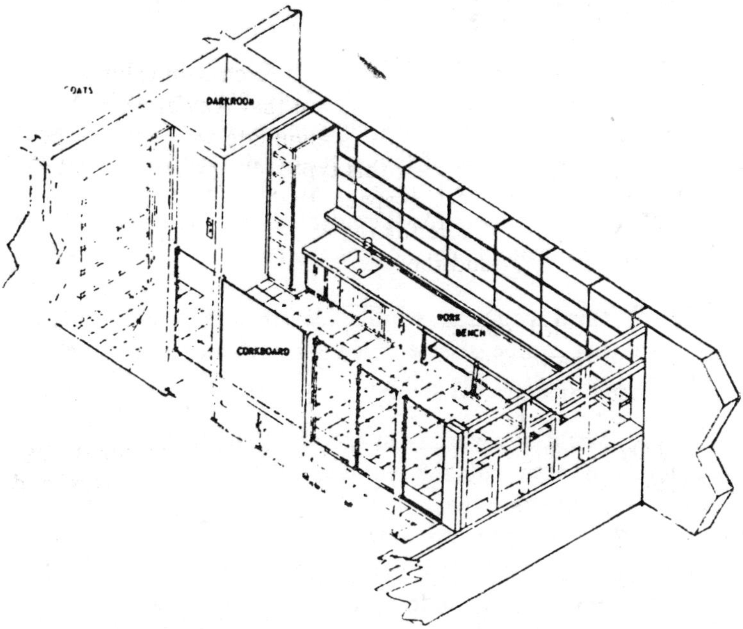

Fig. 2.1. Combined facilities for preparation and storage and for photographic work are provided in this room.

cabinets in the physics classroom-laboratory, (3) a combination of storeroom and built-in units, and (4) movable cabinets and shelving in the classroom. Choices as to which type to use should be made on the basis of the requirements of the individual school. The following suggestions are given as guides for planning of storage facilities.

(1) The separate storeroom is strongly recommended for all schools. The size of this storeroom will be determined by

the type and amount of equipment and materials to be stored and other uses to be made of the room. In many cases the storeroom should be made large enough to provide space for workshop facilities.

The storeroom may be also used as a work center, and possibly as an office for the teacher. The plans in such a storeroom. The plan provides a wide door to the classroom-laboratory, a corridor door, a separate darkroom, and a desk for the teacher.

(2) The advantages of one or more built-in cabinets in the classroom-laboratory for physics are that they are more accessible than separate storerooms, eliminate congestion, and save time. The disadvantage of this type of storage facility is that it takes up so much wall space that, if used extensively, it sacrifices space available for the installation of student desks or other furniture around the walls of the room.

(3) A third common storage device is the wall cabinet or cupboard that can be disassembled and moved. These may be purchased or built at the school.

There should be a variety of specific provisions for storage to meet the needs of the various kinds of apparatus and supplies. Cabinets should have shelves, drawers, and trays. Adjustable shelves provide flexibility in the use of the cabinet, especially if half-shelves are used. Drawers should be shallow and medium in depth, unless special file drawers are needed. For some small items of equipment, light-weight sliding shelves or trays that may be easily removed should be provided. Some apparatus may be hung on hooks and small racks on the backs of doors or on open wall areas. This is especially true of tools. For certain types of stored items, pigeonholes may be used.

Visual materials and equipment require special storage provisions. These materials and equipment include magazines, pictures, charts and posters, slide films, motion picture films, and projectors. Some of this material is in the form of industrial kits of exhibits or samples.

A library-type rack may be used for magazines and bulletins. Open shelving is recommended for the storage of library books. These shelves may be arranged in L- or U-shapes to provide a reading center in the classroom.

Charts and posters are used extensively in physics and chemistry. Charts of the metric system, periodic classification of the elements, electromagnetic spectrum, spectra of certain elements, ammeters, galvanometers, the eye, the camera, and the gasoline engine are common in most physics laboratories. It is usually preferable to keep these charts flat and stored in such a way as to be easily located and used.

PLANS FOR PHYSICS ROOMS

There are many possible plans for rooms for physics and for physics and chemistry. These plans fall into three categories : (1) Single-room layouts ; (2) Classroom-laboratory with accessory rooms ; and (3) Suites of rooms. These three types are considered in the following pages.

Single-Room Layouts

A classroom-laboratory for a physics class of twenty-four students. This plan provides for the use of two-student movable tables which have been modified by the addition of polarized and non-polarized receptacles. In this arrangement all students face the front, but the tables may be rearranged into any desired pattern.

Left-shoulder lighting is provided for shadow-free natural illumination. No sinks or water lines are located at the tables. A large sink is located at the rear of the room for hot and cold water. Electric current is supplied to the tables by flexible cables which connect to floor boxes placed in sub-floor channels at convenient spots. Such cables may be disconnected and put on hooks underneath the tables when the furniture is shifted.

A wall table placed along the outside wall is equipped with gas and air cocks, making it suitable for experiments requiring such facilities. It may also be used for balances, galvanometers, and other instruments. Storage cases for equipment are located on both sides of the wall sink at the rear of the room. If a storage room is adjacent to the classroom, these storage cases should hold only the equipment needed for class demonstrations. If a separate storage room is not available, a storage wall is placed at the front as shown.

The plan is suitable for a small high school, or for very small classes. It utilizes a small, narrow classroom to provide facilities for a class of sixteen students. If Type C desks are used and the wall tables are omitted, the room can accommodate twenty-four students. If the width available is 24 ft., instead of 21 ft., the wall tables may still be used for a 24-student capacity. For the 21-foot width, if a length of 37 ft. is available, the capacity can be expanded to 20 students by the addition of another row of desks. The advantages of this classroom are : all students face the instructor ; it contains essential equipment to make it a relatively satisfactory room.

The Classroom-Laboratory with Accessory Rooms

A major criticism of the conventional science room lies in the lack of flexibility inherent in the fixed furniture usually used for physics and chemistry courses. This limited flexibility in use of equipment results in low utilization. In the modern secondary school, maximum flexibility of facilities is not only desirable but necessary. To attain this goal, modifications of conventional arrangements have been presented by many who are interested in improved facilities for science teaching. Questions similar to those proposed by Clapp and Perkins bring the problem into sharp focus :

"Can we not combine some of these facilities by careful planning ? Will it not be possible to design a science laboratory which can be used for any science as well as for lecture, recitation, or study ? Is there not an instructional trend toward the integration of the sciences ? Why not design a room with laboratory benches around the outside of the room and with space for class seating in the center ?

The plan provides for a Type H desk. This desk is particularly well adapted to arrangement along the walls of a room.

The features of a room using this type of furniture and arrangement include : seating and work space for a class of 24 students in a room of conventional size, the use of bases for storage of individual or general equipment ; the use of the classroom as a homeroom, for science club meetings, or for small group activities, as well as individual seating for viewing films, taking examinations, or participating in demonstrations. The laboratory tables can be used for several experiments or demonstrations at the same time. Economies are effected by the concentration of service facilities in convenient locations with short, easy runs for pipes and wiring. The accessory rooms provide for various kinds of project work as well as preparation, storage, and conference space for the teacher.

The plan illustrates suitable arrangement for a 24-student class in either physics or chemistry, since facilities for both subjects are included within the classroom-laboratory. Noteworthy features of this room are the inclusion of built-in equipment cases for physics storage ; the exhibit case in the corridor ; and the provision of a wall table on the window side with utility connections for experiments. Two-student tables are provided. These are equipped with apparatus support rods. Polarized and non-polarized duplex receptacles connected by flexible plug-in cables into recessed floor boxes are optional facilities. The workroom includes an enclosed darkroom, equipment and tool storage, work bench, and facilities for the teacher.

Figure 2.2. presents a plan for physics laboratory which uses assemblies of standard units. A noteworthy feature of this plan is the provision of both a darkroom and a sound room within the major room. There is a reading corner, and there are facilities for the teacher. A shielded storage and prepration area is provided at the front. Tabletarm chairs and work tables provide flexibility in the use of the room.

Suite Plans

In the larger high schools where several rooms are provided for specialized sciences, it is often thought to be desirable to have such rooms *en suite*. This plan has been followed to some

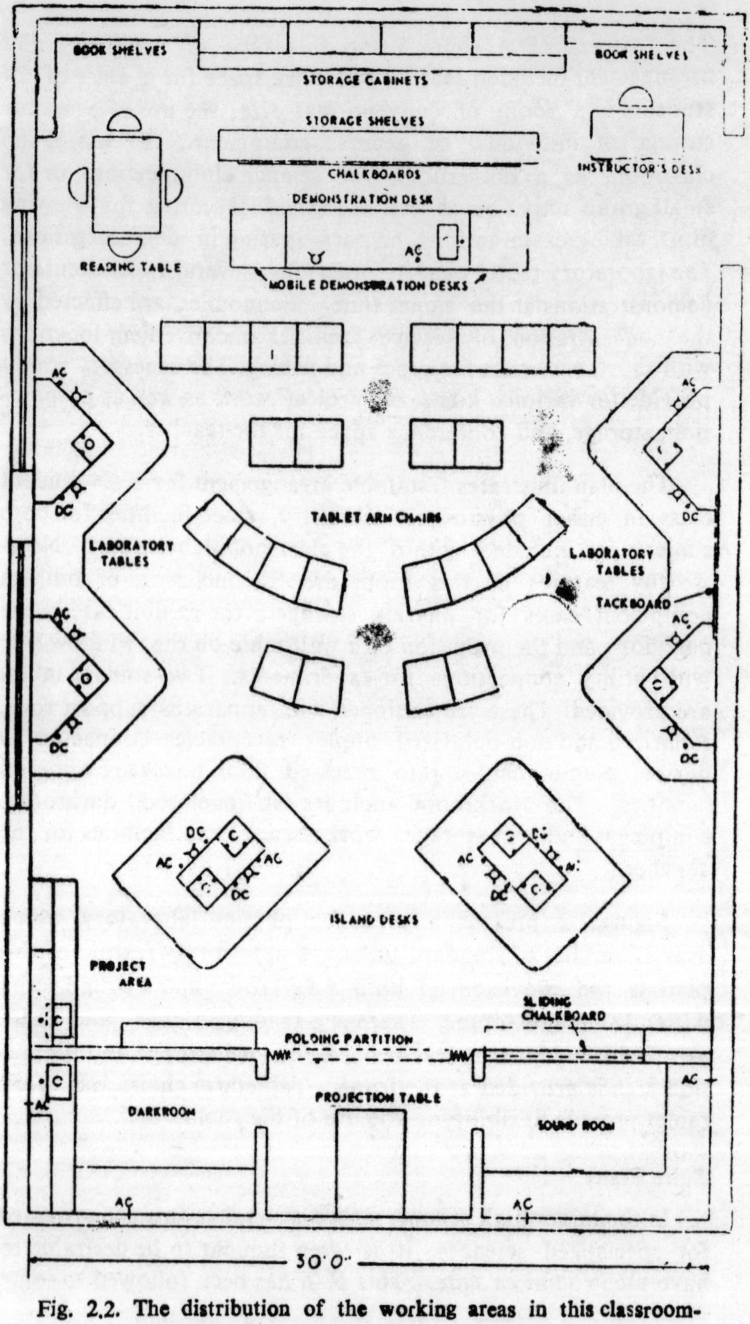

Fig. 2.2. The distribution of the working areas in this classroom-laboratory for physics utilizes the space to full advantage. The plants for the island desks and wall tables.

extent even in small high schools. A weakness of this arrangement in small schools, however, has been pointed out by Clapp and Perkins :

"This has been an area of low utilization in many buildings. Frequently we find separate and distinct laboratories for physics, chemistry, and biology, with one or more science lecture rooms. We have no quarrel with this scheme if there can be effective utilization. This may be possible in larger schools In the smaller schools, however, such a scheme would lead to vacant facilities many hours of the day."

The following plans are presented as examples of the utilization of science suites to facilitate correlation among the sciences. The several proposals contain features found in the previously described facilities. In general, the suites consist of multiples of the single rooms already discussed.

The plan shows a typical physics suite which emphasizes the straight-line arrangement of rooms. The plan is a corner arrangement of rooms for physics and chemistry in a smaller school.

The plan embodies many of the principles which have already been mentioned as being desirable in science rooms. The planning for the unit was done by a group of instructors who would use the facilities. Paramount factors considered in the planning were : flxibility, accessibility, supervision, and the interdependence of the arts and the sciences. These factors were provided for by the following arrangements :

(1) *Flexibility* was secured by the use of semi-movable partitions throughout the unit. Permanent walls were used in the interior only where it was necessary to reduce sound, dust, and fumes. The floor was constructed in such a way that a four-foot pipe space was left below in order that the plumbing might be easily accessible for alteration. Gas, compressed air, and direct and alternating current outlets are spaced to be used wherever there may be a demand for them.

(2) *Accessibility* : As there are no corridors in the unit, students going to and from classes can observe equipment,

demonstration materials, and activities in various areas. Steel and glass partitions which allow observation from many angles contribute to this factor. The laboratories and class sections are also arranged so that they may be used by groups or individuals with a minimum of interference with classes being conducted in other areas at the same time. Opaque shades are provided for the glass partitions.

(3) *Supervision* is facilitated by the central location of the offices with their glass partitions.

(4) *Interdependence of the arts and sciences* is enhanced by the provision of a lobby which is suitable for display of materials from both departments. This lobby is the only corridor between the two departments and is equipped with outlets which enable the construction of operating devices.

Equipment and services of the science unit are designed to give maximum efficiency and to contribute to the purposes of teaching and learning. Light is afforded by four-foot two-tube fluorescent fixtures placed on ten-foot squares. They provide 50 foot-candles at table height with no shadows. The services include natural gas, 110-v. and 220-v. a.c. and d.c., compressed air, and hot and cold running water. Fume hoods are available in the laboratories.

The laboratories have provisions for setting up equipment of a specialized nature when necessary. In the physics laboratory one section has been set aside as a demonstration corner. An optics room and darkroom are also available. The chemistry laboratory contains flattopped tables, with services at the ends and with sinks between. Under the center are three shelves for holding equipment. Four flat-topped tables are placed lengthwise in the chemistry room. Two other tables are placed at a right angle to this long row, leaving space in the center of the room which may be used for projects requiring a large area. It can be used as a reference and study area, being screened by units of shelves for books and magazines. The shelves are 54 in. high. In the general science room, old Type F desks were taken apart and installed around the walls, leaving a free area in the center of the room. Part of the discarded drawers were used to construct an equipment storage cabinet.

OTHER SCHOOL AND COMMUNITY RESOURCES

The close relationship of the teaching of science to the community is expressed in the second principle set forth :

> *School facilities for science should reveal that science is a community as well as a school activity.*

The use of community resources in teaching science is described in *Science Education in American Schools* in the following way :

"... the pupil should be provided with opportunities to expand his classroom experiences with the physical, chemical, and biological phenomena of the environment. By means of his senses he uses acquired learnings continuously to interpret new situations.

Many of the materials of the environment which can aid in the development of this habit of interpretation are permanently fixed and cannot be studied in the science laboratory or brought into the classroom. To do so, even if possible, might interrupt natural existing relationships and reduce the effective use of the materials.

The greatest resource of a community may be its rich soil . . . Other resources available in many communities are forest lands, wild life, and mineral deposits . . . The teacher of chemistry may be anxious to develop an understanding of the properties of metals obtainable from near-by deposits ; a teacher of physics may use the mechanical methods used in removing the metals from below the surface of the ground . . ."

The community is not so remote as it may seem. The school building and grounds are rich sources for physics experiences. The students learn from the household equipment—washing machines, ironers, electric and gas ranges, vacuum cleaners—found in the homemaking department, or from the machines and tools—motors, lathes, drill presses, sanders - in the industrial arts shop. The heating and ventilating, lighting, fire alarm, signal and time control systems of the school are available resources. The projection equipment, the stage lighting and scenery management provisions of the auditorium are sources of physics information. An extensive series of "field trips" can be arranged or an entire unit of study developed around the mechanical arrangements and devices found inside the usual school building.

Many places outside the school in the larger community are available for physics experiences ; a small number is listed. Many more items that are found in each local community can be added to the following list :

- Airport
- Bank vaults, alarm systems
- Electric power plant
- Garages, machine shops
- Gas plant
- Hospital, X-ray equipment
- Industrial plants
- Observatory
- Optical companies
- Photographer
- Planetarium
- Radio repair shops
- Radio station, transmitter
- Railroad shops and yards
- Refrigeration plant
- Shipyard
- Telegraph office
- Telephone exchange
- Television studio
- Theaters, projection equipment
- Water works
- Weather bureau

CHECK LIST OF PHYSICS FACILITIES

1. Does the room orientation meet local needs most satisfactorily with reference to floor location, adjacent resources, and direction the room (or rooms) face ?

2. Is there provision for accessory space for (*a*) the instructor, (*b*) preparation, and (*c*) storage ?

3. Will the type of room layout serve satisfactorily the kinds of activities to be utilized in physics teaching ?

4. Do the room layout and the furniture make possible a ready transition from one kind of activity to another ?

5. Is there provision for centers in the physics room such as those for reading, construction, and weather study ?

6. Do the service facilities provide for running water, gas, and electricity, both a.c. and d.c. at various voltages ?

7. Is there adequate distribution of service facilities in the working areas ?

8. Do the storage facilities provide adequately for all types of stored material ?

9. Are the storage facilities flexible ?

10. What resources of school and community have been provided for in planning for physics facilities ?

11. Has the planning been studied with the safety of students and teachers in mind ?

12. Are the apparatus and materials essential to the teaching of physics provided ?

13. Are adequate audio-visual resources provided ?

BIBLIOGRAPHY

1. American Association of School Administrators, *American School Buildings*. Twenty-Seventh Yearbook. Washington, D. C., The Association, 1949.
2. Behrens, R. H., "The Planning and Equipment of a Photographic Classroom," *American School Board Journal* 114 : 46-47, February, 1947.
3. Clapp, Wilfred E. and Lawrence B. Perkins, "Designing the School Plant for Multiple Use," *The American School and University*. Eighteenth Edition, 1946. pp. 69-74.
4. Committee on Science Education in American Schools, *Science Education in American Schools*. Forty-Sixth Yearbook, Part I, of the National Society for the Study of Education. University of Chicago Press, 1947.
5. Committee on the Teaching of Science, *A Program for Teaching Science*. Thirty-First Yearbook, Part I, of the National Society for the Study of Education. Public School Publishing Company, Bloomington, III., 1932.

6. Dolloff, Norman H. and others, "Facilities for Correlated Work in the Sciences and Arts," *American School and University.* Fifteenth Edition, 1943. pp. 193-195.
7. Engelhardt, N. L., Sr., N. L. Engelhardt, Jr. and Stanton Leggett, *Planning Secondary School Buildings.* New York : Reinhold Publishing Corporation, 1949.
8. National Council on Schoolhouse Construction, Plant Guide Committee, *Guide for Planning School Plants.* The Council, Nashville, 1949.
9. Perkins, Lawrence B. and Walter D. Cocking, *Schools.* New York ; Reinhold Publishing Corporation, 1949.

3

Advanced Physical Science

INTRODUCTION

This course in advanced physical science is designed for those pupils in the eleventh or twelfth grade in the average high school who will probably find it their terminal course in formal science instruction. Their needs are not preparatory for advanced training in science, but are the needs of the average citizen in everyday life. An effort has been made to select subject content and activities that will aid pupils to recognize and solve many problems of daily living by practical applications of science.

There are many high-school pupils who plan to continue their formal education in fields other than science or any of its related fields. Many of these pupils realize the need for some knowledge of science for living in a highly scientific culture. It is the belief of the committee that the technical training of the formal sciences may contribute to the purposes of general education but that a mastery of the mass of theoretical material which they require is not essential in solving most science problems in everyday situations.

There is still another group of pupils that must be served in Missouri. There are many small high schools that do not have enough pupils to warrant the teaching of the more specialized science courses but that do have pupils who are interested in the continued study of the natural sciences. Through a course of this type the pupil in the small school may continue the study of scientific materials useful in his daily living.

The pupil is a potential consumer of countless articles and materials of varying costs, quality, and adaptability which will vitally affect his health, finances, and general well-being. This course is designed to inform the pupil about those products of science which will fulfill his needs to the best advantage. The origin of these products from natural resources and the conservation of resources are developed in parallel. The fulfillment of this objective can be achieved only by carefully developing the scientific method with pupils.

The pupil should secure considerable scientific information and a knowledge of its application in this course in advanced physical science to the end that he may understand more completely the applied science with which he must deal every day and the applications of science that appear in the literature that he will read.

Course Objectives

1. To help pupils develop intelligent attitudes and habits of scientific thinking and behaviour.
2. To develop an appreciation of the cause and effect relationships in nature, so that the individual may be freed from fears, superstitions, and ignorant practices.
3. To acquaint pupils with the contributions of science to their daily lives and to assist in the intelligent use of scientific products.
4. To help pupils acquire a functional understanding of the basic principles of science through old and new experiences.

List of Illustrative Units in Advanced Physical Science

Unit I—Natural Resources and Their Conservation
Unit II—Using Science in Planning and Building a House
Unit III—Using Fuels to Produce Heat and Power

Unit IV—Making Water More Useful
Unit V—Making Electricity Serve Man
Unit VI—Science Aids in Communication
Unit VII—Science Aids in Transportation
Unit VIII—Scientific Facts Man Needs to Know About Textiles
Unit IX—Science Contributes to Health

NATURAL RESOURCES AND THEIR CONSERVATION

I. SCOPE AND PURPOSE

A. Introduction

We are entirely dependent upon nature for all of the things we enjoy. The food we eat and the clothes we wear are produced from plants and animals which depend directly or indirectly upon the soil. Our tools and machines are made from the materials of mines and forests. Our automobiles and airplanes are driven by gasoline and lubricated by oil which comes from the petroleum pumped from great depths below the earth's surface. Even our books and newspapers are made from plant tissue and are therefore indirectly products of the land. Everything that makes our civilization possible is processed from things that grow on the surface of the earth or from minerals stored in its crust. In order to save all the natural resources it would be necessary to stop using them. This would mean that modern peoples would have to give up their present way of living—their great variety of foods, their comfortable homes, their automobiles, trains, and factories—and go back to a primitive civilization. We must use our natural resources, but we must use them wisely; that is, we must use them so as to bring the greatest benefit to the greatest number of people for the longest period of time. The selfish demands of individuals and groups must be controlled.

In our mad haste to utilize the vast resources of the country, we have wasted them; we have depleted our supply of many and almost completely destroyed others. America has earned the reputation of being the most wasteful country in the world. Abundance has been the agency of its own destruction. To the early pioneers, nature's great storehouse seemed inexhaustible. The result has been exploitation instead of efficient utilization.

There are three principal classes of resources : (1) Those which are nondestructible, such as water and air. These resources cannot be conserved because they cannot be destroyed. The central problem is to use them as often and as completely as possible. (2) Those which are destructible and non-renewable—the minerals. (The soil is partly renewable.) We cannot save these materials, but we can use them efficiently. (3) Those which are destructible but renewable—the plants and animals. It is with this group that the great accomplishment of restoration is possible.

Of all the resources the soil is the most important. Nature requires about 500 years to build an inch of top soil, and man can, in two or three generations, render useless the soil which nature has been thousands of years building.

The forests have been used so rapidly that less than half of the original timber is left for future use. However, the forests can be partially restored if the problem is attacked seriously before the soil is too far gone.

In the case of the minerals the two problems are to reduce waste and to prolong the period of usefulness as much as possible. As the mineral resources are depleted it may be necessary to readjust our whole civilization so that we become more dependent on those resources which are renewable and less dependent on those which are non-renewable.

Destruction of natural resources in excess of prudent current consumption is waste. Prudent use of natural resources with restoration whenever possible means conservation. Young persons should recognize and appreciate the need of conservation. Another fifty years like the last half century and it may be too late.

Since no textbook on the secondary level attacks the conservation problem directly, the teacher must use material from many sources. Field trips to farm, woodland, or mine will prove valuable in teaching this unit. A number of learning activities have been suggested and teachers may develop others which are better adapted to the particular interests and needs of their pupils.

B. Unit Objectives

1. To develop in pupils an appreciation of the importance of natural resources to man.
2. To help pupils understand some of the major factors which have been responsible for the depletion of the natural resources of America.
3. To give pupils a working knowledge of some of the principles involved in the conservation, restoration, and management of natural resources.
4. To direct pupils in their efforts to attack conservation problems which exist in their own community.

II. SUGGESTED CONTENT

A. What are the Natural Resources ?

1. What resources are indestructible ?
2. What resources are destructible and non-renewable ?
3. What resources are destructible and renewable ?
4. What is the central problem in the conservation of each of the above classes of resources ?
5. Is our present industrial organization—factories, transporation, mining, etc.—more dependent upon renewable or non-renewable resources ?
6. How is this dependence related to the whole problem of conservation ?

B. What are the Three Main Problems in Dealing with Natural Resources ?

1. What is "conservation" ? In the narrower sense ? In the broader sense ?
2. What is meant by "restoration"?
3. What is "management" ?
4. How are these three special problems related to each other ?

5. What resources cannot be restored ?
6. Explain what is meant by efficient use of resources.

C. How Does the Present Extent of Natural Resources in the United States Compare with the Original Extent of These Resources ?

1. How does the present production capacity of the soil compare with the original production capacity ?
2. What did the pioneer farmer do when his farm began to show a decline in fertility ?
3. What alternatives do present-day farmers have when their soil becomes too poor for profitable cultivation ?
4. Where were the principal original forest areas ?
5. About how much of the original forests remain ?
6. Are the remaining forest lands equal, acre for acre, to the original forest lands on the basis of quantity and quality of the timber ?
7. Compare the original supply of minerals with present available deposits.
8. Which minerals are still most abundant ? Which ones might be depleted in a few more centuries ?
9. Has there been a general increase or decrease in wildlife ?
10. What game animals and birds did the early American colonists find in abundance ?
11. What species have almost completely disappeared ?
12. How do rivers compare with their original fitness for navigation ? As a habitat for water life ?

D. How May the Soil be Conserved ?

1. What is the composition of the soil ?
   (*a*) What are the principal plant nutrients ?
   (*b*) How do rocks become soil ?
   (*c*) What are the two sources of organic matter ?
      (1) How is organic matter related to soil fertility ?
      (2) How is organic matter related to the water holding capacity of the soil ?
2. What are the two factors in the depletion of soil fertility ?

3. What are the two kinds of soil erosion ? Which kind is more common ?

4. What are the factors which determine how badly a soil will wash ?

5. What are the principal methods of checking soil erosion ?

6. How may soil fertility be maintained ?
   - (*a*) What are the characteristics of good crop rotation ?
   - (*b*) What are "green manure" crops ?
   - (*c*) How do legume plants add nitrogen to the soil ? What is inoculation ?
   - (*d*) What advantage has livestock farming over grain farming in the maintenance of fertility ?
   - (*e*) Which of the plant nutrients is most likely to be lacking in Missouri soil ?
   - (*f*) How is soil fertility related to soil erosion ?
   - (*g*) Why is lime so important in improving soil fertility ?
   - (*h*) What are the final criteria in determining whether or not the use of commercial fertilizer on a certain farm is practicable ?

7. What are the three movements of soil water ?
   - (*a*) What is "capillarity" ?
   - (*b*) What is "percolation" ?
   - (*c*) What is "runoff" ?

8. What is the relationship between soil conservation and (1) water conservation, (2) forest conservation, (3) wildlife management, and (4) mineral conservation ?

E. What are Some Major Problems in Conserving Our Water Resources ?

1. What is the "water cycle" ?
2. What are the water resources ?
3. What are the most important uses of water ?
   - (*a*) Why is water directly related to the productivity of the soil ?

(*b*) What is the approximate water content of plant and animal tissue ?

(*c*) What is the importance of water in manufacturing enterprises ?

(*d*) What part does water play in modern transportation ?

4. What are the special problems in the conservation and utilization of water resources ?

(*a*) How can greater uniformity of stream flow be secured ?

(*b*) What are some of the principles involved in flood control ?

(*c*) How can streams be developed for power without destroying their value for other purposes ?

(*d*) How can streams be protected from silting ?

(*e*) What are the principal sources of pollution of water ?

(*f*) How can water power be used to conserve the fuel minerals ?

(*g*) How can streams be improved as habitats for wildlife ?

5. How is water conservation related to ; (1) erosion control, (2) flood control, (3) forest conservation, (4) the conservation of minerals, and (5) wildlife management ?

F. How May Forest Resources be Better Conserved ?

1. What are the principal uses of wood ?
2. How does the annual production of timber compare with the demand for timber products ?
3. What are the principal factors which have been responsible for the depletion of forest resources ?
4. What are some of the principles involved in the conservation and restoration of forests ?
5. How is forest conservation related to : (1) soil conservation, (2) water conservation, (3) conservation of minerals, and (4) wildlife management ?

G. What Procedures are Being Taken for Wildlife Management ?

1. What are the three essentials for the production of all wildlife ?
2. What are the principal ways in which wildlife is of value to man ?
3. Why is destruction of habitat the greatest cause for the depletion of wildlife ?
4. What can individuals and groups do to improve the natural habitat ?
5. Why is man justified in taking for useful purposes all animals in excess of the number which can survive under natural conditions ?
6. Why would the complete abolition of hunting and fishing fail to guarantee a large increase in all wildlife ?
7. Why does restocking an area faill to bring about a permanent increase in the population of a given species when there is not a corresponding improvement in habitat ?
8. Why is the building of power and flood control dams sometimes detrimental to the fish population of streams ?
9. How is wildlife management related to : (1) soil conservation, (2) water conservation, and (3) forest conservation ?

H. What are Some Basic Problems in the Conservation of Minerals ?

1. What are the two general classes of minerals ?
   (*a*) What are the fuel minerals ?
   (*b* What are the metallic minerals ?
2. Why is efficient use rather than conservation the basic problem in the management of fuel minerals ?
3. Why is the conservation of the metallic minerals possible to a greater extent than the conservation of the fuel minerals ?
4. Why is the problem of the conservation of minerals more difficult than the problem of water, forest, and wildlife conservation ?

5. How has civilization become more and more dependent upon mineral resources ?

6. What are some of the major factors which have hastened the depletion of the mineral resources ?
   (*a*) What is meant by exploitation of resources ?
   (*b*) Are most of the mineral deposits under public or private ownership" ?
   (*c*) How is this fact related to the problem of exploitation ?

7. If substitutes are to be used for minerals, from what class of resources must these substances come ?
   (*a*) Why would the increased use of substitutes make the problem of soil conservation more difficult ?

8. What are the principal rock resources ?
   (*a*) For what is limestone used ?
   (*b*) For what is marble used ?
   (*c*) For what is granite used ?

III. LEARNING ACTIVITIES

A. Teaching Procedures

1. Show the film, *Back to Missouri*, Missouri Conservation Commission, three reels, 16 mm. (sound). This film will be excellent in presenting the problem of conservation in Missouri and the work of the Conservation Commission.

2. Take pupils on a field trip to visit a game conservation project or a game preserve if one is nearby.

3. Take pupils on a field trip to a farm where projects on soil conservation such as damming gullies, contour plowing, seeding hillsides, etc. are being carried out.

4. Collect a classroom library of bulletins on conservation issued by the United States Department of Agriculture and the Missouri Conservation Commission.

5. Invite a county agriculture extension agent and a state game conservation agent to speak to the class on soil and game conservation.

6. Organize a class project on game conservation under the Edward K. Love Foundation Program through the Missouri Conservation Commission.

B. Pupil Activities

1. Examine the lower side of a rocky ledge and note the accumulation of small particles of rock. Look for places in which decaying leaves are mixed with the rock materials.
2. Visit a wood and examine the layers of decaying leaves. Take soil samples to a depth of a foot and notice the humus or organic matter, which has accumulated in the soil as a result of vegetable decay.
3. Fill one test tube with air-dried soil from the woods. Put in another test tube the same amount of dry soil from a field which has long been cropped. How do the soil samples compare in colour ? Why ? Pour into each soil all the water which it will hold. Which will hold the most ? Why ?
4. Observe a steep field that has been cultivated for several years. Observe a similar slope which has been kept in grass or timber. Which field shows the greatest extent of erosion damage ?
5. Secure from the College of Agriculture, University of Missouri, a bottle of Comber's acidity reagent and, test soil samples from several fields to determine the calcium content of the land. Compare the tests made on samples from eroded cultivated fields with samples from virgin pastures.
6. Dig up roots of alfalfa, sweet clover, red clover, soy beans, cow peas, or vetch and see if you can find the tiny nodules. What do these nodules contain ?
7. Observe fields on which terracing, strip cropping, or contour farming has been practiced.
8. Observe a steep slope from which the timber has been removed, and observe a similar slope which is still well covered with timber. Which one shows the greater extent of erosion ?

9. Make a survey of the water resources of your community—springs, rivers, creeks, lakes, or large ponds. Do fish or waterfowl inhabit any of these bodies of water.
10. Observe any ponds which farmers in your community may have built for erosion control. What other purposes do these ponds serve ?
11. After a heavy rain visit a ditch which passes through steep land from which the timber has been removed. Observe a similar ditch which has a timbered watershed. Which stream has the greater volume of flow ? Which has the greater velocity of flow ?
12. After a heavy rain observe deposits of silt in a ditch or creek bed. From where did this soil come ?
13. Visit a place where sewage is being emptied into a stream. What effect does this material have upon the life of the stream ?
14. Examine the water in a ditch which drains cultivated land. Examine the water in a ditch leaving a grass and tree covered watershed. What difference do you notice between the water of the two ditches ? Secure a quart of water from each ditch and allow it to settle for an hour. Which contains the more sediment ?
15. Make a check list of all the trees found in your community. How many of these can you identify ? Learn to identify the more common of these trees.
16. Make a leaf chart for your schoolroom.
17. Observe your community to determine the abundance or scarcity of timber. Are there any areas from which the timber has been completely removed ? Is any timber or brush land being cleared for cultivation.
18. Visit a wood and observe the kinds of animals and birds which are present. Do the same for an open field. Which habitat has the more wildlife ?
19. Visit a wood and notice the amount of dead wood on the ground and the number of dead trees. For what purposes could such wood be used ?

20. Learn the proper way to transplant young trees and then set out some young trees at your school or at your homes.
21. Collect samples of various kinds of wood found in your community.
22. Determine what game and fur animals are present in your community.
23. See how many different kinds of animals you can observe.
24. Observe the birds of your community—their colour, markings, songs, nesting places, feeding habits, and habits of migration. Learn to identify some birds with which you are not familiar.
25. Build some bird houses for your school or homes.
26. Put up a feeding table at some appropriate place in the school yard and put out feed for birds during the winter.
27. Visit a fur dealer and find out which pelts are bought in largest numbers. Also find out the comparative values of the various pelts.
28. Secure from the Missouri Conservation Commission a copy of *Wildlife and Forestry Code*. Learn the dates for legal hunting and fishing which apply to the species found in your community.
29. Observe your community to determine whether it is a suitable habitat for wildlife. Note especially the three essentials—food, cover, and water.
30. Start a collection of animal and bird pictures.
31. If there are any mines in your community, learn all you can about the various mining operation.
32. Visit a rock quarry and learn how the stone is prepared for commercial purposes.
33. Examine several pieces of coal and see if you can find pieces of wood which are not completely transformed. Look for traces of leaf marks in the coal.
34. Make a collection of rocks and other minerals.

IV. BIBLIOGRAPHY

A. General References

1. Chase, Stuart, *Rich Land, Poor Land*, McGraw-Hill, 1936.
2. Gustafson, A. F., Guise, C. H., Hamilton, W. J., and Ries, H., *Conservation in the United States*, Comstock, 1936.
3. Heiss, David Elwood, Obourn, E. S., and Manzer, J. G., *Our World of Living Things*, Webster, 1936.
4. Hessler, John Charles, and Shoudy, H. C., *Understanding our Environment*, Sanborn, 1939.
5. Hunter, George William, and Whitman, W. G., *Science in our World of Progress*, American, 1935.
6. Lawson, Floyd Melvin, and Lawson, V. K., *Our America*, Heath, 1938.
7. Moon, *Biology for Beginners*, Henry Holt, 1926.
8. Pieper, Charles John, Beauchamp. W. L., and Frank, O. D., *Everyday Problems in Biology*, Scott, Foresman, 1932.
9. Trafton, Gilbert Haven, and Smith, V. C., *Science in Everyday Life*, Lippincott, 1936.
10. Watkins, Ralph K., and Bedell, R. C., *General Science for Today*, Macmillan, 1936.
11. Watkins, Ralph K., and Perry, Winifred, *Science for Human Control*, Macmillan, 1940.
12. Wheat, Frank Merrill, and Fitzpatrick. E. T., *General Biology*, American, 1932.
13. *World Book*, (see conservation).
14. *Encyclopedia Britanica*, (see conservation).
15. *Encyclopedia Americana*, (see conservation).

B. Soil

1. Baker, O. E., *A Graphic Summary of Physical Features and Land Utilization in the United States*, U. S. Department of Agriculture, Miscellaneous Publication 260.
2. Bauer, *Soil Erosion in Missouri*. University of Missouri Agriculture Experiment Station, Bulletin 349, 1935.

3. *Conserving Corn Belt Soil*, U. S. Department of Agriculture, Bulletin 1795, 1937.

4. *Conserving Soil by Contour Farming*, University of Missouri Agriculture Experiment Station, Bulletin E 399.

5. *Conserving Soils by Strip Cropping*, University of Missouri Agriculture Experiment Station, Bulletin E 368.

6. *Cropping Systems in Relation to Erosion Control*, University of Missouri Agriculture Experiment Station, Bulletin 366.

7. "New Life for a Million Acres," *Readers Digest*, December, 1938.

8. "Silt In Reservoirs," *Nature Magazine*, March, 1938.

9. *Soil and Water Conservation in the Northern Great Plains*, Soil Conservation Service, Region 9, U. S. Department of Agriculture, 1937.

10. *Soil Fertility Losses Under Missouri Conditions*, University of Missouri Agriculture Experiment Station, Bulletin 324.

11. *Terracing, An Important Step in Erosion Control*, University of Missouri Agriculture Experiment Station, Bulletin E 400.

12. *Using Limestone on Missouri Soils*, University of Missouri Agriculture Experiment Station, Bulletin E 399.

C. Water

1. Clark, M. W., *Farm Ponds in Missouri*, University of Missouri Agriculture Experiment Station, Bulletin 351.

2. Ellis, M. M., *Detection and Measurement of Stream Pollution*, Bulletin 48. U. S. Bureau of Fisheries, 1937.

3. Pearson, H. S., *Little Waters—Their Use and Relations to the Land*, U. S. Soil Conservation Service, U. S. Department of Agriculture.

4. Skilling, William Thompson, *Tours Through the World of Science*, McGraw-Hill, 1933.

5. Vogt, William, *Thirst on the Land*, Circular 32, National Association of Audubon Societies.
6. *Water Resources of Missouri*, Missouri Conservation Commission, Jefferson City, 1939.

D. Forests

1. Baker, Arthur O., and Mills, L. H., *Dynamic Biology*, Rand McNally, 1938.
2. Board, W. P., *Forest Conservation*, U. S. Department of Agriculture Forest Service.
3. Edgerton, D. Priscilla, *The Forest : A Handbook for Teachers*, U. S. Department of Agriculture, Miscellaneous Circular 98, 1927.
4. Gabrielson, *The Correlation of Forestry and Wildlife Management*, U. S. Department of Agriculture Biological Survey, 1936.
5. Kinsey, Alfred C., *New Introduction to Biology*, Lippincott, 1933.
6. Mank, Helen, *The Living World*, Sanborn, 1933.
7. Skilling, William Thompson, *Tours Through the World of Science*, McGraw-Hill, 1933.
8. Smallwood, William Martin, Reveley, I. L., and Bailey, G. A., *New General Biology*, Allyn and Bacon, 1929.
9. How to Plant Small Trees, University of Missouri Agriculture Experiment Station, Bulletin E 342.
10. *The Planting and Care of Forest Trees on Missouri Farms.* University of Missouri Agriculture Experiment Station, Bulletin No. E 409.
11. *Tree Planting for Erosion Control*, University of Missouri Agriculture Experiment Station, Bulletin E 345.
12. *Tree Windbreaks for Missouri Farms*, University of Missouri Agriculture Experiment Station, Bulletin E 343.
13. Wheat, Frank Merrill, and Fitzpatrick, E. F., *General Biology*, American, 1932.
14. White, *Forest Trees of Missouri*, Missouri Conservation Commission Bulletin No. 20, 1939.

E. Minerals

1. Ely, N., *Oil Conservation Through Interstate Agreement.* U. S. Federal Oil Conservation Board, Washington, D. C., 1938.
2. Leith, C. K., "Mineral Resources and Peace," *Foreign Affairs*, Vol. 16, April, 1938.
3. McQueen and Grohshopf, *Mineral Production in Missouri*, Missouri Geological Survey, Bulletin, 1935.
4. "National Mineral Policy Proposed," *Engineering and Mining Journal* ; Vol. 136, 1938.
5. Public Relations Program for the Mining Industry, *Engineering and Mining Journal*, Vol. 139, 1938.
6. Skilling, William Thompson, *Tours Through the World of Science*, McGraw-Hill, 1933.

F. Wildlife

1. Baker, Arthur O., and Mills, L. H., *Dynamic Biology*, Rand McNally, 1938.
2. Bennitt, Rudolph, *An Introduction to Bird Study in Missouri*, Missouri Conservation Commission, Jefferson City, 1939.
3. Bennitt, Rudolph, *List of Missouri Mammals*, Missouri Conservation Commission, Jefferson City, 1939.
4. Kinsey, Alfred C., *New Introduction to Biology*, Lippincott, 1933.
5. McAtee, W. L., *Usefulness of Birds on the Farm*, U. S. Department of Agriculture, Farmers Bulletin 1682, 1931.
6. McAtee, W. L., *Groups of Plants Valuable for Wildlife Utilization and Erosion Control*, 1936.
7. Mank, Helen, *The Living World*, Sanborn, 1933.
8. Nagel, W. O., "Objectives for the Education of Youth in Wildlife Conservation," *School and Community*, March, 1940.

V. EVALUATION

A. Observational Questions in Terms of Objectives

1. Do pupils seem aware of the need for conservation of our natural resources ?

2. Do pupils recognize the significance of natural resources to our national economy ?
3. Are pupils familiar with the work of the United States Department of Agriculture in soil conservation ?
4. Are pupils familiar with the purposes and program of the Missouri Conservation Commission ?
5. Are pupils familiar with the services of the College of Agriculture of the University of Missouri in conservation work ?
6. Have pupils shown enough interest in conservation to undertake any projects in this work ?
7. Do pupils recognize the interrelationship of soil, forest, game, and other conservation problems ?

B. Sample Testing Items and Procedures

True-false statements

......1. Conservation means the wise use of resources.

......2. Three fourths of the original forests in America still remain.

......3. All of our food and clothing comes directly or indirectly from the soil.

......4. Destructible resources cannot be renewed.

......5. Civilization may need to become more dependent upon renewable resources and less dependent upon non-renewable resources.

......6. Exploitation means excessive and wasteful use of resources for selfish interests.

Completion items

1. Legumes add...........to the soil through the action of bacteria.
2. The two kinds of erosion are :

   (*a*) ....

   (*b*) ....
3. The releasing of artificially reared animals on an area is known as...........
4. The damaging of streams by sewage, mine seepage, and industrial wastes is known as...........

UNIT I

4

Using Science in Planning and Buiding a House

1. SCOPE AND PURPOSE

A. Introduction

Many people have occasion at some time or other to build or remodel a house. Building is one of the biggest industries in the world and employs a large number of draftsmen, engineers, mechanics, and laborers. Because nearly everyone will have an opportunity to do or to have done some type of home construction work (building, reparing, or redecorating) and because of the importance of the building industry, this unit is presented to acquaint pupils with some of the problems of building and with the contributions of science to building.

It is not the purpose of this unit to present highly technical information or to attempt to develop specialized skills used in building. It is designed primarily to assist pupils to become more intelligent consumers of building materials and of the services of architects, contractors, and building mechanics. It is also designed to familiarize pupils with some of the principles of science used in building and with the composition and methods of manufacturing building materials.

Such things as insulating a house, humidity control, heating, prevention of wall cracking, roof construction, proper bracing and foundations, types and costs of materials, planning a house, sources of advice and information, judging a good mechanic, decorating, and protecting against decay and other deterioration can be intelligently attacked with the aid of science.

B. Unit Objectives

1. To acquaint pupils with sources of advice and information on problems related to the construction and repair of houses.
2. To acquaint pupils with materials used in building a house.
3. To present some of the scientific principles and information essential in house construction.
4. To assist pupils to gain a knowledge of types of design and construction for houses.
5. To acquaint pupils with methods of financing the building or purchase of a house.
6. To acquaint pupils with the parts of a house and the construction problems peculiar to each part.

II. SUGGESTED CONTENT

A. What are the Problems to be Studied and Sources of Information in Planning a House ?

1. Problems to consider
   (*a*) Size and type of house desired
   (*b*) Location and cost of lot—zoning requirements
   (*c*) Estimated costs of house
   (*d*) Means of financing—per cent of income required
   (*e*) Developing plans—employing an architect
   (*f*) Finding a reliable contractor.

2. Sources of information
   (*a*) Current periodicals, books, and government bulletins on housing
   (*b*) A competent architect
   (*c*) Dealers in lumber and other materials
   (*d*) A competent contractor
   (*e*) Home owners who have built recently.

B. What Are Some Properties, Advantages, and Limitations of Various Building Materials ?

1. Wood
   - (*a*) Properties which make wood a good building material
   - (*b*) Some limitations of wood as a building material
   - (*c*) Kinds of wood used in building houses
   - (*d*) Grades of lumber.
2. Brick, tile, and concrete blocks
   - (*a*) Methods of making different types of bricks
     - (1) Advantages of bricks for houses
     - (2) Limitations of bricks for houses
     - (3) Chemical properties of bricks.
   - (*b*) Methods of making tile, and kinds of tile
     - (1) Advantages of tile
     - (2) Limitations of tile
     - (3) Chemical properties of tile.
   - (*c*) Methods of making, and kinds of concrete blocks
     - (1) Advantages of concrete blocks
     - (2) Limitations of concrete blocks.
3. Concrete, cement, and plaster
   - (*a*) Uses for concrete and cement in building a house
   - (*b*) Proper mixtures for concrete and cement
   - (*c*) Composition of concrete and cement
   - (*d*) Uses of plaster in building a house
   - (*e*) Kinds of plaster—proper mixtures for plaster
   - (*f*) Composition and manufacture of lime.
4. Natural stone
   - (*a*) Sources and kinds of natural stone
   - (*b*) Advantages of natural stone in building houses
   - (*c*) Limitations of natural stone in building houses
   - (*d*) Chemical properties of natural stone used in building.
5. Metals
   - (*a*) Uses for metals in building a house
   - (*b*) Kinds of metals used in building a house

- (*c*) Methods of mining and preparing metals used in building a house.

6. Special composition materials
   - (*a*) Types of wallboard and uses
   - (*b*) Types of insulating materials and uses
   - (*c*) Types of roofing
   - (*d*) Types of flooring
   - (*e*) Advantages and limitations of composition materials
   - (*f*) Methods of manufacturing various composition materials.
7. Glass
   - (*a*) Manufacture and composition of glass
   - (*b*) Uses of glass in building a house.

C. How Are Houses Classified According to Construction ?

1. Frame
   - (*a*) Advantages
   - (*b*) Limitations.
2. Nonfireproof
   - (*a*) Advantages
   - (*b*) Limitations.
3. Fireproof
   - (*a*) Advantages
   - (*b*) Limitations.

D What Are the Parts of a House which Require Major Attention in Building ?

1. Building the basement
   - (*a*) Planning the basement
   - (*b*) Excavating
   - (*c*) Finishing the basement—types of walls—thickness of walls—use for foundation
   - (*d*) Provision for proper drainage.
2. Building the foundation
   - (*a*) Planning—load to be carried—size of footings
   - (*b*) Use of basement walls for foundation
   - (*c*) Materials for the foundation

(1) Concrete
(2) Concrete blocks
(3) Brick
(4) Tile.

(*d*) Use of beams, pillars, and bridging

(1) Types of beams—stress and strains to be resisted—relative strength of beams of different shapes and sizes—wooden, steel, and concrete beams
(2) Bridging—types of geometrical figures for maximum rigidity.

3. Building the walls and roof

(*a*) Frame walls
(1) Construction
(2) Insulating
(3) Advantages and limitations.

(*b*) Brick veneer walls
(1) Construction
(2) Insulating
(3) Advantages and limitations.

(*c*) Solid walls—brick—stone.

(*d*) Pre-fabricated
(1) Steel
(2) Cement
(3) Others.

(*e*) Constructing the roof
(1) Materials
(2) Types of construction.

(*f*) Painting and preserving walls and roofs
(1) Types of outside paint—composition of good paints—manufacture of lead and linseed oil, uses—costs
(2) Roof stains—composition—uses—costs.

4. Windows

(*a*) Types of windows—costs
(*b*) Methods of preventing drafts

(*c*) Placing windows and ratio of window space to floor space
(*d*) Storm windows and doors—costs
(*e*) Screens—costs.

5. Plumbing
(*a*) Planning arrangement of fixtures, drains, traps, vents, etc.
(*b*) Types of metals used in plumbing
(*c*) Costs of pipes and fixtures
(*d*) Plumbing regulations.

6. Electrical wiring and outlets
(*a*) Planning the location of outlets—types of outlets
(*b*) Metals used in wiring
(*c*) Kinds of wiring—parallel—series—safeguards
(*d*) Wiring for power, for heating, and for lights
(*e*) Costs of electricity for power, heating, and lights
(*f*) The construction of switchboards, meters, fuses, etc.

7. Making walls beautiful
(*a*) Kinds of plaster
(*b*) Finishes for plaster—smooth, sand, special
(*c*) Types of lathing—metal—wood
(*d*) Composition wallboard
(*e*) Painting.
(1) How paints are made
(2) Composition of good paints—interior
(*a*) Pigments—composition of white lead, etc.
(*b*) Vehicles—composition of linseed and synthetic oils
(*c*) Driers—Japan, turpentine, synthetic.
(3) Number of undercoats and finishing coats needed
(4) Water colours and sizing—composition and application
(5) Kinds of wall finishes—flat, gloss, tiffany, etc.
(*f*) Papering
(1) Manufacturing and composition of wallpaper
(2) Types of hanging—lap work and butt work
(3) Oilcloth and canvas.

8. Making woodwork and floors beautiful
   (*a*) Kinds of woods used for woodwork—soft and hard woods
   (*b*) Kinds of woods used for floors
   (*c*) Finishing woodwork
      (1) Shellac and varnishes—manufacture and composition—uses
      (2) Enamels—manufacture and composition—uses
      (3) Lacquers—manufacture and composition—uses
      (4) Stains—composition—kinds—uses.
   (*d*) Finishing floors
      (1) Hardwood— sanding— filling— finishes, wax and varnish
      (2) Softwood—sanding—base—varnish
      (3) Linoleum—manufacture— composition— uses —costs
      (4) Tile—uses—costs.
   (*e*) Importance of good sub-flooring and method of laying.
9. Methods of heating the house
   (*a*) Hot air—advantages and limitations—types of systems—costs
   (*b*) Stoves—advantages and limitations—costs
   (*c*) Hot water—advantages and limitations—costs
   (*d*) Steam—advantages and limitations—costs
   (*e*) Gas and oil—advantages and limitations—costs
   (*f*) Fireplaces—advantages and limitations—construction.

E. How are Buildings Made Strong ?

1. Principles of mechanics to be considered
   (*a*) Forces acting on a house or building
   (*b*) Geometrical designs which secure rigidity
   (*c*) How braces strengthen a house
   (*d*) How arches give strength
   (*e*) How trusses support weight.
2. How parts of buildings are held together.

III. LEARNING ACTIVITIES

A. Problems to be Studied and Sources of Information in Planning a House

1. Teaching procedures
   (*a*) The teacher should enlist the aid of trained and competent builders who are available in most communities in teaching this unit. Invite an architect, contractor, carpenter, mason, electrician, plasterer, painter, and plumber to visit the class problems in their fields in building a house.
   (*b*) Collect books, magazines, and bulletins issued by the United States Department of Commerce and by manufacturers for a classroom library.
   (*c*) Ask a person in your community who has recently built a house to discuss some of the problems from the viewpoint of the owner or consumer.
   (*d*) A number of films and slides are available on construction work. Show one or two of these as a means of stimulating interest in the unit.
   (*e*) Invite the industrial arts instructor of the local school to give some elementary instruction in drawing plans and reading blueprints.
2. Pupil activities
   (*a*) Sketch front and side elevations for a five-room house.
   (*b*) Draw rough floor plans for a five-room house.
   (*c*) Make a report on the building regulations for your city.
   (*d*) Report on zoning restrictions in different parts of your city.
   (*e*) Prepare a list of factors which affect the valuation of residential properties.
   (*f*) Report on the training, wage scales, seasonal employment, working conditions, and other factors to be considered for some building trade.
   (*g*) Make a list of tradesmen needed to build a house.
   (*h*) Report on factors which affect building costs in different parts of the nation ; in the state.

(*i*) Visit a house under construction and sketch details of the various phases of construction such as the foundation, joists, beams, bridging, cross section of walls, roof construction, flooring, wiring, plumbing, heating system, etc.

(*j*) Make a model framework for a house.

3. Additional activities

(*a*) Draw plans for a recreation room in your basement.

(*b*) Draw plans for a sum porch for your house.

(*c*) Draw up a model building code for houses for your city.

(*d*) Draw plans and make blueprints for a double garage.

(*e*) Take snapshots of some attractive houses in your city and arrange them for a poster display.

B. Some Advantages and Limitations of Various Building Materials

1. Teaching procedures

(*a*) Take the class to visit a lumberyard, plumbing shop and paint store. Have someone who is familiar with the materials handled explain grades, quality, and prices of various materials to the class. Prepare carefully for these trips—give pupils study questions or outlines before the trips and request written reports or give an informal quiz after the trips.

(*b*) Work up improvised devices for testing crushing strengths and tensile strengths of various building materials. Test tensile strength of copper wire, steel, etc.

(*c*) Take a field trip to a brick or tile plant if one is near by. Have pupils report on the various processes observed.

(*d*) Demonstrate some of the means for purifying metals such as copper by means of electrolysis.

(*e*) Demonstrate the fireproof qualities of different types of building materials.
(*f*) Demonstrate the heat insulating properties of different building materials.
(*g*) Conduct experiments on cement and concrete. Use different types of mixtures and demonstrate relative strengths of these products.

2. Pupil activities

(*a*) Bring samples of various types of native building stone found in your neighbourhood to class. Test for chemical composition and crushing strength.
(*b*) Conduct an experiment to show the expansion of different metals used in building. Use a regular expansion apparatus from the physics laboratory if one is available.
(*c*) Make a brick or a piece of pottery. Try to put a glaze on it.
(*d*) Make some cement from limestone and clay.
(*e*) Heat some marble or limestone and test for carbon dioxide.
(*f*) Make a small reinforced concrete "T" beam and a square beam. Compare their tensile strengths. Compare also with wooden beams of the same sizes and shapes.
(*g*) Make a report on the manufacturing of cement in Missouri.
(*h*) Report on the mining of metals in Missouri which are used in building.

3. Additional activities

(*a*) Make a collection of various types of bricks used in building and arrange a display for the school.
(*b*) Make a collection of tile made in Missouri and arrange them for a school display.
(*c*) Make a concrete block.
(*d*) Make a report on the methods of testing building materials used by the United States Bureau of Standards.
(*e*) Report on the manufacturing of steel.

(*f*) Report on the manufacturing of white lead.

(*g*) Report on native lumber for building purposes found in Missouri.

(*h*) Report on glass manufacturing in Missouri.

C. How Houses Are Classified by Type of Construction

1. Teaching procedure

(*a*) Take the class to visit a frame house under construction.

(*b*) Take the class to visit a brick veneer house under construction or examine one in the community which is completed.

(*c*) Visit a solid stone or brick building under construction or examine one in the community which is completed.

(*d*) Visit an all-steel house or building.

(*e*) Invite the fire chief to discuss types of fireproof construction.

2. Pupil activities

(*a*) Build a small model of a wall for a frame house and test it for fire resistance.

(*b*) Heat pieces of sheet steel, concrete, brick, and stone. Note effects of high temperatures and sudden cooling.

(*c*) Report on fire losses for a one-year period in Missouri and secure data for the types of construction suffering the greatest losses.

(*d*) Survey your community and tabulate the number of houses and buildings of different types of construction.

(*e*) Secure estimates from lumber dealers and contractors on the relative costs of houses of different types of construction but of the same size.

D. Parts of a House

1. Teaching procedure

(*a*) Visit a building or house under construction and note the construction of the foundation and basement. Show methods of bracing and reinforcing a house. Note the footing used for the foundation. Try to find a house or building using steel beams ; point out the size and shape of these beams.

(b) Demonstrate the advantages of certain geometrical figures to secure rigidity. Call attention to the use of these figures in house construction and engineering.

(c) Have some of the boys of the class demonstrate how to lay bricks for a foundation out in the schoolyard.

(d) Ask some of the boys to construct a concrete bench or some other useful object as a special project.

(e) Take the class over the school building to note the type of construction, especially the frameworks, foundation, floors, and roof.

(f) Have some members of the class finish different types of lumber as a class demonstration.

(g) Have some members of the class test different kinds of paint for covering qualities, speed of drying, effect of sunlight, dull or gloss finish, etc.

(h) Build a $6' \times 8' \times 5'$ three-wall model room, with a two by two frame and wallboard walls, in the laboratory and wire it for various electrical outlets and switches. Demonstrate both parallel and series wiring.

(i) Pupils might finish the walls of this room and the woodwork as a class laboratory project.

(j) Demonstrate the electrical conductivity and resistance of different metals.

(k) Demonstrate the insulating properties against electricity of various substances.

2. Pupil activities

(a) Visit the basement of your home and draw a cross-sectional diagram showing method of construction.

(*b*) Visit the attic of your home and draw a cross-sectional diagram of its construction.

(*c*) Make a collection of different types of roofing and arrange them for a school display.

(*d*) Make a report on the suitability of various metals for plumbing.

(*e*) Test the rust resisting properties of iron, steel, stainless steel, copper, brass, lead, galvanized iron, and tin.

(*f*) Report to the class on methods for the purification of aluminum.

(*g*) Make some solder and solder flux in the laboratory. Use them in making a simple tin box, cookie cutter, or some other object.

(*h*) Test the degree of refraction for different types of glass.

3. Additional activities

(*a*) Make a model plumbing system for a five-room house from glass tubing.

(*b*) Report on methods of making shatterproof glass.

(*c*) Collect samples of different kinds of wallboard and arrange for a classroom display.

(*d*) Report on the manufacturing of turpentine.

(*e*) Report on the source and uses of tung oil.

(*f*) Mix some exterior paint from white lead and linseed oil. Add drier and colour it.

(*g*) Mix some interior flat wall paint.

(*h*) Visit a wallpaper shop and report on price range and quality of wallpaper.

(*i*) Report on the manufacturing of linoleum.

(*j*) Report on ways of eradicating termites and methods of protecting a house against termites.

IV. BIBLIOGRAPHY

1. Bush, George L., Ptacek, Theodore M., and Kovats, John, *Senior Science*, American, 1937, pp. 427-499.
2. Beery, Pauline, *Chemistry Applied to Home and Community*, Lippincott, 1926.

3. Beery, Pauline, *Stuff*, Appleton-Century, 1930.
4. Bulletins of the U.S. Bureau of Standards, Washington, D.C.
5. Clarke, Beverly L., *Marvels of Modern Chemistry*, Harpers, 1935, pp. 214-224.
6. Darrow, F.L., *The Story of Chemistry*, Harpers, 1932, pp. 423-428.
7. Foster, William, *The Romance of Chemistry*, Appleton-Century, 1936, pp. 173-187.
8. *How to Judge a House*, U.S. Dept. of Commerce Bulletin, 1931.
9. Howe, H.E., *Chemistry in the World Work*, Van Nostrand, 1926.
10. Hubbard, T.K., and Hubbard. H. V , *Our Cities Today and Tomorrow*, Harvard University Press, 1929.
11. Meade, R.K., *Portland Cement, It's Composition, R. Materials, Manufacture, Testing and Analysis*, Chemical Publishing Company, 1926.
12. Nole, J., *City Planning*, Appleton, 1916.
13. Riegel, E.R., *Industrial Chemisty*, Chemical Catalogue Company, 1933.
14. Rogers, Allen, *Manual of Industrial Chemistry*, Macmillan 1932, pp. 405-444.
15. Sadtler, S.S., *Chemistry of Familiar Things*, Lippincott, 1931.
16. Spring, L.W., *Nontechnical Charts on Iron and Steel*, Stockes, 1927.
17. *Tentative Standards*, American Society for Testing Materials, 1936.
18. *The Cost of Comfort*, National Lumber Manufacturer's Association, 1929.
19. *Thermal Insulation of Buildings*, U.S., Bureau of Standards, 1929.
20. Thorp, F.H., *Outlines of Industrial Chemistry*, Macmillan 1929.

V. EVALUATION

Observational check list

1. Have pupils learned where to go for reliable information on building and repairing houses ?
2. Do pupils seem to show an appreciation of the problems of architects, contractors, and building mechanics in building a house ?
3. Do pupils know where to go for reliable assistance in financing a house ?
4. Do pupils have a general knowledge of costs, kinds, and qualities of building materials ?
5. Do pupils know the more common types of house construction ?
6. Do pupils know the chemical properties of common building materials ?
7. Do pupils know the scientific principles of mechanics, heat, and light used in constructing a house ?
8. Do pupils seem to show an interest in sometime building homes of their own ?

ADVANCED PHYSICAL SCIENCE

TEACHER EVALUATION AND SUGGESTIONS FOR IMPROVEMENT

Unit...

(*Number*) (*Title*)

Notice to Teacher : As a result of your experiences in teaching this unit, please make suggestions for improvement and send to Lloyd W. King State Superintendent of Public Schools. Use an additional sheet if necessary.

Scope and Purpose

Suggested Content

Learning Activities

Evaluation

UNIT II

5

Using Fuels to Produce Heat and Power

I. SCOPE AND PURPOSE

A. Introduction

Man uses and controls heat to keep warm, to keep cool, to provide transportation for himself, to do much of his heavier labour, and to maintain his health.

Heat is a form of radiant energy which can be produced by man from various fuels existing or created by man from substances of the earth. The study of heat energy is a fascinating study. The measurement of heat and temperature, the effects produced by adding or subtracting heat, and the transmission of heat energy are interesting and vital phenomena.

The study of the production, chemical and physical properties, and uses of various fuels is also a fascinating study. How man has developed gas, coke, gasoline, kerosene, fuel oils, ethyl gasoline, synthetic gasoline, and other fuels is a tribute to his genius, just as the misuse of these fuels is indicative of his social inadequacy.

It is the purpose of this unit to assist pupils to understand better the nature and control of heat, to know the sources of fuels, their many uses, and how to use them most economically in the home.

B. Objectives

1. To acquaint pupils with the different ways man controls heat.
2. To show pupils how heat and temperature may be measured.
3. To develop an appreciation in pupils of the need for conserving natural fuels.
4. To show how man uses heat energy to do work.
5. To acquaint pupils with the types, sources, and chemical properties of fuels.
6. To give pupils certain information which may make them more intelligent consumers of fuels.

II. SUBJECT CONTENT

A. How Does Man Use Fuels ?

1. Heating homes and buildings
   (*a*) Fireplaces
      (1) Heating by convection and radiation
      (2) Advantages and disadvantages of fireplaces
      (3) Proper construction of a fireplace.
   (*b*) Stoves
      (1) Heating by convection and radiation
      (2) Types of stoves used for heating
      (3) Advantages and disadvantages of stoves—costs.
   (*c*) Furnace systems
      (1) Hot air—construction—heating by convection—advantages and disadvantages—operation—special types, such as gas and oil—costs
      (2) Hot water—construction—heating by radiation and convection—advantages and disadvantages—operation—costs

(3) Steam—construction—heating by radiation—advantages and disadvantages—operation—costs.

(*d*) Special methods—gasoline, kerosene.

2. Developing power for transportation

(*a*) Operating automobiles, trucks, and buses,

(1) Gasoline—various types

(*a*) Construction and operation of gasoline engines—measuring power

(2) Special fuels—wood, synthetic gasoline, substitute fuels

(3) Extent of gasoline consumption in the United States annually

(4) The automobile industry—production and maintenance—its contributions to American economy and standard of living.

(*b*) Operating airplanes

(1) Fuels used in airplane motors

(2) Construction and production of airplane motors—types of motors used

(3) The invention and development of the airplane

(4) The airplane in national defense.

(*c*) Operating tractors

(1) Fuels used in tractors

(2) Construction and production of tractors

(3) Use of tractors on the farm and in industry.

(*d*) Operating railroads

(1) Fuels used by railroads

(2) Steam locomotives—their construction and uses

(3) Diesel-electric locomotives—the streamliner

(4) Electric locomotives

(5) The development of the railroad industry and its place in American economy.

(*e*) Operating ships and boats

(1) Fuels used by ships and boats

(2) Steam turbines—their construction and uses.

(3) Diesels—their construction and uses
(4) Gasoline motors—outboard and inboard.

3. Cooking
   (*a*) Coal and wood stoves
   (*b*) Kerosene and gasoline
   (*c*) Gas—natural and artificial.

4. Manufacturing
   (*a*) Preparing metals
      (1) Iron and steel
      (2) Copper, lead, zinc, aluminum, etc.
      (3) Gold and silver
      (4) Blast furnaces—construction and operation
      (5) Smelters—construction and operation
      (6) Types of fuels used in preparing metals.
   (*b*) Manufacturing bricks, tile, cement, etc.
      (1) Methods of heating bricks and tile
      (2) Methods of making cement.
   (*c*) Manufacturing glass
      (1) Use of fuels and processes for making glass
      (2) Making big lenses and mirrors—cooling process.
   (*d*) Operating power machinery
      (1) Electricity
      (2) Steam
      (3) Diesel
      (4) Many uses for power machinery in various industries.
   (*e*) Manufacturing electricity
      (1) Steam turbines for generating electricity
      (2) Diesel engines for generating electricity.
   (*f*) Home and farm power
      (1) Small gasoline power engines—their uses and construction
      (2) Small Diesels—their uses and construction.

B. How Does Man Obtain Different Types of Fuels ?

1. Coal and coke
   - (*a*) Composition of various kinds of coal
   - (*b*) Location of coal deposits in the United States and in Missouri
   - (*c*) Methods of mining coal
   - (*d*) Methods of manufacturing coke
   - (*e*) Coal tar and its many derivatives.
2. Wood
   - (*a*) Kinds of wood used for fuels
   - (*b*) Kinds of wood found in Missouri which make good fuel
   - (*c*) Uses for wood as a fuel in industry
   - (*d*) Preparation and uses of charcoal
   - (*e*) Fractional distillation of wood and its products.
3. Gas
   - (*a*) Kinds of gas used for fuels—natural, coal, water, and producer
   - (*b*) Chemical and physical properties and sources of natural gases
   - (*c*) Chemical and physical properties and methods of production of artificial gases.
4. Oil
   - (*a*) Methods of obtaining petroleum
   - (*b*) Fractional distillation of petroleum—methods of refining
   - (*c*) Chemical properties of petroleum
   - (*d*) Products of petroleum and their physical and chemical properties
   - (*e*) Uses of the various products from petroleum
   - (*f*) The problem of conserving our oil supply
   - (*g*) "Cracking" process in producing gasoline and the preparation of ethyl gasoline.

C. What is Heat and How May it be Controlled ?

1. Heat is a form of radiant energy—the kinetic molecular hypothesis

   (*a*) Early beliefs about the nature of heat
   (*b*) Various theories of the nature of heat
2. Units for measuring heat
   (*a*) Definition of the calorie
   (*b*) Definition of the British thermal unit.
3. Measuring temperature
   (*a*) Boiling point and freezing point of water
   (*b*) Fahrenheit and Centigrade scales
   (*c*) Absolute zero
   (*d*) The thermometer, thermostat, and pyrometer.
4. Expansion caused by heat and its applications
   (*a*) Expansion of gases—Charles' law and Boyle's law
   (*b*) Expansion of liquids—peculiar behaviour of water when it freezes
   (*c*) Expansion of solids—determining coefficient of linear expansion—its use in building and engineering.
5. Changes of state in matter caused by heat .
6. Transfer of heat
   (*a*) Convection
   (*b*) Conduction
   (*c*) Radiation.
7. Producing cooling effects
   (*a*) Cooling from evaporation
   (*b*) Humidity and evaporation
   (*c*) Insulating against heat—methods
   (*d*) Ice, gas, and mechanical refrigeration
   (*e*) Air conditioning—means—construction of units—costs.

III. LEARNING ACTIVITIES

A. How Does Man Use Fuels ?

1. **Teaching procedures**
   (*a*) **Show a film on the manufacturing of steel to illustrate the use of coal and coke in blast furnaces.**
   (*b*) Take the class on a field trip to any near-by industries for preparing metals if available.

(*c*) Examine with the class various types of heating systems—hot air, steam, gas, and hot water.

(*d*) Construct a simple stove and demonstrate the operation of drafts, etc.

(*e*) Examine the construction of a gasoline engine with the class. If one is not available in your laboratory, buy one from a near-by junk dealer and strip it down for demonstration purposes.

(*f*) Visit a railroad shop and examine the construction of steam locomotives. If a railroad shop is not available, examine a model of a steam engine or a toy steam engine. Have pupils diagram the steam cylinder, valves, and piston.

(*g*) Take the class to visit a near-by light plant. Observe the steam turbines or Diesel engines.

2. Pupil activities

(*a*) Make a model hot air heating system.

(*b*) Make a model hot water heating system.

(*c*) Make a model of a small gasoline motor for an airplane.

(*d*) Construct a model airplane with a gasoline motor (boys).

(*e*) Report on the development of the automobile industry.

(*f*) Debate, "Resolved : That man would be economically better off if automobiles were abolished."

(*g*) Report on the Wright brothers.

(*h*) Report on the development of railroads in America.

(*i*) Compare the cooking of a roast in an ordinary roaster and in a pressure cooker. Explain your findings to the class.

3. Additional activities

(*a*) Go on a weiner roast or steak fry and use charcoal for cooking. Report your results to the class.

(*b*) Make up a diet designed to increase your weight and one designed to reduce your weight. Justify your selection of foods in terms of their heat values.

(*c*) Examine and report on the way electricity is manufactured for your community.

(*d*) Report on the use of fuel to do work on the farm.

B. How Does Man Obtain Different Types of Fuels ?

1. Teaching procedures

(*a*) Conduct a demonstration to show the kindling temperatures of different fuels : coal, wood, oil, etc.

(*b*) Run a rough fractional distillation of powdered soft coal to show production of gas, coke, and coal tar.

(*c*) Take the class to visit a near-by coal mine. Prepare carefully for the trip. Use study questions and follow up with reports and discussion.

(*d*) Demonstrate a coal dust explosion to show dangers encountered by miners.

(*e*) Test the heat production value of different types of wood and coal.

(*f*) Take the class on a field trip to a farm where firewood is being cut. Note the various kinds of native timber used for fuel and how it is processed.

(*g*) Show the film (or one similar), *Energy and Its Transmission*, University of Chicago Series, one reel, 16mm., sound.

2. Pupil activities

(*a*) Make a collection of products of coal tar and arrange them for a display.

(*b*) Make a collection of the products of petroleum and arrange them for a display.

(*c*) Make a collection of different kinds of native wood used for fuel. Arrange them for a display.

(*d*) Make some charcoal. What are its chemical and physical properties and uses ?

(*e*) Report on forest conservation in Missouri.

(*f*) Report on the manufacture of wood alcohol.

(*g*) Report on the methods of drilling for oil.

(*h*) Report on the methods of transporting crude oil.

3. Additional activities

(*a*) Report on the octane rating of gasolines and what it means.

(*b*) Report on the making of ethyl gasoline.

(*c*) Report on the products of petroleum and how they are obtained.

(*d*) Make a report on the manufacture and uses of asphalt.

(*e*) Make a report on the sources and uses of natural gas.

C. What Is Heat and How May It Be Controlled ?

1. Teaching procedures

(*a*) Demonstrate the effect of air pressure and pressure of vapour molecules by heating a small amount of water in a flat gallon can, sealing it, and permitting it to cool.

(*b*) Demonstrate the expansion and contraction of metals by a simple ball and ring apparatus, compound bars, etc.

(*c*) Demonstrate the transfer of heat by convection by placing a lighted candle in the bottom of a flask. The candle will soon go out because of lack of oxygen. Insert a trip of bent metal in the flask so that the bent part is just above the flame. This will cause convection currents to be set up within the flask and the candle will continue to burn.

(*d*) Demonstrate absorption of heat by black bodies by placing a burner equidistant between two air thermometers. Coat one of the thermometers with soot and note the difference in the levels of the liquids.

(*e*) Demonstrate the transfer of heat by conduction by heating one end of different kinds of metal rods. Permit different members of the class to conduct the experiment.

(*f*) Demonstrate how heat may change substances from one state to another by heating ice, water, wax, lead solder, iodine crystals, etc.

2. Pupil activities

(*a*) Conduct a laboratory experiment to show the heat of fusion of ice and the heat of vaporization of water.

(*b*) Conduct a laboratory experiment on the cooling effect of evaporation with an air thermometer and a piece of cheesecloth tied to the bulb. Dip the cheesecloth into water, alcohol, carbon tetrachloride, etc., and fan. Note changes in the level of water in the thermometer.

(*c*) Conduct an experiment to measure the relative humidity in the air by means of a dry-bulb and wet-bulb thermometer.

(*d*) Construct a simple pyrometer apparatus by use of two kinds of wire (alumel and chromel) fused together and connected to a galvonometer. Heat the fused ends of the two wires and note the degree of deflection of the galvanometer needle.

(*e*) Conduct a simple experiment to show the expansion of gases by heating the bulb of a glass flask with a glass tube attached and immersed in water. Note bubbles caused by expansion of air and the rise of water in the tube when the air in the flask cools and contracts.

(*f*) Visit an ice plant and note how ice is made. Trace the cycle of the refrigerant through the apparatus.

(*g*) Make a report on methods and materials used for insulating a house against heat.

(*h*) Collect samples of heat insulating materials and arrange into a display.

(*i*) Report on the construction and uses of various types of air conditioning machines.

3. Additional activities

(*a*) Conduct an experiment to check the fixed points of a Fahrenheit and a Centigrade thermometer.

(*b*) Examine and note the construction of a thermostatically controlled valve used in automobile cooling systems.

(*c*) Show the expansion of metals when heated by stretching a long iron wire between two supports and suspending a weight from it. Pass an electric current through it and note the sag in the wire.

(*d*) Report on the development of the thermometer.

V. BIBLIOGRAPHY

A. General References

1. Beauchamp, Wilbur, and others, *Science Problems, Book 3*, Scott, Foresman, 1939, pp. 531-544.
2. Bush, George L., Ptacek, T. W., and Kovats, John, *Senior Science*, American, 1937.
3. Clark, John A., Gorton, Frederick Russell, and Sears, Francis W., *Physics of Today*, Houghton Mifflin, 1938.
4. Corwin, Walling, and Corwin, M. J., *Science of Discovery and Invention*, Wagner, 1931, pp. 270-352.
5. Hausrath, Alfred H., Jr., and Harms, John H., *Consumer Science*, Macmillan, 1939, pp. 327-346.
6. Hopkins, B. Smith, and others, *Chemistry and You*, Lyons and Carnahan, 1939, pp. 425-461.
7. Trafton, Gilbert Haven, and Smith, V. C., *Science in Daily Life*, Lippincott, 1936, pp. 30-82.
8. Watkins, Ralph K., and Perry, Winifred, *Science for Human Control*, Macmillan, 1940, pp. 391-499.

B. Special References

1. Beery, Pauline, *Stuff*, Appleton-Century, 1930, pp. 98-194.
2. Clarke, Beverly L., *Marvels of Modern Chemistry*, Harpers, 1935.
3. Darrow, Floyd Lavern, *The Story of Chemistry*, Harpers, 1932.
4. Foster, William, *The Romance of Chemistry*, Appleton-Century, 1936.

5. Goldblatt, Leo Arthur, *Collateral Readings in Inorganic Chemistry*, Appleton-Century, 1937.
6. Holmes, Henry N., *Out of the Test Tube*, Emerson, 1937.
7. Morrison, Abraham Cressy, *Man in a Chemical World*, Scribners, 1937.
8. Rogers, Allen, *Manual of Industrial Chemistry*, Macmillan, 1932.
9. Tilden, Sir William Augustus, *Chemistry and Discovery and Invention in the Twentieth Century*, Dutton, 1936.
10. Williard, Lester R., *Experiences in Physics*, Ginn, 1939.

C. Film References

1. *Black Gold Beyond the Rio Grande*, Pan-American Union, Washington, D. C.
2. *Know Your Coal*, Department of Interior, Washington, D. C., one reel, 16 mm., sound.
3. *Refining of the Crude*, Bureau of Mines, Washington, D. C., one reel, 16 mm., sound.
4. *The Story of Coal*, Y. M. C. A. Film Bureau, one reel, 16 mm., sound.
5. *The Story of Gasoline*, Bureau of Mines, Washington, D. C., 2 reels, 16 mm., sound.
6. *Wild Wood, A Hundred Per Cent Mechanized Mine*, Bureau of Mines, Washington, D. C., three reels, 16 mm., sound.

V. EVALUATION

Below are some illustrative test items.

A. *True-False*

T F 1. Peat is a common fuel in America.

T F 2. Coal is deposited in the earth in unlimited quantities.

B. *Completion*

1. Coke is made from..............coal.
2. The Diesel engine burns..............

C. *Multiple Choice.* Underline the correct answer.

1. The most common type of heating system in the small home is : hot air, hot water, steam.
2. A common coal tar chemical is : benzine, benzene, naphtha, gasoline.

D. *Selection of Definitions.* Put the number of the correct definition in the parentheses after the word.

1. Anthracite	( )	1.	Coal with high carbon compound content
2. Benzine	( )	2.	Coal having high uncombined carbon content
3. Bituminous	( )	3.	A distillate of coal tar.

ADVANCED PHYSICAL SCIENCE

TEACHER EVALUATION AND SUGGESTIONS FOR IMPROVEMENT

Unit...
(*Number*) (*Title*)

Note to Teacher : As a result of your experiences in teaching this unit, please make suggestions for improvement and send to Lloyd W. King, State Superintendent of Public Schools. Use an additional sheet if necessary.

Scope and Purpose

Suggested Content

Learning Activities

Evaluation

UNIT III

6

Making Water More Useful

I. SCOPE AND PURPOSE

A. Introduction

Water constantly affects our daily tasks and pleasures. It makes up seventy per cent of our bodies and an even larger percentage of the animal and vegetable matter which we use for our food.

The rise and decline of civilization has closely followed the abundance or the scarcity of water. Climatic changes involving water have been responsible for mass migrations which have had great bearing upon the history of mankind.

Through experience the pupil has gained much knowledge about water. It is the purpose of this unit to interpret the pupil's experiences with water to the end that he may better understand and appreciate its value and usefulness.

The several problems of the unit may be presented in any sequence. The season of the year, some unusual current event, or the teacher's or pupil's interests should determine the order of presentation. Each topic should be introduced by an explanation or demonstration that is interesting, thought provoking, and pertinent. Teacher demonstrations and pupil experiments should be performed largely with inexpensive or improvised apparatus and interpreted in a way that will encourage individual experimentation outside the classroom.

B. Unit Objectives

1. To show the importance of water in sustaining animal and plant life.
2. To show how water affects weather and climate.
3. To show how man controls water to make it useful rather than destructive.
4. To help pupils to understand how water may be converted into power.
5. To show how water may be purified for man's use.

II. SUGGESTED CONTENT

A. What Is the Importance of Water as It Relates to Urban and Rural Life ?

1. Water has played an important role in the development of our civilization. Trace the history of some famous rivers and the civilizations which grew up along their banks.
2. Some modern cities flourish hundreds of miles from the nearest satisfactory water supply. How has science made this possible ?

B. What Is the Importance of Water to Animal and Plant Life ?

1. Compare the animal and plant life in arid and semiarid regions with regions of abundant rainfall.
   (*a*) What has been the effect of the scarcity and abundance of water upon the kinds of animals found ?
   (*b*) What has been the effect of water upon the abundance or scarcity of animal and vegetable life ?
2. What are three ways that water serves plant life ?
3. What are three ways that water serves the human body ?

C. How Can Man Control Water to Make It Useful and Non-destructive ?

1. Study the expansion of freezing water and note that it may be useful but that it is harmful if we do not learn to control it.
    (*a*) How can we protect water pipes and wall footings from the expansive force of freezing water ?
    (*b*) Study antifreeze solutions and the principles controlling their use.
    (*c*) Study the energy changes involved in the freezing and thawing of water.
        (1) The effect of water in preventing too sudden and too severe changes in weather
        (2) The use of frozen water in refrigeration
        (3) The freezing of water in cracks of rocks to aid in the formation of soil.
2. Methods for control and utilization of water
    (*a*) Flood control through use of reservoirs and dams
    (*b*) Use of reservoirs to maintain river commerce
    (*c*) Use of impounded water to develop power.

D. How Does Man Make Water Pure and Store It for His Use ?

1. The cistern and the well
    (*a*) Their construction and use
    (*b*) Simple and reliable ways for testing a water supply.
2. Spring and surface water and precautions which should be taken in their use
    (*a*) How to tell a "wet weather" spring from a real one
    (*b*) Simple and safe ways to treat surface water or doubtful spring water to make it safe for use.
3. Study of hardness in water and methods used in its removal
    (*a*) Nature of calcium and other minerals which cause hardness
    (*b*) The effect of hard water on soaps
    (*c*) Simple and effective ways of removing hardness

4. Study of the processes for removing sediment and bacteria from surface water
   (*a*) Applying the principles of sedimentation with the use of chemicals and settling basins
   (*b*) The use of sand filters
   (*c*) The study of reservoirs, lakes, and standpipes for storing water supply.

III. LEARNING ACTIVITIES

The nature of learning activities must depend upon the interests and abilities of the members of the class, the available reference materials suitable opportunities for field trips, and time available for the unit. These sample activities are some that have been used successfully and are offered as suggestions to help teachers plan and carry out programe of their own.

A. Importance of Water

1. Ask different pupils to make reports on the famous rivers of the world.
2. Have pupils report on the history of the development of our own state, calling attention to the importance of water courses.
3. The story of the development of the water supply systems of St. Louis and Los Angeles will show how science has simplified the problem of water supply. Have pupils report on these systems.

B. Ways in Which Water Sustains Plant and Animal Life

1. Make field trips to ponds, woods, and pasture and to note the importance of water in determining the types and abundance of plant and animal life.
2. Have pupils weigh samples of different kinds of foods and place in a drying oven. After twenty four hours reweigh and compute the percentage of water in the original samples.
3. Determine the amount of water evaporated by a potted plant during one week.
4. Demonstrate the importance of water to plant cells by reviving a wilted stalk of celery or a leaf of lettuce or

spinach. (Water gives plant cells rigidity and when it leaves the plant the cells collapse and the plant wilts.)

5. Both plant and animal food is dissolved in water before it can be utilized. Test the solubility of common plant and animal foods.

6. The cooling effect of the evaporation of perspiration can be demonstrated by the use of wet and dry bulb thermometers. The bulb of one thermometer is covered with cloth or cotton and moistened. The difference in the temperatures of the two bulbs is due to the evaporation of the water. The cooling effect of evaporation can be easily demonstrated by pouring a little ether or carbon tetrachloride in the palm of the hand.

C. Control and Utilization of Water

1. The destructive force of freezing water can be demonstrated by placing a test tube half full of water in a salt and ice mixture. Within a few minutes the test tube will burst. Another tube of water protected by insulating materials will resist freezing for some time.
2. Antifreeze solutions of different strengths can be prepared and tested in freezing mixtures. Different kinds of antifreeze mixtures can be tested and compared. The use of the hydrometer in determining the freezing point of these solutions may be demonstrated.
3. If near by, flood control and power dams should be visited by the class. If this is not possible pupils may prepare and make reports to the class on these projects.
4. The use of chemical solutions to replace soil in growing plants is interesting and can be carried out in glass jars in the school room or laboratory.
5. The plant itself may be set in a mass of excelsior or straw with the root crown about an inch from the surface of the water. An excellent guide to this work is the book by William Gericke, *Soilless Gardening*.

D. Purification and Storage of Water

1. Cisterns and wells can still be found in most communities. Visit these and consult some person who is

engaged in the work of making cisterns or wells. It is very difficult to test water for the bacteria which are harmful but quite easy to test for the presence of organic matter which is always present along with bacteria. Place a teaspoonful of a one per cent solution of potassium permanganate in a quart of the water being tested. If after twenty-four hours the water has retained its purple colour there is no organic matter, and therefore no bacteria, present. If organic matter is present the purple colour will have disappeared and a brown sedimentation formed. The time taken for this change is an indication of the amount of organic matter present.

2. A field trip to a water treating plant is usually possible. Sometimes one pupil or a committee may make the trip and return to demonstrate water purification to the class Samples of the chemicals used at the water plant can be procured and used in the demonstration.

IV. BIBLIOGRAPHY

1. Chase, Stuart, *Rich Land, Poor Land*, McGraw-Hill, 1936.
2. Powers, Samuel R., Neuner, E.F., and Bruner, H.B., *This Changing World*, Ginn, 1934.
3. Caldwell, Otis William, and Curtis, F.D., *Science for Today*, Ginn, 1936.
4. Bush, George L., Ptacek, Theodore W., and Kovats, John, *Senior Science*, American, 1937.
5. Weed, H.T., Rexford, F.A., and Carroll, F.B., *Useful Science for High School*, Winston, 1935.
6. Eckels, Charles F., Shaver, C.B.. and Howard, B W., *Our Physical World*, Sanborn, 1938.
7. Watkins, Ralph K., and Perry, Winifred, *Science for Human Control*, Macmillan, 1940.
8. Obourn, Ellsworth Scott, and Heiss, E.D., *Modern Science Problems*, Webster, 1936.
9. Skilling, William Thompson, *Tours Through the World of Science*, McGraw-Hill, 1933.

10. Regenstein, Anna B., and Teeters, W.R., *Science at Work*, Rand McNally, 1935.
11. Wilson, Sherman R., *Descriptive Chemistry*, Henry Holt 1936.

V. EVALUATION

1. Do pupils recognize the importance of water to all animal and plant life ?
2. Do pupils know how water affects weather and climate ?
3. Do pupils understand how water may be controlled so that it is useful rather than destructive ?
4. Do pupils know how water may be treated to make it safe for drinking purposes ?
5. Do pupils know how water may be converted into power ?
6. Do pupils know how water may be stored conveniently for man's use ?

ADVANCED PHYSICAL SCIENCE

TEACHER EVALUATION AND SUGGESTIONS FOR IMPROVEMENT

Unit...

(*Number*) (*Title*)

Note to Teacher : As a result of your experiences in teaching this unit, please make Suggestions for improvement and send to Lloyd W. King, State superintendent of Public Schools. Use an additional sheet if necessary.

Scope and Purpose

Suggested Content

Learning Activities

Evaluation

UNIT IV

7

Science Aids in Communication

I. SCOPE AND PURPOSE

A. Introduction

This unit has been developed to assist the pupil to gain a better knowledge of communication as it does and may affect his daily life. The pupil should be stimulated to develop an interest in the contributions of science to the development of communication. The development of scientific principles as such is not the primary purpose of this unit. The principles are presented only as they may lead the individual to understand better the various methods of communication.

B. Unit Objectives

1. To develop an appreciation of the contributions made by the several means of communication to man's day-by-day living.
2. To point out the underlying scientific principles of the field of communication.
3. To encourage the wise and efficient use of the means of communication.
4. To widen the individual's occupational knowledge of the field of communication.

II. SUGGESTED CONTENT

A. How Does Communication Affect Everyday Habits of Living ?

1. The historical development of communication
   (*a*) What were the earliest forms of communication ?
   (*b*) What have been the main steps of advancement in communication ?
   (*c*) Why was scientific advancement in communication so slow for many centuries ?
   (*d*) What has contributed to the many recent improvements in communication ?
2. How do the various means of communication affect our daily lives ?
   (*a*) What services do systems of communication extend to the individual ?
   (*b*) What are the methods of communication which we have at our disposal ?
   (*c*) To what extent has communication contributed to our happiness and business effectiveness ?
   (*d*) Would modern civilization be possible without communication ?
   (*e*) To what extent would the modern business world be impaired without communication ?
   (*f*) What would happen to our daily living if all of the means of communication were suddenly closed ?
3. What research facilities are maintained in the field of communication ?
   (*a*) Where are the great research centers ?
   (*b*) What problems are being worked on ?
   (*c*) What are the general obstacles involved in research work ?

B. What Are the Common Methods of Communication and Their Underlying Principles ?

1. What is man's natural means of communication ?
   (*a*) What are the organs of speech ?
   (*b*) How is sound produced ?

(*c*) How is sound transmitted ?
(*d*) How does the ear receive sound ?
(*e*) What are the physical qualities of sound ?

2. What has made man's vast storehouse of knowledge possible ?
   (*a*) What would the word "printing" have meant to man 500 years ago ?
   (*b*) What educational facilities were available to the average man when printing was first introduced ?
   (*c*) What are some of the changes printing produced ?
   (*d*) What are some of the evolutionary steps in the development of printing ?
   (*e*) What are some of the difficulties or problems that printing has produced ?
   (*f*) What are some common terms used in the printing industry ?
   (*g*) How are scientific developments affecting the printing industry ?

3. What service does the telegraph offer to man ?
   (*a*) What is meant by the term telegraph ?
   (*b*) What scientific principles are embodied in the telegraph ?
   (*c*) What are some common terms used in telegraphy ?
   (*d*) What circumstances led to its invention ?
   (*e*) What are the means of obtaining telegraph circuits ?
   (*f*) What is a neutral telegraph system ?
   (*g*) What is the nature of currents in neutral systems ?

4. How was the telephone developed and how does it operate ?
   (*a*) What circumstances led to the invention of the telephone ?
   (*b*) What training did Bell have that made it possible for him to invent the telephone ?
   (*c*) What were some of the earlier technical difficulties that had to be overcome ?
   (*d*) What is the scientific explanation of sound ?

(*e*) How are the peculiar characteristics of sound utilized in the construction of a telephone ?
(*f*) What are the common terms used in telephone communication ?
(*g*) How is a simple telephone circuit constructed ?
(*h*) How does a speaker's voice cause the electrical current to vary in intensity in a telephone circuit ?
(*i*) What is the purpose of the telephone transmitter ?
(*j*) How does a simple magneto exchange operate ?
(*k*) What is a simple battery telephone ?
(*l*) What happens in the telephone circuit when a call is made ?

5. What contributions has radio made to communication and how does it operate ?
(*a*) What means of communication were in use preceding the introduction of the radio ?
(*b*) What scientific facts had to be known before the advent of the radio was possible ?
(*c*) What contributions did the early scientists make to the radio ?
(*d*) Why was the radio developed ?
(*e*) What are some common terms used in radio ?
(*f*) How does a radio transmitter operate ? A radio receiver ?

6. What seem to be the possibilities in television ?
(*a*) What is television ?
(*b*) What is the present status of television ?
(*c*) What problems must be solved before television may be operated on a wide scale ?
(*d*) What is the possibility offered by the coaxial cable ?
(*e*) What are the more common terms in television ?
(*f*) What would television mean to the average person if successfully introduced ?

C. How Can Man Secure the Greatest Services from Systems of Communication ?

1. Of what value is the telephone ?
(*a*) Is a telephone essential in the home ?

(*b*) Is a telephone essential in a place of business ?
(*c*) What services can we expect of the telephone ?
(*d*) What procedures should be taken if our telephone service is unsatisfactory ?
(*e*) How should we use the telephone to secure the best service ?
(*f*) What should the telephone company expect of us as users of the service ?

2. What problems should be considered in using and buying a radio ?
(*a*) What is the purpose of radio broadcasting ?
(*b*) Who sponsors our broadcasts ? Who pays for them ?
(*c*) What factors should be considered in determining whether a person should have a radio ?
(*d*) What determines the cost of a radio receiving set ?
(*e*) How may we judge a good radio ?
(*f*) What precautions must be observed in buying a radio ?
(*g*) How may we operate a radio to insure maximum efficiency ?

3. What services can we secure from telegraph companies ?
(*a*) What situations may require use of the telegraph ?
(*b*) What services can we expect from telegraph companies ?
(*c*) What is the cost of telegraph services ?

4. What can we expect of television ?
(*a*) How may television be of value to man ?
(*b*) What factors should influence us in deciding on the purchase of a television set ?
(*c*) Is television possible on a large scale ?
(*d*) What precautions must be observed with an instrument still in the experimental stage ?

D. What Does the Field of Communication Offer as a Vocation ?

1. Where may you go for information about occupations in the field of communication ?

(*a*) Where can you find a list of all the vocations in this field ?

(*b*) Do you know how to find vocational information in books and magazines ?

(*c*) What are some of the values of studying biographies of successful people ?

(*d*) How may you obtain information from successful people ?

(*e*) Where may you get firsthand information on jobs available and working conditions in the communication industries ?

2. How should you go about getting a communication job ?

(*a*) Do you know what type of work you are interested in and for which you have talent ?

(*b*) Do you know the time and cost of training for this job ?

(*c*) Do you know where to find employers in your line of work ?

(*d*) Do you know how to interview an employer ?

(*e*) Do you know how to plan an interview with an employer ?

3. What does it take to advance on a job in communications ?

(*a*) Do you know the kind of workers employers want ?

(*b*) Do you know how employers choose persons for advanced positions ?

(*c*) Do you know what personal traits employers like ?

(*d*) Do you know for what reason employees are dismissed ?

(*e*) Do you have the preparation for advancement ?

(*f*) What are the opportunities for advanced study in communications ?

III. LEARNING ACTIVITIES

A. Teaching Procedures

1. Raise questions with the class which may stimulate interest ?

   (*a*) What were our first means of communication ?

   (*b*) What means of communication did the founders of this nation have ?

   (*c*) How did their methods of communication compare with earlier methods ?

   (*d*) Compare their methods of communication with methods used today.

2. Suggested teacher demonstrations.

   (*a*) Resonance of electrical circuits may be demonstrated through use of the Leyden Jar.

   (*b*) Sympathetic vibration may be demonstrated through use of two tuning forks.

   (*c*) Phenomena of beats may be demonstrated by means of so-called "singing tubes."

   (*d*) Vibrating air columns may be shown by means of pipes and vibrating strings.

   (*e*) Demonstrate the fundamental tone and the overtones of a vibrating string.

   (*f*) Demonstrate the laws of vibrating strings.

   (*g*) Show how a vacuum tube can be used for amplification.

   (*h*) Compare reflection of sound with rebound of elastic bodies and with the reflection of light.

   (*i*) Test the acoustic properties of a room.

3. Field trips

   (*a*) Make a trip to a railroad station and study the telegraph.

   (*b*) Make a trip to a radio broadcasting station.

   (*c*) Make a trip to the local newspaper and study the procedures and mechanics used in publishing a newspaper.

B. Pupil Activities

1. Pupils may make investigations and reports on the history and importance of communication.

   (*a*) History and evolutionary development of communication

   (*b*) The history of the first printing press

   (*c*) The lives of Faraday, Maxwell, Hertz, Edison, Bell, and Morse

   (*d*) History of communication as shown by collecting clippings, pictures, and diagrams

   (*e*) Development of the radio

   (*f*) Recent developments in television.

2. Pupils may conduct a number of experiments under the direction of the teacher.

   (*a*) Radiometer
   (*b*) Vacuum tube
   (*c*) Cathode tube
   (*d*) Speed of sound
   (*e*) Wave length and resonance
   (*f*) Laws of vibrating strings
   (*g*) Overtones and beats
   (*h*) Operation of telegraph system
   (*i*) Operation of telephone system.

3. Group activities

   (*a*) Make a list of factors to be considered in selecting a radio.

   (*b*) List the advantages of putting telephone wires underground in urban centers.

   (*c*) Secure a radio and make a study of its parts and operation.

   (*d*) Make a study of the telephone system in the local community.

   (*e*) Compare telephone rates in surrounding towns.

4. Vocabulary

   The following are some of the words that the pupils should learn during a study of this unit :

acoustics	longitudinal waves	radio frequency
audio frequency	loud speaker	radio reception
chromatic scale	overtone	refraction
Doppler effect	phonodeik	resonance
echoes	pitch	telegraph
frequency	compression wave	telephone
grid	decibels	television
harmony	diatonic scale	transatlantic
intensity	discord	telephony
interference	quality	transverse wave
kilocycle	radio	tuning

C. Additional Activities

1. Special studies for those interested in importance of communication
   (*a*) Make a study of the number of languages used.
   (*b*) Make a study of the number of telephones in use in the United States in comparison with the rest of the world.
   (*c*) Determine the amount of money invested in the field of communication.
   (*d*) Determine the number of people employed by the field of communication.
2. Special studies on methods of communication and their underlying principles
   (*a*) Make a study of the separate steps required to publish a newspaper.
   (*b*) Make a study of the relationship of sound waves and radio waves.
   (*c*) Make a complete and detailed study of a radio set.
   (*d*) Locate and repair some minor trouble in a radio set.
3. Special studies on using communication services
   (*a*) Make a list of desirab.e features in a radio set.

(*b*) Make a study of the means of communication available to other communities in Missouri.
(*c*) Determine factors of desirable telephone service.

4. Special studies of vocations in the field of communication
   (*a*) Determine sources of materials for study.
   (*b*) Make a study of vocational opportunities in the field of communication.
   (*c*) Make an intensive study of a group of vocations in the field of communication.

IV. REFERENCES

A. General References

1. Black, Newton H. and Davis, H.N., *Elementary Practical Physics*, Macmillan, 1938.
2. Bush, George L., Ptacek, Theodore W., and Kovats, John, *Senior Science*, American, 1937.
3. Clark, John A., Gorton, Frederick Russell, and Sears, Francis W., *Physics of Today*, Houghton Mifflin, 1938.
4. Davis, Watson, *Science Today*, Harcourt, Brace, 1931.
5. Dull, Charles F., *Modern Physics*, Henry Holt, 1939.
6. Eyring, Carl Ferdinand, *A Survey Course in Physics*, Prentice-Hall, 1936.
7. Foley, Arthur Lee, *College Physics*, Blakiston, 1937.
8. Henderson, William D., *New Physics in Everyday Life*, Lyons and Carnahan, 1930.
9. Holley, Clifford, and Lohr, V.C., *Mastery Units in Physics*, Lippincott, 1932.
10. Kallet, Arthur, and Schlink, F.J., *100,000,000 Guinea Pigs*, Vanguard Press, 1933.
11. Osborn, Frederick Arthur, *Physics of the Home*, McGraw-Hill, 1935.
12. Van Buskirk, Edgar Flandreau, Smith, E.L., and Nourse, W.L., *The Science of Everyday Life*, Houghton Mifflin, 1936.

13. Watkins, Ralph K., and Bedell, R.C., *General Science for Today*, Macmillan, 1936.

B. Selected References

1. American Radio Relay League, *The Radio Amateur's Handbook*, New Hartford, Connecticut.
2. "Aviation Altitude," *Radio News*, February, 1940.
3. Brewer, John Marks, *Occupations*, Ginn, 1936.
4. Bryan, George S. and Knopf, Alfred A., *Edison, The Man and His Work*, 1926.
5. By leaders in world affairs, *Achievement*, American Educational Press, 1928.
6. Chase, Stuart, *Men and Machines*, Macmillan, 1929.
7. Dalton, Edward F., *Selling Yourself*, Ripon, 1930.
8. Davis, James John, and Wright, J.C., *You and Your Job*, Wiley, 1930.
9. Durand, William F., *Robert H. Thurston*, American Society of Mechanical Engineers, 1929.
10. Faris, John Thomson, *Winning Their Way*, Stokes, 1909.
11. Fancher, Albert, *Getting a Job and Getting Ahead*, McGraw-Hill, 1931.
12. Hammond, John W., *A Boy's Life of Steinmetz*, Century, 1924.
13. Hammond, John W., *Charles P. Steinmetz—A Biography*, Century, 1924.
14. Kilduff, Edward Jones, *How to Choose and Get a Better Job*, Harpers, 1921.
15. Kitson, Harry Dexter, *How to Find the Right Vocation*, Harpers, 1929.
16. Lemon, Harvey Brace, *From Galileo to Cosmic Rays*, University of Chicago Press, 1935.
17. Mackenzie, Catherine, *Alexander Graham Bell—Biography*. Houghton Mifflin, 1928.
18. Marshall, Leon Carroll, *The Story of Human Progress*, Macmillan, 1925.
19. Parker, Willard Eagleson, *Books About Jobs*, American Library Association, 1936.

20. Pitkin, Walter Boughton, *New Careers for Youth*, Simon and Schuster, 1934.
21. Rosengarten, William, *Choosing Your Life Work*, McGraw-Hill, 1936.
22. "The Miracle of Talking by Telephone," F. Barrows Colton, reprinted from *National Geographic*, 1937.

C. Films

1. The following silent films may be secured from Bray Picture Corporation, 729 Seventh Avenue, New York.
   How We Hear, $\frac{1}{8}$ reel.
   Sound Waves, $\frac{1}{4}$ reel.
   How the Telephone Talks, $\frac{1}{2}$ reel.
   The Human Voice, $\frac{2}{3}$ reel.
2. The following sound films may be secured from Erpi Picture Consultant, Inc., 250 West 57th St., New York
   The String Choir.
   The Woodwind Choir.
   The Percussion Group.
   Sound Waves and their Sources.
   Fundamentals of Acoustics.
3. *Wizardry of Wireless*, 2 reels, 16 mm., sound, General Electric Company, Schenectady, N.Y.
4. The following one-reel sound films may be secured from the University of Missouri, Visual Education Service, Columbia, Missouri.
   Network Broadcasting.
   Voices in the Air.
   Sound Waves and their Sources.
5. Radio Literature and Pictures of Tubes and Radio Sets :

   R.C.A. Manufacturing Co.
   R.C.A. Victor Division, Camden, N.J.

   Silent and Sound films on Telephone Communication
   Northwestern Bell Telephone Co.

   Library of Sound and 350 Silent Subjects and 50 Sound
   Motion Picture Bureau of Y.M.C.A., 19 S. La Salle. St., Chicago, Illinois.

V. EVALUATION

A. Check List in Terms of Objectives

1. Do pupils appreciate the importance of communication ?
2. To what extent has the class developed scientific methods of thinking ?
3. Do the members of the class understand the operation of the radio ?
4. Do the pupils know the factors which determine a wise and efficient use of the various means of communication ?
5. Do the pupils appreciate the contributions of the early scientists ?
6. Have I widened and deepened the interests of my pupils in the field of communication ?

B. Illustrative Testing Exercises

1. True-false items

...............a. Sound waves have their origin in vibrating matter.

...............b. The velocity of sound in air at 0° C. is 1190 ft. per second.

...............c. A frequency which is a multiple of the overtone is called a fundamental.

...............d. There is but one type of ether wave.

2. Completion exercises

(*a*) Sound waves are transmitted to the ear through some

(*b*) Sound waves may be reflected, producing............

(*c*) Discord is a phenomenon of............

(*d*) Radio waves are long waves, varying in length from a few meters to...........or more meters.

3. Matching exercise

( ) 1. A device used to study the law of strings — 1. Triode vacuum tube

( ) 2.	A device used to study sound waves	2. Sonometer
		3. Bell
( ) 3.	A device used as a generator of radio waves	4. Vibrograph
		5. Edison
( ) 4.	The inventor of the telephone	6. Siren disc

ADVANCED PHYSICAL SCIENCE

TEACHER EVALUATION AND SUGGESTIONS FOR IMPROVEMENT

Unit..

(*Number*) (*Title*)

Note to Teacher : As a result of your experiences in teaching this unit, please make suggestions for improvement and send to Lloyd W. King, State Superintendent of Public Schools. Use an additional sheet if necessary.

Scope and Purpose

Suggested Content

Learning Activities

Evaluation

UNIT V

8

Science Aids in Transportation

I. SCOPE AND PURPOSE

A. Introduction

The unit on transportation offers an interesting study of the application of machines to our daily lives. It is intended that this unit bring out the principles of construction and operation of the steam, gasoline, Diesel, and Diesel-electric engines as applied to transportation.

This work should be made practical by the study of the actual machines wherever possible. The study of the automobile should be from the standpoint of the consumer, with a definite attempt made to create an attitude of careful investigations and intelligent use of the automobile as a means of transportation.

B. Unit Objectives

1. To develop an appreciation of the contribution of science to the development of modern methods of transportation.
2. To develop practical knowledge of principles of construction and operation that will be useful to consumers and operators of the modern automobile.

3. To develop attitudes and ideals of safety in regard to the operation of motor vehicles, based upon a knowledge of scientific principles.

II. SUGGESTED CONTENT

A. What Contributions Has Rail Transportation Made to Society ?

1. How did the steam engine transform the transportation methods of the world ?
   - (*a*) How did primitive man transport materials ?
   - (*b*) What progress had man made in transportation by the end of the 18th century ?
   - (*c*) How did steam transportation develop ?
   - (*d*) Why have transportation methods developed so much more rapidly during the past 100 years ?
   - (*e*) What is the status of transportation today ?
2. How is steam used for power ?
   - (*a*) What is the mechanical equivalent of heats ?
   - (*b*) How can heat be made to do work ?
   - (*c*) What is the source of the energy of steam ?
   - (*d*) How does the volume increase when water is changed to gas ?
3. How is the power of expanding steam applied to the locomotive ?
   - (*a*) What is the principle of the reciprocating type of steam engine ?
   - (*b*) How is the reciprocating motion changed to rotary motion ?
   - (*c*) In what way is the drive wheel like a lever ?
   - (*d*) What are the advantages of a steam turbine ?
4. How has the air brake contributed to modern rail transportation ?
   - (*a*) How were trains originally stopped ?
   - (*b*) How much power is necessary to stop a moving object ?
   - (*c*) How do air brakes work ?
5. Why is the Diesel-electric power plant replacing steam for transportation ?

(*a*) How does the Diesel engine compare with the steam engine ?
(*b*) What are the advantages of the Diesel-electric power plant ?
(*c*) Why is streamlining necessary for modern trains ?

B. How has the Development of Automobile Transportation Affected Modern Living ?

1. What have been the outstanding steps in the development of the automobile ?
   (*a*) Who were the pioneers in the development of the automobile ?
   (*b*) What problems had to be solved before the automobile was successful ?
   (*c*) Why is the gasoline engine rather than the steam engine more practicable for automobiles ?
   (*d*) What were the early automobiles like ?
   (*e*) Why has automobile transportation developed so rapidly in America ?
   (*f*) What is the status of automobile transportation today ?

2. How does the automobile work ?
   (*a*) What happens inside the cylinder of a gasoline engine ?
   (*b*) How does a fcur-cycle engine work ?
   (*c*) What is the work of the carburetor ?
   (*d*) How is power transmitted to the drive wheels ?
   (*e*) Of what does the electrical system of an automobile consist ?
   (*f*) How is the automobile made to stop quickly ?
   (*g*) How have automobile designers attempted to overcome wind resistance ?

3. What are the factors to be considered in the selection of an automobile ?
   (*a*) What machine will give the most value for the money ?
   (*b*) What is the average fuel and oil consumption ?
   (*c*) Are repairs available ?

   (*d*) What is the cost of repairs over a long period of time ?
   (*e*) Is the machine made by a reliable, well established company ?

4. How can the automobile be most efficiently operated ?
   (*a*) What are the principles of economical and careful driving ?
   (*b*) What is the relation between careless driving and costs of repairs ?
   (*c*) Why does gasoline and oil consumption increase so rapidly with speed ?
   (*d*) How can maximum mileage be secured from fuel and oil ?
   (*e*) How can maximum service be secured from tires ?
   (*f*) How can the life of brake linings be increased ?

5. What are the precautions necessary for safe driving ?
   (*a*) Why does safe driving require good tires ?
   (*b*) Can driving be safe without good brakes ?
   (*c*) How does a good steering mechanism contribute to safety ?
   (*d*) What are the light requirements for safe driving ?
   (*e*) Why is the driver the most important factor in safe driving ?
   (*f*) How does one's attitude toward traffic laws affect safety on the highway ?
   (*g*) What rules for safe driving on highways should be followed ?
   (*h*) What are Missouri's driving signals ?

C. What are the Principles and Significance of Water Transportation ?

1. Why do bodies float in water ?
   (*a*) What is meant by density ?
   (*b*) What is specific gravity ?
   (*c*) What is the principle of Archimedes ?
   (*d*) In what way is the center of gravity related to the stability of a boat ?

2. What are the methods of water transportation that have been used ?
   (*a*) How was the use of oars probably developed ?
   (*b*) In what way are oars used as levers ?
   (*c*) How did the development of sailing vessels depend upon a knowledge of the laws of physics ?
   (*d*) How has the magnetic compass affected navigation ?
   (*e*) What it the gyroscope and how does it work ?
   (*f*) What has been the development of steam navigation ?
3. How has water transportation kept pace with land transportation ?
   (*a*) To what extent is the steam turbine being used as power for steamships ?
   (*b*) Is the Diesel-electric power plant adaptable to sea craft ?
   (*c*) What are some of the world's great ships ?
   (*d*) What are some recent developments in navigation ?
   (*e*) What is the future of water transportation ?

D. What are the Important Steps in the Development of Air Transportation ?

1. What is the story of lighter than air machines ?
   (*a*) What is the meaning of "lighter than air ?"
   (*b*) What is the value of these machines for transportation ?
   (*c*) What is their value to the study of science ?
2. How does the airplane fly ?
   (*a*) How is a kite kept aloft ?
   (*b*) How is the glider like a box kite ?
   (*c*) What has been the development of the airplane ?
   (*d*) How has the success of the airplane depended upon an understanding of the laws of physics ?
   (*e*) Upon what does the lifting force and speed of an airplane depend ?
   (*f*) How are planes supported in flight ?
   (*g*) What are the types of airplanes ?

(*h*) Why has the airplane been accused of being an "enemy of civilization" ?

3. What are the principal features of the airplane ?
   (*a*) How does the engine compare with the automobile engine ?
   (*b*) How is the body or fuselage constructed ?
   (*c*) How do the stabilizers and controlling surfaces operate in controlling flight ?
   (*d*) How does a parachute operate ?
4. What scientific aids have been developed to make air transportation practicable ?
   (*a*) How is the weather studied and reported to pilots ?
   (*b*) What has been done to make night flying practicable ?
   (*c*) How is the course of airways marked by radio signals ?
   (*d*) How does the pilot determine his altitude ?
   (*e*) How can "blind flying" be accomplished ?
5. What is the probable future of air transportation ?
   (*a*) What experiments have been made in high altitude flying ?
   (*b*) What is the variable pitch propeller ?
   (*c*) How is the variable supercharger an aid to high altitude flying ?
   (*d*) How have slow landing wings made high speed planes practicable ?
   (*e*) What is the probable future of aviation ?

III. LEARNING ACTIVITIES

A. Teaching Approach

1. Present a challenging question that will stimulate interest
   (*a*) What would happen to us if our community had no transportation facilities ?
   (*b*) How did your grandfathers come to Missouri ?
   (*c*) How did their transportation methods compare with earlier methods ?

(*d*) Why did it take Columbus and the explorers so much longer to cross the Atlantic than it requires today ?

(*e*) What did Charles Dickens have to say about American roads ?

(*f*) How long does it take to cross the Atlantic on the Atlantic Clipper ?

2. Present a news item, magazine article, or statement that will arouse interest.

(*a*) A story of the first locomotive

(*b*) The story of the contest between steam and electric locomotives.

(*c*) The story of Sir Malcolm Campbell, the noted English racer.

(*d*) Such stories as those of Admiral Byrd and Lindbergh.

(*e*) A statement such as : "So popular had the horseless carriage become by 1900 that more than four thousand were manufactured in that year."

3. The teacher should present a number of special demonstrations.

(*a*) Boyle's Law
(*b*) Showing that air has weight
(*c*) Showing that air exerts pressure
(*d*) Demonstration of the barometer
(*e*) Types of levers
(*f*) The wheel and axle
(*g*) The effect of pressure on the boiling point
(*h*) Archimedes' Principle
(*i*) Pascal's Law
(*j*) Density
(*k*) Laws of friction.

4. The teacher should arrange for a number of field trips.

(*a*) Make a trip to the railroad station and study a locomotive.

(*b*) If possible take the class through a streamlined train.

(*c*) Make a trip to the local garage to study an automobile which has been torn down for repairs.

B. Pupil Activities

1. The pupils should make investigations of the history of transportation.

   (*a*) Present the story of the first steam engine.
   (*b*) Prepare reports on the lives of Newcomen, Watt, Stephenson, and others.
   (*c*) Make a study of the use of rails in transportation.
   (*d*) Trace the history of transportation by collecting pictures and clippings.
   (*e*) Report on the first steamboat and the life of Robert Fulton.
   (*f*) Investigate and report upon the development of the automobile.
   (*g*) Make a study of the development of aviation.
   (*h*) Collect figures and statistics concerning transportation today ; make reports, summaries, and predictions for the future.
   (*i*) Make a survey of the number of automobiles in the community.

2. Pupils should perform a number of experiments under the guidance of the teacher.

   (*a*) Archimedes' Law
   (*b*) Experiments to determine density
   (*c*) Types of levers
   (*d*) Inclined plane
   (*e*) Wheel and axle
   (*f*) Specific gravity
   (*g*) Laws of friction
   (*h*) Operation of a model steam engine
   (*i*) Exploding a mixture of gasoline vapour and air.

3. Students should make individual studies and reports.

   (*a*) Trace the changes that are now taking place in transportation systems and methods and summarize these changes.

(*b*) Make a study of bus and truck transportation ; explain why these types have become such serious competitors of railroads and streetcars.

(*c*) Make a report on the signaling system and safety devices used by railroads.

(*d*) Study the airbrake—its operation and effect upon the speed of the train.

4. Classroom activities (To be worked out by teacher and pupil.)

(*a*) Make a study of the factors to be considered in selecting a new automobile ; a used automobile.

(*b*) Make a study of the chemistry of burning fuel in the automobile.

(*c*) Secure a carburetor and study its parts and operation.

(*d*) Secure other parts of the automobile such as the clutch, gears, differential, etc., and make a study of their operation.

(*e*) Make a study of the construction, chemistry, and use of the storage battery.

(*f*) Make a detailed study of one or more of the system of the automobile—power, electrical, lubricating, cooling ; etc. ; use pictures, charts, and diagrams.

(*g*) Make a detailed study of automobile lubrication ; study and test various kinds of motor oils. Make similar studies of motor fuels and of tires.

(*h*) Make a list of common causes of automobile troubles suggest methods of prevention.

(*i*) Formulate a set of rules for the good driver ; study traffic laws and regulations.

5. Vocabulary

The following are some of the words that the students should learn during a study of this unit.

altimeter
amphibian
carburetor
center of gravity
clutch
crankshaft
cylinder
density
Diesel engine
Diesel-electric
differential
energy
force
friction
fulcrum
fuselage
gyroscope
horsepower
ignition
mechanical advantage
octane selector
parachute
piston
power
specific gravity
streamline
supercharger
transmission

C. Additional Activities

1. Special studies for those interested in railroads
   (*a*) Make a study of air conditioning in trains.
   (*b*) What are the safety devices used by railroads ?
   (*c*) Make a study of grades in roads and their relationship to power necessary to pull loads.
   (*d*) Report on the electrification of railroads—its advantages and disadvantages.
   (*e*) Make a model steam engine or locomotive.
   (*f*) Compare the speed of sound with the speed of a train at 100 miles per hour.

2. Special studies on the automobile
   (*a*) Make a study of the relationship between speed, wind resistance, and gasoline consumption.
   (*b*) Make a survey among friends who own automobiles to find average gasoline mileage. Report your findings to the class.
   (*c*) Make a detailed study of the electrical system of an automobile. Report using diagrams and charts.
   (*d*) Make a set of suggestions for securing more mileage from brake linings ; from tires ; from gasoline.

(*e*) Make a set of suggestions entitled, "Characteristics of a Good Driver," to be given to young people just learning to drive.
(*f*) Locate and repair some minor automobile trouble.
(*g*) Show the film, *The Automobile*.
(*h*) Other films : *Land Transportation* ; *Transportation* and *Gas Engine, Four-Stroke Cycle*.

3. Special activities on water transportation
   (*a*) Make a model steam turbine.
   (*b*) Build a ship model.
   (*c*) Make a special report on the gyroscope.
   (*d*) Investigate methods used to determine the depth of the ocean.
   (*e*) Make a study of the Panama Canal or other waterway.
   (*f*) Show the film, *Steam Power*.
4. Activities on air transportation
   (*a*) Make and fly a model airplane.
   (*b*) Report on the use of airway radio fences.
   (*c*) Make a detailed study of the forces acting upon an airplane in flight ; show how it is kept aloft and controlled.
   (*d*) Report on the qualifications required of pilots, mechanics, and air hostesses.

IV. REFERENCES

A. General References

1. Black, Newton H., and Davis, H.N., *Elementary Practical Physics*, Macmillan, 1938.
2. Bush, George L., Ptacek, Theodore W., and Kovats, John, Jr., *Senior Science*, American, 1937.
3. Chase, Stuart, *Men and Machines*, Macmillan, 1929.
4. Davis, Watson, *Science Today*, Harcourt, Brace, 1931.
5. Hausrath, Alfred H., Jr., and Harms, John H., *Consumer Science*, Macmillan, 1939.
6. Marshall, Leon Carroll, *The Story of Human Progress*, Macmillan, 1925.

7. Millikan, Robert A., Gale, Henry G., and Coyle, James P., *New Elementary Physics*, Ginn, 1936.
8. Williard, Lester R., *Experiences in Physics*, Ginn, 1939.

B. References on Rail Transportation

1. Coolidge, Ann, and Di Bona, Anthony, *The Story of Steam*, Winston, 1935.
2. Flaxman, Edward, *Great Feats in Engineering*, Blackie and Son, 1931.
3. Fraser, Chelsea Curtis, *Story of Engineering in America*, Goodheart-Wilcox, 1935.
4. Jackson, George Gibbard, *Triumphs and Wonders of Modern Engineering*, Sampson, Low, Marsten, 1931.
5. Jackson, George Gibbard, *The Book of the Locomotive*, Longmans, Green, 1924.
6. Jackson, George Gibbard, *The Romance of the Railway*, Raphael Tuck, 1929.
7. Little, W.B., *The World's Book in Industry*, Pitman, 1931.
8. Parkman, Mary, *Conquests of Invention*, Century, 1931.
9. Starr, John William, *One Hundred Years of American Railroading*, Dodd, 1928.
10. Van Metre, Thurman William, *Trains, Tracks, and Travel*, Simmons-Boardman, 1931.

C. References on Automobile Transportation

1. Dyke, Andrew Lee, *Automobile and Gasoline Engine Encyclopedia*, Goodheart-Wilcox. 1935.
2. Epstein, R.C., *Automobile Industry*, Shaw, 1928.
3. Floherty, John J., *Youth at the Wheel*, Lippincott, 1937.
4. Hawks, Frank Monroe, *Speed*, Harcourt, Brace, 1931.
5. Reck, Franklin Mering, *Automobile from Start to Finish*, Crowell, 1935.
6. Sherman, Ray Wesley, *If You Are Going to Drive Fast*, Crowell, 1935.
7. Strouse, C.R., *Starting and Lighting : Lighting Devices*, International Textbook Company, 1931.
8. Whitney, Albert Wurts, *Man and the Motor Car*, National Bureau of Casualty and Surety Underwriters, New York.

9. Wright, John Calvin, *Automotive Construction and Operation*, Wiley, 1933.

10. General Motors Publications, Detroit
    (*a*) *Automobile Users Guide.*
    (*b*) *Diesel, the Modern Power.*
    (*c*) *Transportation Progress.*
    (*d*) *When the Wheels Revolve.*

11. Magazine Articles
    (*a*) Billings, C., "When You Drive Fast," *Harpers*, July, 1936.
    (*b*) Klemin, A., "Are Modern Cars Safe ?" *Scientific American*, August, 1936.
    (*c*) Drum, R.W., "Who Have the Highway Accidents ?" *Scientific American*, July, 1938.
    (*d*) Peck, A.P., "Motor Car Engine Takes Form," *Scientific American*, March, 1938.
    (*e*) "What Makes an Automobile Run ?" *Scholastic*, October 17, 1936.

D. References on Water Transportation

1. Chartwright, Charles E., *Boy's Book of Ships*, Dutton, 1925.
2. Darrow, Floyd Lavern, *The Boy's Own Book of Great Inventions*, Macmillan, 1924.
3. Holland, Maurice, *Industrial Explorers*, *Harpers*, 1928.
4. Mott-Smith, Morton, *This Mechanical World*, Appleton-Century, 1925.

E. References on Air Transportation

1. Bryan, Leslie Aulis, *Aerial Transportation*, Anderson, 1925.
2. Collins, Archie Frederick, *Aviation and All About It*, Appleton-Century, 1929
3. Collins, Archie Frederick, *The Boy's Book of Model Aeroplanes*, Appleton-Century, 1936.
4. Hamburg, Merrill, *Beginning to Fly*, Houghton Mifflin, 1930.
5. Hawks, Ellison, *Romance of Transport*, Crowell, 1931.

6. Kneen, Orville Hayter, *Everyman's Book of Flying*, Stokes, 1930.
7. Philip, Charles G., *The Conquest of the Stratosphere*, Pitman, 1937.
8. Simmons, Ralph, *All About Aircraft*, Cassell, 1915.
9. Wilkins, Harold Tom, *Marvels of Modern Mechanics*, Dutton, 1932.
10. Magazine Articles
    (*a*) Cleveland, R.M., "Wings That Turn," *Scientific American*, July, 1935.
    (*b*) Klemin, A., "Airship Plus Helicopter," *Scientific American*, November, 1935.
    (*c*) Klemin, A., "Engines for Light Planes," *Scientific American*, June, 1938.
    (*d*) Klemin, A., "What is the Power of an Engine ?" *Scientific American*, November, 1935.
    (*e*) Klemin, A., "Ultimate in Resistance Reduction," *Scientific American*, October, 1935.
    (*f*) Wilkinson, P.H., "Diesel in the Air," *Popular Mechanics*, August, 1938.

F. Films

The following films are all 16 mm, silent and may be secured on rental basis from the University of Missouri, Visual Education Service, Columbia, Missouri.

1. *Along the Firing Line*, two reels. (Illustrates the use of spark plugs in gasoline engines).
2. *Automobile Lubrication*, one reel.
3. *Evolution of Oil*, four reels.
4. *Gas Engine, Four-Stroke Cycle*, one reel.
5. *Land Transportation*, one reel.
6. *Rubber*, one reel.
7. *Simple Machines*, one reel.
8. *The Automobile*, one reel.
9. *Transportation*, one reel.

G. Additional Films

These all are 16 mm. silent films and may be secured from the U.S. Bureau of Mines, 48C0 Forbes St.. Pittsburg, Pennsylvania.

1. *Story of Gasoline.*
2. *Story of the Gasoline Major.*
3. *Story of a Storage Battery.*
4. *The Evolution of the Oil Industry.*
5. *The Metals of a Motor Car.*
6. *Transportation.*

H. Free Flat Pictures, Bulletins, and Charts

1. *Aeronautical Mechanics.* The new 1000 H.P. Wright cyclone engine to show mechanics of the airplane. Wright Aeronautical Corp., Patterson, New Jersey.
2. *Automotives.* Bulletins describing Zenith carburetors Zenith Carburetor Co., 696 Hart Ave,, Detroit, Mich.
3. *Locomotives : The Modern Trends in Railway Motor Power.* American Locomotive Co., 30 Church St., New York.
4. *Rubber : Samples of materials.* Firestone Tire and Rubber Co., Firestone Park, Akron, Ohio.
5. *Storage Batteries.* A chart 41 in. by 82 in. showing the construction of storage batteries. Electric Storage Battery Co., Philadelphia, Pa.

V. EVALUATION

A. Check List in Terms of the Objectives

1. Does the class have a better appreciation of the contribution of science to the problems of transportation ?
2. Do the students have an appreciation of the work of individual scientists ?
3. To what extent has the class developed scientific methods of thinking ?
4. Have the pupils improved in their attitudes toward safety on the streets and highways ?
5. Have I succeeded in teaching my pupils the principles and rules for good automobile drivers ?

6. Have I succeeded in developing any interests in the class ?
7. Do the students understand the working principles of the gasoline engine ?
8. Have I improved my technique of teaching ?

B. True-False Items

............1. The first locomotive was built by James Watt.

............2. The Diesel engine is more efficient than the steam turbine.

............3. The power stroke of a four-cycle gasoline engine occurs once in every two revolutions of the fly-wheel.

............4. The motor of an automobile should be raced to warm it up quickly.

C. Completion Exercises

1. The fuel most commonly used in the Diesel engine is...........
2. The energy of a moving vehicle is changed into......... energy in the brake drums when the brakes are applied.
3. The equipment of an automobile consisting of battery, wires, spark plugs, coils, and distributor points is known as the.....................system.
4. Steam under high temperature and pressure is known as..................steam.

D. Matching Exercises

( )	1. An automatic device used to control temperature	1. Carburetor
		2. Carbon monoxide
( )	2. A device which stores mechanical energy	3. Thermostat
		4. Battery
( )	3. A deadly gas produced by an automobile engine and given off in the exhaust	5. Differential
		6. Transmission
( )	4. The device which regulates the mixture of air and gasoline entering the cylinder of an automobile engine	

ADVANCED PHYSICAL SCIENCE

TEACHER EVALUATION AND SUGGESTIONS FOR IMPROVEMENT

Unit..

(*Number*) (*Title*)

Note to Teacher : As a result of your experiences in teaching this unit, please make suggestions for improvement and send to Lloyd W. King, State Superintendent of Public Schools. Use an additional sheet if necessary.

Scope and Purpose

Suggested Content

Learning Activities

Evaluation

UNIT VI

9

Scientific Facts Man Needs to Know About Textiles

I. SCOPE AND PURPOSE

A. Introduction

The study of this unit should help a pupil to be able to buy clothing and textiles more intelligently and wisely, to know why some materials are cheap and some expensive, why some garments are cool and some warm, and why some wear longer than others. He should be able to obtain information from labels on materials and be able to recognize adulteration of fabrics. The pupil should learn to recognize the different textiles and a few of the fabrics and should learn how to remove stains and to care for clothes correctly.

B. Unit Objectives

1. To help pupils to be able to buy textiles more intelligently.
2. To show pupils how to care for textiles.
3. To help develop an appreciation for beautiful materials.

II. SUGGESTED CONTENT

A. Where Are Each of the Textile Fibers Obtained and How Are They Manufactured ?

1. What are the vegetable fibers ?
   (*a*) How is cotton grown and manufactured ?
   (*b*) What is linen ? How is it made into material ?
2. What are the animal fibers ?
   (*a*) How is silk produced ?
   (*b*) From what animals is wool obtained ?
3. What are the synthetic fibers ?
   (*a*) What is rayon made out of and how is it manufactured ?
   (*b*) How is Nylon manufactured and what is it used for ?
   (*c*) From what is lanital made ?
   (*d*) How is fiberglas made ?
4. Why is rubber useful in the textile field ?
5. How is leather made ?
6. What furs are commonly worn for wearing appearel ?

B. How Are Materials Woven, Bleached, and Dyed ?

1. How does the weave influence the kind of fabric ?
2. How are materials bleached ?
3. How is dye applied to material ?

C. What Are the Characteristics of Textile Fibers ?

1. What does "affinity for dye" mean ?
2. Which of the textile fibers is the longest ?
3. Which fiber has the greatest luster ?
4. Which fiber conducts heat the best ?
5. Which fiber is the most elastic ?
6. Which fiber absorbs the most water ?

D. How Are Materials Adulterated ?

1. What is sizing ?
2. What is weighting ?
3. Why are cheaper fibers mixed with better ones ?

4. What kinds of materials are reworked ?
5. What does shoddy mean ?

E. What Information Is Placed on the Labels of Materials ?

1. How can one tell when materials will not fade ?
   (*a*) What does washable mean ?
   (*b*) Does tubfast mean that the material will not fade ?
   (*c*) What does colourfast mean ?
2. What does mercerized mean ?
3. Which materials have weighting added ?
4. How does the thread count influence the quality of material ?
5. What is shrinkage ?
   (*a*) Will pre-shrunk material shrink when washed ?
   (*b*) How is material sanforized ?
   (*c*) What does needlized mean ?
6. How much wool must be in material before it can be labeled "part wool" ?
7. What is meant by tensile strength ?

F. How May the Different Textiles Be Recognized ?

1. What fibers can be identified by the burning test ?
2. How is the ink test made ?
3. What appearance and "feel" does each of the textiles have ?
4. What chemical tests are used to identify fibers ?
   (*a*) Which fibers can be identified by the five per cent sodium hydroxide ?
   (*b*) Which fibers does concentrated hydrochloric acid dissolve ?
   (*c*) Which fibers can be identified with Milon's Reagent ?
   (*d*) Which kind of rayon does acetone dissolve ?
5. How does each of the fibers look under the microscope ?

G. How Can Stains Be Removed ?

1. Which stains can be removed with absorbents ?
2. Which fluids are used in dry cleaning ?
3. Which materials should be dry cleaned ?

H. How Should Textiles Be Cleaned ?

1. What steps should be followed in laundering ?
2. Which fluids are used in dry cleaning ?
3. Which materials should be dry cleaned ?

I. How Can Clothes Be Protected From Moths ?

1. What are some effective ways of preventing moths ?
2. How should clothing be stored to keep it away from moths ?
3. What household pests, other than moths, bother clothing ?

III. LEARNING ACTIVITIES

A. Teaching Procedures

1. This unit may be introduced by showing one of the motion picture films on manufacturing textiles.
2. The teacher may have on hand some good quality materials and some poor quality materials. Let the pupils examine them and see if they can detect the things which make the difference in the quality of the materials ?
3. A field trip may be made to a textile factory or tailor shop to examine different fabrics.

B. Pupil Activities

1. Pupils may give reports on the growth and manufacture of various textiles.
2. Identify unknown samples of materials with various identification tests.

   (*a*) Burning test
   (*b*) Ink test
   (*c*) Chemical tests
   (*d*) Microscopic test.

3. The teacher may prepare slides of the various textile fibers for study under the microscope.
4. With charts or small looms, demonstrate the most common weaves.
5. Have materials stained several different ways and let the class remove the stains.
6. The teacher may have some adulterated materials for display and may show how the adulteration can be detected.
7. Discuss the characteristics of various fibers and then draw conclusions as to the use each should have.
8. Make a trip to a laundry or a dry cleaning establishment.
9. Study the different substances used as protection against moths.
10. Bring several of the most common materials to class and learn to identify the different fabrics by name—muslin, dimity, etc.
11. Dye some materials made of various textile fibers.
12. Terms which will be helpful in the study of this unit.

acetate	benzene	Javelle water
adulteration	damask	mercerized
affinity	dimity	mildew
broadcloth	jacquard weave	napping
needlized	serge	tensile strength
Nylon	sericulture	thread count
pupa	shoddy	viscose
pre-shrunk	sized	warp
reeling	synthetic	weighted
retting	tanning	woof
sanforized		

C. Additional Activities

1. Give special reports on the origin, production, manufacture, and uses of our five most commonly used fibers. The reports may also include the life and customs of the different people who produce these fabrics, as for example, the silkworm raisers.

2. Study how soap is made and find which brands are best for laundering.
3. Better students may be given more materials to identify, or more stains to remove, etc.

IV. REFERENCES

1. Balderston, Lydia K., *Laundering*, Lippincott, 1923.
2. Bush, George L., Ptacek, Theodore W., and Kovats, John, Jr. *Senior Science*, American, 1937.
3. Donovan, Dulcie G., *The Mode in Dress and Home*, Allyn and Bacon, 1935.
4. Dooley, Henry, *Textiles*, Heath, 1924.
5. Dyer, Elizabeth, *Textile Fabrics*, Houghton Mifflin, 1923.
6. Gibbs, Charlotte Mitchel, *Household Textiles*, Whitcomb and Barrows, 1922.
7. Giles, Nathan B., and Ellis, D.G., *Science of the Home*, Wiley, 1929.
8. Hunter, George William, and Whitman, W.G., *Civic Science of the Home*, American, 1921.
9. Justin, Margaret M., and Rust, L.M., *Home Living*, Lippincott, 1935.
10. Kinne, Helen, and Cooley, A.M., *Shelter and Clothing*, Macmillan, 1926.
11. Matthews, Mary Lockwood, *Clothing, Selection and Care*, Little, Brown, 1936.
12. Nystram, Paul Henry, *Textiles*, Appleton, 1916.
13. Pieper, Charles J., and Beauchamp, W.L., *Everyday Problems in Science*, Scott, Foresman, 1936, Unit 8.
14. Rathbone, Lucy, and Tarpley, Elizabeth, *Fabrics and Dress*, Houghton Mifflin, 1937.
15. Wilson, Sherman Ray, *Descriptive Chemistry and Physics*, Henry Holt, 1936, Chapter 7.
16. Woolman, Mary (Schenk), *Clothing*, Lippincott, 1926.
17. Woolman, Mary (Schenk), and McGowan, E.A., *Textiles*, Macmillan, 1927.

18. **Films**

    (*a*) 16 mm. sound film, *Clothing*, one reel.

    (*b*) 16 mm. silent films :

    Cotton, 1 reel.
    Cotton Growing, 1 reel.
    Cotton—From Seed to Cloth, 2 reels.
    From Flax to Linen, 1 reel.
    Leather, 1 reel.
    Rubber, 1 reel.
    Woolen Goods, 1 reel.
    From Cocoon to Spool, 1 reel.

V. EVALUATION

A. Observation Questions

1. Can the pupils identify the different textile fibers ?
2. Have I taught the pupils to buy materials more wisely ?
3. Can each one read the labels on material intelligently ?
4. Can the students detect adulteration of materials ?
5. Do the students know how to remove the most common stains ?
6. Do the students know the correct procedures for laundering and dry cleaning ?
7. Do the students know how to protect clothing from moths ?

B. Illustrative Testing Items and Procedures

True-false questions

.... 1. The silk worm eats mulberry leaves when it is in the pupa stage.

.... 2. Linen is obtained from the stem of the flax plant.

.... 3. Chemists have been able to produce a cheap synthetic rubber.

Completion items

1. Wool smells like...........when it burns.
2. When cotton material is sized,...........is added to the material to give it more body.

3. ....is put in the rinse water for white things to make them look white.
4. Fruit stains may be removed by pouring........... ....over them.
5. Most of our silk comes from...........

ADVANCED PHYSICAL SCIENCE

———

TEACHER EVALUATION AND SUGGESTIONS FOR IMPROVEMENT

Unit...

(*Number*) (*Title*)

Note to Teacher : As a result of your experiences in teaching this unit, please make suggestions for improvement and send to Lloyd W. King. State Superintendent of Public Schools. Use an additional sheet if necessary.

Scope and Purpose

Suggested Content

Learning Activities

Evaluation

10

The Education of Science Teachers

INTRODUCTION

The philosophy basic to establishing the science offerings in our schools has been presented. It has set forth the principles which provide the criteria for determining the material requirements such as rooms, furnishing equipment and supplies for the teaching of science. Other chapters have dealt with the physical facilities for science instuction under various school conditions for the elementary school and the secondary school.

The facilities and materials which are indicated as essential or desirable are of value in instruction only to the extent that the teacher is competent to use them effectively and to discriminate wisely in his choice of science activity in a given situation. Teacher competence is developed, in part, through experience with the materials of science instruction in surroundings that are equivalent to school conditions.

Courses in the basic sciences and in the psychology, philosophy, and methodology of teaching are essential to teacher preparation. Where class groups in the science courses can be composed entirely of prospective teachers, attention should be given in both the classroom and the laboratory to problems of instruction as well as to the content. As subject matter is being taught, good procedures for the teaching of science in the elementary and secondary schools should be emphasized. Where prospective teachers of science participate in classes with students of engineering, arts and sciences, pharmacy, medicine, and law, it is evident that they must have the opportunity through professional courses, professionalized subject-matter courses, and laboratory facilities to learn to do those things essential to effective teaching.

The facilities described in this chapter should be used extensively in the pre-service phase of teacher education and should be so organized and administered as to encourage continuous in-service use. The science teacher with a feeling of professional responsibility will use such facilities voluntarily to help him to develop new techniques and procedures, new ideas relative to instructional materials, and to avail himself of the opportunity to use specific pieces of equipment under laboratory or demonstration conditions. Informal "open-house" days when science teachers use the facilities, planned science teacher conferences, and credit courses will contribute to the in-service teacher use of the facilities.

The institution that assumes responsibility for the preparation of science teachers must provide instruction and laboratory experience in the use, manipulation, building and maintenance of the facilities and materials required for science teaching. Such resources should be organized in the form of a professional laboratory for science teachers. This chapter describes such laboratories, their resources and their organization, and various aspects of their administration.

ADMINISTRATIVE ORGANIZATION OF FACILITIES

An adequate program for the preparation of science teachers is a joint responsibility of educators and scientists. It is as important to have the prospective science teacher study with and come to know competent scientists who are also good teachers, as it is that he study the principles of teaching with competent educators.

The laboratory and materials center may be housed by the departments of science, or by the school or department of education as considered best in the local institution. Whatever the plan, the nature of the facilities and the methods and procedures for their use will be essentially the same. There are advantages in each type of arrangement that which is most effective in the local situation for increasing the competence of the prospective teacher should, of course, be utilized.

Organization through Academic Departments

Active cooperation between departments of education and the subject-matter departments most closely related to high school science may result in joint responsibility for the appointment of staff, the determination of curricular offerings, and in the provision of space in the science building for the laboratory and materials center, with ready access to the facilities and resources of the department or departments. This arrangement is particularly desirable in institutions where all sciences are housed in one building. In larger instutions it may be better to provide a life science laboratory for science teachers separate from a corresponding laboratory for teachers of the physical sciences, each being established in the building which houses the associated science department or departments. It is not recommended that separate laboratories be established in the individual sciences, as, for example, botany and zoology. In large institutions where the departments of sciences are housed separately it is still possible to provide cooperatively for both materials and instruction. This is done in at least one institution where the phyical science teachers' laboratory is housed in the physics building and where a member of the chemistry staff is appointed as a consultant and authorized to provide the teachers' laboratory with needed apparatus and supplies from chemistry stores. A single teachers' laboratory is probably the most desirable plan for the preparation of teachers for the areas of elementary and general science.

Disadvantages may result from this type of organization. Where the laboratory is placed in the building housing a single subject matter department, care must be taken to avoid overemphasis of the one field. This kind of organization may tend to place emphasis on content as such, with too little concern for the professional selection, organization and use of content ; however, the establishment and maintenance of subject-matter competence among science teachers is based upon the active participation of scientists in the education of science teachers. Mutual understanding and appreciation by scientists and educators of the values to be obtained by the coordinated presentation of pertinent content in each field can be important byproducts of this type or organization.

Organization through Departments of Education

A major advantage in organizing the laboratory for science teachers within the department of education is that teachers may understand more fully the relation of science teaching to the teaching in other fields such as mathematics education. Similarly, the probability of comparable emphasis on the various fields of science is greater than it may be where the laboratory is a function of a single academic department. These outcomes do not follow as a matter of course in either plan of organization but must be striven for if they are to be achieved.

Disadvantages may be found in this type of organization. There may be a loss of contact with the departments which can supply personnel as well as physical resources. The academic departments, by reason of the physical separation, may readily lose interest in and concern for the preparation of science teachers.

Where the laboratory is housed within the department of education, cooperative arrangements may be made with the subject-matter departments for the use of such facilities as a greenhouse and for the loan of special pieces of apparatus with which the teacher should be familiar ; however, constant access to sources of science teaching materials may not be so easily arranged.

Use of the Campus or Cooperating School

An advantageous placement of the laboratory for science teachers is in the campus or cooperating school. Here the materials serve the needs of a school laboratory as well as those of teacher preparation. The real atmosphere of the school situation tends to give stimulus and direction to the activities of teacher education. There is less tendency to plan and work in an abstract, unrealistic manner. The disadvantages found in certain other types of organization have their counterparts in this arrangement: there is loss of contact with other personnel of the institution, and physical resources tend to be less accessible.

The most desirable plan seems to be that in which the science teachers' laboratory is so established and administered as to have the joint support of scientists and educators. This will usually involve placement in either a science building or the education building.

The Laboratory in Relation to Student Teaching

Where the laboratory is established in the department of education or in a department of science, an adequate materials and preparation center should be provided in the school where student-teachers in science do their work. If this is an elementary school the facilities described in the chapter dealing with the elementary school will be adequate, especially if a room is set aside as a science center. If the laboratory is established in a junior or senior high school the requirements will depend on the number of student-teachers in the field of science. In some instances student-teachers are assigned to full-time duty under the direction of a supervising teacher. In this case the facilities indicated in the previous chapters will probably be adequate.

In large institutions the student-teachers are often assigned to cooperating public schools, only one or two being under the direction of any one science teacher. There are situtations, however, where a student-teacher assumes responsibility for a single class for an entire semester, this being under the direction of a supervising teacher. Here as many as six student-teachers may be required to make independent preparations for as many separate classes, all under the direction of one supervising teacher. For this the same type of equipment will be needed as before but a greater quantity of each item will be required. Likewise more preparation space will be needed.

Organization Through Facilities for General Education

The facilities desirable for the laboratory for the prospective science teacher are similar in many respects to those of a laboratory designed to serve courses in science for general education. The possibilities of providing a multipurpose laboratory to serve both functions should be explored. Such a laboratory can justify the utilization of more space than can either laboratory alone. Likewise, a broader range of facilities is possible in the dual-purpose laboratory.

NATURE OF THE PROFESSIONAL LABORATORY

That there is a need for a professionalized laboratory for science teachers has long been agreed upon by science educators. Recommendations have been reported in the literature. The specific features of the laboratory will vary somewhat from one college to another; however, there are certain general qualities that should be common to most laboratories.

The equipment of the laboratory should be realistic; it should provide opportunities for varied and rich experiences for those teachers served, and should be based upon activities characteristic of the usual school. This laboratory should aid the prospective teacher in making the transition from student to teacher, i.e., from one who has received a great deal of direction to one who is responsible for planning and directing. The laboratory should provide facilities which will enable the teacher to plan subject matter content, appropriate demonstrations and laboratory work, to assign reference materials, to design, build, and repair equipment, and engage in the various other activities necessary to effective teaching.

The laboratory should provide, in general, for easy access to equipment and materials. While resources should be readily accessible there should be provision for orderly care, and for the development of responsibility on the part of the prospective teacher for such care. Attention must be given to the conservation and replenishment of materials and supplies.

The several kinds of provisions that should be made in the science teachers' laboratory include the following :

(1) There should be supplies and apparatus for a broad range of experimentation; this should go beyond the conventional "experiments" of fundamental courses in science, and should accommodate the needs for project work in high school science and of special teacher interests. This laboratory should inspire teachers to encourage and direct creative extra-class activity among their students.

(2) There should be provision for the construction, repair, and adjustment of apparatus. Such work requires work space, materials, and tools.

(3) There should be provision for designing and building new apparatus. This requires a library rich in source materials and ideas. There must be tools, work space, test instruments, raw materials, and miscellaneous hardware.

(4) There should be demonstration and laboratory equipment and supplies, and for on-going projects.

(5) There should be adequate gas, electrical, and water services.

(6) There should be appropriate tools for field work such as collecting apparatus, soil augers, plant presses, geology hammers, and soil testing equipment.

(7) There should be abundant storage space for equipment and supplies, and for ongoing projects.

(8) There should be audio-visual resources such as projectors and recorders, charts, models, slides, recordings, and materials for making charts, and slides.

(9) There should be library resources such as reference materials, textbooks, laboratory manuals, catalogs, manufacturers' bulletins and books to encourage free reading of both teacher and student.

(10) There should be a good demonstration desk equipped with gas, water and electrical services. Additional facilities for demonstration and laboratory work may be provided through the use of movable tables.

(11) The facilities should be such that the arrangement of the room is flexible.

(12) Depending upon the area to be served, there may be need of provisions for growing plants and animals, and other biological activities.

INSTRUCTIONAL CENTERS

Much of the competence essential to the laboratory and demonstration aspects of science teaching is acquired in science courses at both high school and college level. The contribution which has come from extra-class science activity, science club work, science fairs, science hobbies and out-of-school activities should also be emphasized. The education of the science teacher is based on the assumption that basic courses in science contribute materially to the development of laboratory abilities essential to the teaching of science in the elementary and secondary schools. Experience has demonstrated conclusively that this instruction is not adequate. In addition, the prospective and inservice science teacher must have experience based on the needs which derive from the science activities of the elementary or high school student.

Although the numbers of prospective teachers to be accommodated at one time may be large it is not desirable, in general, to provide multiple sets of apparatus and facilities so that many, or all students can have the same laboratory experiences at the same time. This might actually defeat much of the purpose of the teachers' laboratory where importance is placed on the development of creative leadership and not on the performance of another "cook book" activity. Many different activities may be under way at any given time in the science teachers laboratory. With perhaps a few exceptions, provisions for various types of activities can be made through establishing instructional centers within the laboratory. Such areas, or centers, may be chosen, equipped, arranged, and used as the needs of a particular institution warrant.

Characteristics of Centers

An instructional center is a work area equipped to provide for a given kind of activity or a group of related activities.

The center is supplied with most or all of the necessary apparatus, supplies, and services normally used in connection with the activities for which the center is developed.

In many centers such services as running water, gas, and electricity are essential. In some instances one or more of these is not necessary. In most instances provision for good, natural or artificial illumination is desirable. For more specialized work, such as plant growth or photography, provision for darkening is necessary.

A center should provide adequate storage for the equipment and supplies unique to a given center or commonly used there. Equipment and supplies needed for several centers may profitably be grouped in a common storage space.

In general, the centers should be available for use at any time with few or no preliminaries. Ready use should be characteristic of the reference and curriculum center, the photographic center, and the materials center. In various centers, of course, preliminary activity such as reading, planning, obtaining supplies and assembling equipment is necessary. In some cases it is necessary to schedule the use of a center, such as a darkroom.

In some institutions it is not possible to develop the most desirable floor plan nor to have the space necessary to meet all the requirements listed here because existing rooms must be converted into the laboratory for science teachers. It may be necessary to use the storage cases, tables and the like which are available, so compromises must be made. Such compromises may be turned to advantages. Whereas the prospective teacher's previous experience has usually been in laboratories especially designed for a specific purpose, he now has firsthand experience in seeing how it is possible to improvise and make the most effective use of available space, material and equipment. The two laboratories described briefly in this chapter and other laboratories for science teachers[1] have been established by the appropriate adaptation of existing rooms.

Kinds of Center

The choice of centers and their combination for a laboratory for science teachers obviously depends upon the needs of a particular institution. Similarly the nature of a center is determined by the circumstances of the local situation. A laboratory for the preparation of teachers of biological science will be composed of a combination of the centers necessary for providing the experiences essential to the competence of the biology teacher, whereas a laboratory specifically for the preparation of the chemistry or physics teacher will include a different combination of centers. In some situations two or more of the centers suggested in the following pages can be combined ; in others, a center may be more specialized than the listing and brief descriptions suggest.

I. General Centers

Centers within this category are appropriate to the laboratory for science teachers regardless of the particular filed or fields of science teaching to be served.

Reference and Curriculum Centers

In this center are found such materials as reference books, current literature, magazines and other periodicals, pamphlets, textbooks, laboratory manuals, courses of study, unit plans, and tests. There is provision for reading and writing, and for adequate storage and filing of materials. This center should be so located as to be quiet and clean.

Conference Center

This center, which may be the office, should provide adequate space for two or more to sit in conference. There should be a table for writing, and storage of at least certain of the records of the prospective teacher. This center should provide a certain amount of privacy because of the personal nature of many conferences. If this center also serves as the instructor's office it should be provided with a desk and comfortable chairs for visitors, a typewriter desk and chair file cabinet, office supply storage cabinets, and telephone. A spirit duplicator should be available nearby in the laboratory.

Audio-Visual Center

Equipment. Projectors (opaque, filmstrip, lantern-slide, overnead, motion-picture, micro-projector), radio-phonograph, recorder, camera, films, filmstrips, slides, recordings, screens.

Arrangements should be made to borrow films from the departments of science and the audio-visual center of the college or university. In some instances similar arrangements must be made for the use of projection equipment and will usually be necessary if the use of a variety of projectors is to be taught.

Supplies. Cardboard, paint, pens, brushes, and the like for chart making, lantern slide cover glasses, ink, crayons, cellophane, and the like for slide-makings ; materials for preparing tackboards and making mock-ups.

Museum and Display Materials. Display cabinet, tackboard, display rail, materials for mounting and background, label materials ; prepared exhibits for the preparation of displays.

Files of Prepared Material. Charts, graphs, maps and mounted materials for tackboard or other use are filed for the use of the prospective teacher.

Reference Materials Center

This center may be a part of the reference and curriculum center or may be separate. In it are placed such materials as pamphlets, trade journals, commercial exhibits, magazines, and government publications.

Construction Center

In this center apparatus and equipment are built, adjusted, and repaired. The center provide, for accessory operations such as those in connection with the preparation of displays and demonstration equipment.

The construction area should have available the common hand tools for woodworking and metalworking. Where there is adequate supervision, power tools of the kinds that would usually be available in the wood- and metal-working shops of high schools are specially desirable in the laboratory for prospective high school science teachers. A power grinder, drill press, wood and metal lathes, circular saw, band saw, and scroll saw are in this category. Where the laboratory is in the science building or a part of the physics department student shops will usually be available. The use of these student shops may be quite desirable since this procedure frees space in the laboratory for other purposes.

Appropriate workbenches, metal and wood vises, mounting boards and drawers for hand tools, drawers and cabinets for the storage of hardware and raw materials are essential. There should be the necessary tools and equipment for soldering. Gas, compressed air, and electrical outlets for 110-v., a.c. are necessary. Glassworking requires a hot-wire glass cutter, a blast lamp with a compressed air source, and tools for drilling holes in glass. An oxygen tank with a reduction valve is desirable for the glass-working bench.

Materials such as wood, plastic sheet and rod, sheet metal, metal tubing, nails, screws, glass, cardboard, and glue should be provided. The accumulation of an extensive amount of such materials requires that a variety of storage facilities be provided.

Photographic Center

This center may be a darkroom, or may be essentially a part of the major room set aside for photographic activity if the entire room can be satisfactorily darkened. The resources should include such items as one or more cameras, developing trays, enlarger, printing box, films, photographic paper, and corresponding supplies. Provision for making enlargements, photographic lantern slides and filmstrips is desirable.

Most science buildings are equipped with darkrooms. The possibility and desirability of using one of these rooms in connection with the science teachers' laboratory should not be overlooked.

II. Elementary Science Center

In some institutions a separate science center for elementary teachers is provided. This center provides for most of the activities suggested in the foregoing discussion of General

Centers. In addition, the elementary science center makes provision for activities in the general fields of biological and physical science. Provisions for centers for these activities are suggested in the following sections.

The elementary science center may be divided into areas for the study of scientific topics. For example, apparatus and supplies for experiments with electricity, heat, water, plants, and many other topics may be provided in specific laboratory work areas. One table with appropriate storage space may house the experimental materials for the study of heat in the elementary school, another, light, another, sound ; and another, plant growth. Because the quantity of apparatus and materials needed in the elementary school is generally not so great as in the high school it is possible to use storage boxes for each category if storage space is not available in tables.

Attention should be given to materials which are in common use in the homes of elementary school students. Much science can be taught by the use of "home" and "ten-cent-store" equipment.

If the professionalized science laboratory serves both elementary and secondary teachers, some of the material can be used for both.

In general, great care must be taken to provide the materials which are actually used by teachers in the teaching of science in the elementary schools. In the joint laboratory for elementary and secondary science teachers each center should provide all essential materials and the teacher will choose those which fulfill his requirements. This is a realistic approach, for this is what teachers of science must do in preparing for a period of instruction where experimental or reference materials are to be used. Each center is supplied with those resources (books, apparatus, supplies) that are unique to the field of elementary science.

III. Biological Science

Plant Center

There should be facilities for the germination and growth of plants, including seed flats and pots, and for the culturing of microscopic plants. There should be soil bins, sand, fertilizer, sphagnum and peat moss. A sterilizer is desirable and running water is necessary. There should be provisions for varying the source and intensity of light. The problem of the storage of projects in progress is particularly acute in this field ; particular attention shoud be given to such facilities.

Plant presses should be accessible. A herbarium of preserved plants may be a part of the museum and display resources.

The plant center may be provided as a greenhouse, or a separate plant room. In some institutions provisions for such activities as those described are made in the greenhouse.

Animal Center

Living Animals. Provisions should be made for the care of at least four groups of living animals worms, insects, aquatic animals, and mammals. In certain instances there may be provisions for birds and snakes. The necessary types of provisions for the animals include those for food and water, cages and aquaria, and bedding and cleaning. The arrangements of cages and aquaria should be made in the light of good observation conditions.

The laboratory facilities should provide for incubation, and for breeding and nutrition experiments. There should be facilities also for collecting living animals.

For both living plants and living animals there may be provisions for controlled habitat. This can be provided to a certain extent by such a device as the familiar terrarium. For teacher education it may be desirable to provide a large case with temperature and humidity controls.

Preserved Animals. There should be killing jars for insects, preservatives for animals and dissection equipment. Preserved animals may be a part of the museum and display resources.

Microtechnique Center

A separate and somewhat removed workspace should be provided for this center because of the desirable freedom from disturbance. The space should be well lighted.

Blank and prepared slides, stains and fixers, and running water should be available. The equipment should include a microtome, tweezers, a microscope, and a microprojector. Teachers should learn to use pieces of apparatus such as the microtome, even though they may not have an instrument of this nature in the high school laboratory.

General Facilities

There should be adequate separate storage for chemicals, glassware, equipment and miscellaneous supplies needed for the biological area. The laboratory should be supplied with centers for construction, audio-visual facilities, and references as described in the previous sections.

In view of the requirements for growing plants and animals and of the need to make use of the materials of the biological science department it seems advisable to have the laboratory for the preparation of biology teachers closely associated with the biology or life science building or with a subject-matter department, such as zoology. The common use of this laboratory by the general education classes in the biological sciences and the prospective biology teachers may be seriously considered.

IV. Physical Science

Chemistry Center

In this center should be found a broad range of reagents, chemical glassware and apparatus. Such commercial products as soaps, fabrics, paints, and oils should be accessible. Reserve supplies of the most used chemicals should be on hand. The experience in college chemistry courses deals largely with principles; preparation for high school science teaching must provide competence in the application of principles.

Semi-micro technique is particularly desirable in the small high school where chemistry is taught only one or two periods per day and where it is not possible to establish a laboratory to be used only for chemistry. Since a large majority of teachers begin their work in small schools they should have practical experience with this procedure, especially if they have not had college laboratory courses in which the semi-micro technique was applied.

Electrical Center

The electrical center is at once an area to assist the teacher in building, assembling, servicing, and maintaining electrical equipment; in developing demonstration and laboratory materials for the teaching of the principles of static and current electricity; and a service area where electricity is available to assist in other phases of science teaching. The center should provide 110-v., a.c. at several points, and by means of transformers and rheostats or "variacs" should provide higher and lower voltages. A d.c. generator should be available to provide voltages of 24 to 30 volts. If the laboratory is in the science or physics building it should be serviced from the distribution panel in that building and thus have available both alternating and direct current at any desired potential. A circuit panel may be incorporated as a part of this center. Safe conditions must be provided for the use of electrical equipment.

Provisions should be made for the study of radio and common home appliances, as well as for electrochemistry.

Aeronautics Center

Facilities are provided in the aeronautics center for studying elementary aeronautics, aerodynamics, navigation, power plants and meteorology. Wind tunnels, model planes, engine models, navigation instruments, and meteorological instruments are accessible. Models, mock-ups, charts, and other visual devices may be included.

Meteorological Center

In some institutions it may be desirable to establish a center for weather study without provisions for the field of aeronautics, as such. The usual weather instruments should be provided. Weather maps should be received daily by the laboratory. In many institutions an official weather station may serve as the center, or may be utilized for supplementary experiences. This center should be at least partially developed in order to provide the necessary background for instruction in general science and physics.

Earth Science and Astronomy Center

The centers for earth science and for astronomy may be separate or combined. Such centers should include provisions for studying soil and rock sample., historical geology and erosion, and for observing and demonstrating astronomical phenomena.

A planetarium of the "Spitz" type is desirable, especially for the preparation of teachers of general science. Such an instrument can be used cooperatively with other departments of the college.

General Provisions

The provision of centers may be extended as far as circumstances warrant. Regardless of the physical organization of facilities, there should be provision for the prospective teachers to become acquainted with and use the apparatus commonly found in schools. Much of the equipment found in the college laboratory is designed for preresearch instruction. While there are certain ends gained through the use of this apparatus, the teacher who knows only such apparatus is poorly prepared. There is a considerable array of demonstration and laboratory apparatus for high school use ; the professionalized science laboratory should be equipped so as to provide competence in the use of such resources for teaching.

Unique Needs of the Laboratory School

In those situations where several student teachers must depend upon the same preparation room and resources for science teaching at the same time, attention should be given to their separate needs. This problem may be found in a laboratory school which accommodates all the student teaching for a large department of education.

The preparation of demonstration and laboratory materials requires not only the resources commonly recognized, but also space and time. To facilitate the preparation of demonstration materials, duplicate piers are placed in the classroom and in the preparation room. These piers are stationary and contain the essential utilities such as running water, sink and drain, gas, electricity and fume hood connections. The demonstration desks are mounted on wheels and are moved to a position alongside the pier in the preparation room for making the "set-up." For the teaching period the table is moved to the pier in the classroom, where the utility outlets are identical. The number of mobile demonstration desks and the length of the service pier in the preparation room is determined by the probable number of student teachers to be served.

A distinct advantage of this arrangement is in the fact that the student teacher who is also carrying a schedule of college courses can have access to the preparation room during the hours when he is free. He can work on the preparation of demonstration materials well in advance of the class period when they are to be presented.

DESCRIPTIONS OF TWO PROFESSIONAL LABORATORIES

As specific examples of the type of organization of facilities suggested, the laboratories for science teachers in two institutions are described. There is no implication that these two laboratories should be prototypes for other institutions ; the descriptions are intended only to show that steps can be taken to meet the needs of science teachers. In both instances the laboratories were developed in existing rooms without extensive changes of walls plumbing, or other services.

In one institution the laboratory for teachers of general and physical science is a function of the Department of Education ; the instructors in charge of the laboratory hold their appointments in this department. The laboratory is housed in a converted building, with relatively adequate space, but with a minimum of utilities. Windows in the roof as well as those in the walls provide abundant illumination. The offices, reading center, project room and storage room are separated by permanent partitions. The major space remaining is separated into areas for laboratory and class work by movable cabinets, thus providing considerable flexibility. Centers are developed as need, insight, and resources indicate.

In this laboratory certain centers have been developed and others are in the process of development. An audio-visual center is provided, with facilities for making charts, posters, and hand-made slides; it includes a darkroom for photographic work as well as for other operations requiring a darkened area. The center has available a selection of filmstrips and lantern slides for use in secondary school science. There are projectors for these, as well as a microprojector, a motion picture projector and an opaque projector. Mock-ups and working models are used by students. A spirit duplicator is available for student use.

A chemistry center provides common reagents and apparatus. The construction center includes provisions for woodworking and metalworking. The power tools include a circular saw, scroll saw, drill press, lathe, and grinder. There are cabinets of hand tools and supplies for construction such as screws, bolts, wire, and the like. A materials center is located in the class area. It includes a twelve-foot length of tackboard, files of pamphlets and mounted clippings, a display rack for pamphlets shelves for professional magazines, panels for chart display and storage, a case for arranging exhibits and a display stand with panels for tackboard materials. The facilities are available for students to plan and present demonstrations as a part of their preparation for teaching.

Other resources include a library of textbooks and reference books and cabinets of equipment and supplies. These resources are typical of the apparatus and materials commonly found in high school laboratories Additional resources for science teachers are provided in two separate rooms. In one room there are specialized provisions for on-going construction, including the storage of long-term projects. The other room is used primarily for the operations concerned with inexpensive printed materials. The ordering, receiving, and storing of pamphlets center in this room. Reserve stocks of multiple copies are set aside to be loaned to student-teachers for their use in the class-room.

This laboratory serves several scores of prospective and in-service science teachers each year. All undergraduate students who have a major teaching field in general science, physics, or chemistry, are required to register for the course, Laboratory Practicum for Teachers of Science, which utilizes the laboratory. Many other students with the corresponding minor areas and others with a major or minor teaching field in biological science take this course as an elective. The laboratory serves also the courses. Special Methods in the Teaching of Science. Materials for Science Teaching (study of printed and audio-visual materials) and provides resources for the student-teachers. Nearly all graduate students in science education make use of the laboratory in the course of their work. A comparable laboratory for teachers of biological science is maintained by the Department of Zoology.

In a second institution a laboratory for physical science teachers is established in he Department of Physics.[2] The plan of the laboratory in shown in Figure 10.1. The room is an appropriately equipped customary elementary physics laboratory A general view of the room, with cabinets for equipment in the background, and a blueprint cabinet for the storage of charts, sheet metal, cardboard, and radio tubes. Reading tables and tablet-arm chairs are provided for study and class use. The construction area with power tools and a generous array of hand tools is along the outside wall of the room. A small parts and apparatus cabinet containing small drawers is located near the blueprint cabinet.

In spite of limitations of floor area, certain centers have been developed. The demonstration area as is the shelving for periodicals in science and science education and for trade and industrial pamphlets. A chemistry center has essential apparatus and supplies for both macro-and semi-micro techniques. Nearby benches contain tools and a variety of small supplies for construction and for glassworking.

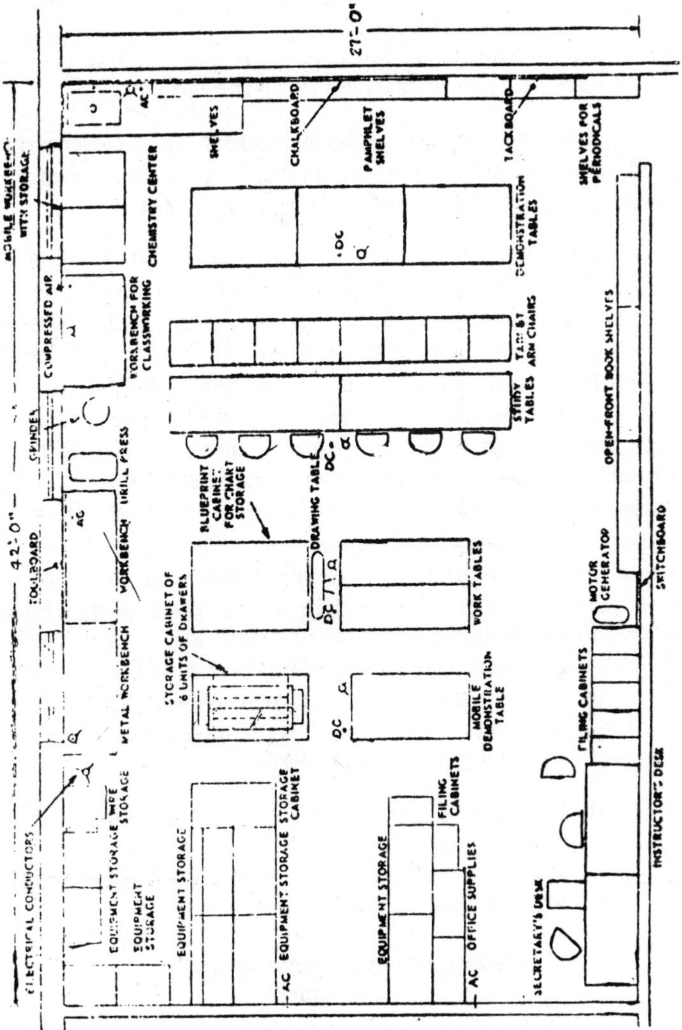

Fig. 10.1. Prospective teachers have many professional experiences in this laboratory for teachers of physical science.

An extensive library of text and reference books in the fields of physics, chemistry, general science, and elementary science. There are also books for the encouragement of free reading and reference books of particular use to high school science students. Several of the files contain bulletins of an educational nature produced by business and industrial organizations. These are open to teachers using the laboratory.

The apparatus available in the laboratory is representative of good, typical equipment for high school science teaching. Prospective teachers learn how to use these resources.

This laboratory serves the science teachers of the state as well as those who are prospective teachers. The instructor in charge of the laboratory serves as counselor for physical science for the state. Open house in the laboratory is held on one Saturday of each month ; many teachers avail themselves of the opportunity to meet informally with other science teachers to discuss common problems, to browse through the library of the laboratory, to repair equipment or use the facilities of the laboratory to develop new demonstration and laboratory equipment for their own use. The materials of the laboratory, including the books of the library, are available to science teachers on a loan basis, so that the teacher who is interested in determining how best to spend his budget allowance may determine, how appropriate certain pieces of equipment or other materials are to his own school. The student shop and darkroom facilities within the buildings are used to supplement the facilities of this laboratory.

A similar workshop for biology teachers is maintained in the Department of Biological Science. In both cases the instructors hold joint appointments in their respective departments and in the Division of Education.

COMMUNITY RESOURCES

As the teaching of science in the elementary and secondary schools is related to the community of which the school is a part, so should the education of the science teacher be a community function. The community utilized for this purpose includes the college or university campus, the surrounding area, and the home communities of the science teachers.

The Campus Community

The usual college or university campus has many resources of value to prospective science teachers that are often neglected because of the nature of the courses and the length of the period of preparation. In many institutions there are research operations of various kinds in progress, but these are not accessible to the undergraduate. While the actual performance of scientific research is usually not possible in the program for the preparation of the science teacher, at least not at the undergraduate level, an understanding of and familiarity with a few representative on-going research operations is highly desirable. Such resources should be a part of the planned program for the education of science teachers.

Prospective science teachers may well serve as guides for groups that are touring research and instructional laboratories of the institution. Such service requires that the guide be familiar with the activities in the laboratories, and it gives experience in an activity related to and of direct benefit to the elementary and high school teacher.

Resources of Surrounding Area

It is difficult, if not impossible, to imagine an area surrounding a college campus without resources of value to the prospective science teacher. In many large communities there are such resources as industrial operations, research laboratories, commercial projects such as green-houses, farms, stone quarries, forests mines, radio transmitters, or fisheries. The preparation of the science teacher should include experience with a broad range of such resources. In many instances it is possible to provide in the laboratory on the campus reference materials, guides, samples and models of the materials to be studied in the field.

Teacher Education Camps

Several institutions provide facilities for the education of teachers at off-campus points that may be broadly classified as camps. One of the major emphases of study at these camps is conservation. Such an area of concern has values for teachers from various fields—elementary, secondary, and college. The science teacher in particular is concerned with conservation.

The camps are variously organized, administered, and named. In some institutions the camp is administered by the department of education, in others by a department of science. Such names as Conservation Camp[3], Conservation Laboratory[4], and Regional-Community Study Workshop[5] are applied. In general, the experiences provided are directed to the study of problems of conservation and ecology. With full-time study available in a natural seting the studies take on genuine significance as the teachers become informed about the natural environment and competent in its use and conservation.

Human Resources in Science Teaching

A significant resource of the surrounding area is the body of science teachers in the schools. The services of these teachers in conferences and as supervisors of student teaching are of great assistance in the education of the prospective science teacher. The laboratory on the campus is an appropriate center for at least a portion of these activities. The improvement of science teaching becomes a two-way process at such a point.

The laboratory should serve as a materials center for the in-service teachers of the region. Open-house days provide for the development of new demonstration and experimental materials to be used in the schools ; equipment can be repaired, the library materials studied, and new apparatus and audio-visual equipment tried. It is through such occasions and opportunities that in-service teachers are able to approach their problems of teaching directly, and pre-service teachers become acquainted with the problem and participate in their solution.

BIBLIOGRAPHY

1. Blough, Glenn O. and Paul E. Blackwood, *Science Teaching in Rural and Small Town Schools*, Washington,

D.C. : U.S. Government Printing Office (Federal Security Agency, Office of Education, Bulletin No. 5, 1949).

2. Blough, Glenn O. and Albert J. Huggett, *Elementary-School Science and How to Teach It*, New York : The Dryden Press, 1951.
3. Bruce, Guy V., *Science Teaching Today* ; *Experiments with Water, Experiments with Air, Experiences with Fuels and Fire, Experiences with Heat, Experiences with Sound, Experiences with Magnetism and Electricity, Experiences with Light and Colour* (seven volumes). Washington, D.C. : National Science Teachers Association, 1950-1951.
4. Committee on the Teaching of Science, *A Program for Teaching Science*. Thirty-first Yearbook of the National Society for the Study of Education, Part I. Public School Publishing Co., Bloomington, Illinois, 1932.
5. Committee on Science Education in American Schools, *Science Education in American Schools*, Forty-sixth Yearbook of the National Society for the Study of Education, Part I, University of Chicago Press, 1947.
6. Fowles, G., *Lecture Experiments in Chemistry*, Third Ed , The Blakiston Co., 1947.
7. Heiss, Elwood D., Ellsworth S. Obourn and Charics W. Hottman, *Modern Science Teaching*, Macmillan Co., 1950.
8. Lynde, C.J., *Science Experiences with Home Equipment, 1949. Science Experiences with Inexpensive Equipment, 1950, Science Experiences with Ten-Cent Store Equipment*, 1950. Scranion ; International Textbook Company.
9. Miller, David F. and Glenn W. Blaydes, *Methods and Materials for Teaching Biological Sciences* New York : McGraw-Hill Book Co., Inc., 1938.
10. Richardson, John S. and G.P. Cahoon, *Methods and Materials for Teaching General and Physical Science*, New York : McGraw-Hill Book Co., Inc. 1951.

11. Richardson, John S., G.P. Cahoon, and Ralph W. Lefler, "Facilities for Science Teacher Education," *The American School and University*, Twenty-fourth Edition, pp. 299-308, 1953.

12. Sutton, Richard M., *Demonstration Experiments in Physics*, New York: McGraw Hill Book Co., Inc., 1938.

13. Weisbruch, Fred, *Lecture Demonstration Experiments for High School Chemistry*, St. Louis, Educational Publishers, Inc., 1954.

References

1. For example, the laboratories at Harvard University and at Boston University.
2. At Purdue University.
3. Iowa Teacher College.
4. Ohio State University.
5. Teachers College, Columbia University.

11

The Course in Physics

A long note at the beginning : There was a teacher who gave her students an assignment, a review of a book on penguins. In order to stimulate clear thinking, as well as brevity, she asked that the review be couched in one sentence. From one boy she got this statement : "This book tells me more about penguins than I care to know."

Probably teachers of physics would say, and with justice, that they have been told more about the need for revision of physics courses than they care to know. Yet another way of putting it in one sentence would be : Physics has a tremendous impact on society, but too little impact on enrollment. This is a pity, because physics is useful ; it is interesting, and it is necessary equipment for boys and girls who would understand modern society.

Why, then, do a great number of students shun the physics classroom ? Let us deal only with three major myths which affect physics teaching (and for that matter chemistry teaching).

The myth of the selected student body. An examination of courses of study and methods of teaching now employed indicates that physics teachers seem to think the high school population is entirely composed of individuals with I.Q.'s of 110 or more, all interested in becoming physicists.

Obviously this is one so.[1] Yet the course generally given is intended for such students. And this course seems to be even unsatisfactory for the physicits-to-be.

Most students in our schools cannot learn a vast assortment of facts unrelated to their present lives and combined with a private shorthand, a private mathematics, high levels of abstraction, often symbolic, as well as the laboratory skills which comprise the existing course in physics. Enrollments in such physics courses cannot be high, because the number of students who can cope with such a course is limited. Yet the solution is clear.

1. For those who are to become experts in physics, or who are capable of this even though the interest has not yet been aroused, the course in physics as given now ought to be extended and enriched. It ought to be made, if you wish, more abstract, more esoteric, and more delightful and exciting to those whose gifts enable them to do more.

2. For those who are not to become experts in physics, a physics course suited to their needs and interests is also possible and, indeed, necessary. Such a course would deal with the problems these boys and girls will face as citizens ; with topics such as the automobile, T.V. electric currents, the H bomb, the bicycle, and so forth. Surely atomic energy would be dealt with in such a course, but on a level which satisfies the curiosity of such students, explains theory sufficiently for them to understand newspaper accounts, yet does not require them to write nuclear reactions and to understand fully the theory behind them.

Is this physics ? Or is it watered-down physics ? This leads us to the next myth which affects our thinking about the teaching of physics.

The myth of the "watered-down course." Let us make short shrift of this. If you examine collegiate physics courses, including those for graduate students, you will not find a single course (even the most advanced) which was not "watered down" ; watered down, that is, from the existing body of knowledge. Every teacher selects from the body of knowledge, and every course is necessarily "watered down" or "slected" to fit the student body.

Surely it is no academic sin to fit one course to students who might be physicists or scientists (to modify a college course if need be), and also to fit a course to students who will not be physicists, by selecting materials which will help them solve the problems in physics which they will face as human beings. Or will one course do for both, a course suited to modern science and modern life ?

There is all the difference in the world between teaching physics as an end in itself and teaching it as a help in solving problems of living. The first helps the experts ; the second helps both the experts and those who will cooperate with them.

The myth of the physics teachers' strait jacket. Talks with many teachers indicate that they do want to introduce courses which fit both the expert-to-be and the citizen-layman-to-be ; that is, they want to introduce courses to fit both special education and general education. However, they point out that courses of study set by state Boards of Education and the College Entrance Examinations are among many pressures which, they feel, restrict their flexibility. Little innovation seems present in textbooks which are quite similar. Agreed, these factors do exist, but they need not exist forever.

A firm and steady pressure by teachers will influence state courses of study and examinations. Not everything in the textbook need be taught ; the book is a basic reference, not a strait jacket. Texts will change as the demand is felt. Yet even the existing texts have a great deal of material from which intelligent selection can be made. Through the efforts of many committees of both college and high school teachers, the large-scale examinations such as the Regents Examination in New York State and the College Entrance Examinations are already being modified. All the restraining factors are man-made and will respond to a polite form of sincere rebellion in the interests of children.

If you could visit simultaneously many classes in physics early in September, you would find nearly everyone undertaking the same series of topics ; measurement, then machines, and so on. It would seem that some ordained series of events goes on throughout the land. Yet the time is coming when each course will be designed for the type of community in which the school is located, for the kind of lives the children will lead, and for the ingenuity of the teacher.

Surely we can agree that physics is important to modern life and living. Likewise we can agree that children cannot be convinced of the importance of physics if they never come to the physics classroom. The conclusion seems obvious : revision of physics along two lines. One would result in physics being more attractive to the expert-to-be. The other would attract those who will live in a world of experts and make choices affecting their personal affairs.

America today is a land of millions of automobiles, millions of homes, and millions of refrigerators; mechanical devices abound on all sides, from can openers to cranes, from electric mixers to giant transformers. Yet, relatively few in our population understand why the brakes are called "hydraulic brakes", and how they operate ; why the claw hammer is constructed as it is ; how a thermostat operates ; what the ignition coil does in an automobile ; how a fuse operates and why it should not be replaced by a penny ; how an electric motor or gas flame cools a refrigerator ; how the gas and electric meters should be read ; and so on. These are part of physics. So are $F=ma$, $E=mc^2$, $I=E, R$. So are many other basic principles which have helped make our present age the Age of Science and the Age of Satellites.

Yet the *percentage* of high school students enrolled in physics has *declined* over the past fifty years[2]. Will examining the nature of physics courses and physics teaching in the country help us understand why this has occurred ?

The development of the course in physics

The development of courses in physics in America parallels closely that of chemistry. Physics, however, appeared earlier (as natural philosophy) than chemistry, because it was already established as a science (especially as Newtonian mechanics) when chemical facts, theories, and laws were few and poorly organized.

The physics course offered one hundred years ago would not be unfamiliar to teachers and students today. The organization of content into the broad subdivisions still in use was already established. Instruction was, however, almost entirely by means of recitation, apparently intended "... to anticipate all needs and questions of the reader so that he would never have to do any thinking on matters of physics."[3]

Then in the 1860's the establishment of the land-grant-colleges placed an emphasis on the vocational aspects of science. At about the same time, and as part of the "social climate," the influence of foreign practices in teaching physics and training specialists began to emphasize the desirability of intensive laboratory instruction. Once again the influence of Harvard University weighed heavily : first, with the recognition in 1872 of mathematics and physics as an optional admission program in place of the classics ; and second, with the issuance in 1886 of The Descriptive List of 40 standard experiments which the applying student could offer for admission, and on which he was tested in the college laboratory.[4]

The immediate beneficial result, that of stabilizing the high school physics course, was followed in the next decades by a curious swing of the pendulum. From an extreme textbook, catechetical basis, the physics course swung to an almost purely laboratory course, ignoring textbooks and recitations. But what happened in chemistry who also inevitable in physics.

By 1910, the laboratory had not solved the problems of physics teaching chiefly because both teachers and texts were of poor quality ; passing examinations was the prime purpose of the work ; and the laboratory work was not *real*—it was mainly quantitative and abstract.[5]

The unsuitability of the course as it had "rigidified" was further high lighted at the turn of the century by a changing high school population. Various professional committees began the re-examination of the aims and objectives of physics, with its attendant content and methodology ; a shift away from the laboratory course was under way by 1915. Recitation and discussion periods reappeared ; laboratory time decreased and demonstrations became customary.

What is the picture with respect to physics courses today ?[6] Physics instruction in the high schools continues to be intended principally for the college-bound student with an interest in science......

1. Courses in physics are offered more in the 12th than in the 11th grade.

2. The mathematics associated with the college preparatory course is often a prerequisite or coincident study.

3. Boys enrolled outnumber girls by more that 2 to 1.

4. Enrollment in physics represents about 13 per cent of the students in the 11th and 12th grades.

5. The actual number of students taking physics has not changed significantly through the [recent] years although the percentage is smaller than in earlier years.

A leading textbook of physics in use one hundred years ago included the following topics of study :

matter and its properties	electricity
gravity	voltaic electricity
the laws of motion	magnetism
the mechanical powers	electromagnetism
regulators of motion (pendulum, governor)	telegraphy
	the electrotype process
hydrostatics	magnetoelectricity
the steam engine	thermoelectricity
optics	astronomy

The present-day teacher of physics would be completely at home in this course, but he would have to add many new devices, facts, and principles that have since appeared, without

Table 11.1. "What's wrong with high school physics," 1923 and 1947.

*1923**	*1947†*
The content of the modern physics course is not objectionable in itself, but is too bulky and needs to be cut down. The highly abstract and theoretical, the incidental and insignificant—*whatever is entirely foreign to the pupils' present purposes, present knowledge, and daily experience, and cannot be connected up with them through significant problems in whose answers they can be vitally interested—should be dropped out.* There must be a change in emphasis that will result in paying most attention to the "big dynamic things" in physics and to those facts and minor principles which are exemplified in the students own locality, and which are therefore significant because they raise questions in whose answers the students can see some use. Minor and special principles must be justified before the pupils are required to learn them...... In other words, definitions, principles, and generalizations are justified by leading up to them inductively through concrete problems that arise out of the pupils' previous knowledge and their spirit of wonder or intellectual curiosity.	The number of topics or units taught during the year must be reduced. For years, physics teachers have been bewailing the steady increase in the amount of material in their courses. New material is often added ; little is ever dropped. It is time to realize that it is far better to leave out *whole* sections... than to teach so much poorly. The course should be organized largely or entirely about problems. This principle suggests a method of work rather than material to be taught. Class activities—demonstrations, experiments, discussion—as well as student activities outside the classroom are carried on in order to obtain answers to certain larger questions which have been accepted by the class as defining worthwhile problems.... Physics teaching at the high school level should largely reject the college preparatory function and stress the contributions of physics to the general education of American youth.
*G.R. Twiss. *Principles of Science Teaching*, Macmillan. N.Y., 1923. pp. 325-26.	†National Society for the Study of Education. *Forty-Sixth Yearbook*, Part 1. *Science Education in American Schools*, U. of Chicago Press, Chicago, 1947, pp. 210-11

dropping much from this list. The telephone, radio, television, jet propulsion, photoelectricity, the "expanding universe", atomic energy, space satellites—to name only a few—have added to physics enough content to provide at least a whole semester's work in themselves. Physics has experienced the typical growth of a course in the science curriculum, with more having been added than removed. This process has been going on for many years, and people have been aware of it. (Table 11.1 shows comments on the situation made in 1923 and 1947. Can you distinguish one from the other ?) Yet the pattern of physics teaching has remained essentially unchanged.

Unfortunately, the sort of physics course proposed by both Twiss (1923) and the NSSE (1947) requires a degree of *leisure* in both teaching and learning which is not provided by syllabuses preoccupied with facts—particularly facts whose recall will be the major part of examinations to come.

Here, as in the teaching of chemistry, we encounter a major dilemma. Teachers are advised, and sometimes agree, that science courses should be taught inductively around problems significant to the students. Yet former experience, texts, tests, and "pressures" encourage a continuation of the traditional, teacher-dominated, systematic course.

The failure of the laboratory-centered course of the 1890's, in which the student was expected to operate entirely by induction, seems obvious. The student was supposed to re-create the classical results of physics, in the same context in which the original discovery was made. But this was impossible. The student was not Boyle or Newton or Faraday. What is more, he could read what they had found ; why, therefore, should he pretend to go through the same operations which had no significance to him ? A clean distinction should be made between the effort to have students practice induction and the context within which they were to practice this important process. The failure was not in the attempt to have inductive study, but in the formal, academic context within which it was to be practiced. This point is still significant in current discussions, as we shall see.

Teachers currently approaching the apparent dilemma often take an easy approach : One pattern, the systematic review of past physics, is known to them ; the other, based on student problems, is at best hazy and unknown, with many potential pitfalls. So course modification waits until someone else has pioneered the way. Such a reaction is understandable. Yet the need for modification is intense. In the following discussion of present course patterns and possible bases for changes, there may be suggestions which will encourage evolutionary if not revolutionary changes in your courses.

Patterns of present courses in physics

The organization of content in physics courses has shown less change in the past one hundred years than in any other science course. The classical pattern remains in courses and textbooks : mechanics, heat, sound, light, and electricity. The past few years have brought the addition of a sixth division : nuclear energy. While such organization may be defended on the ground that these areas are coherent, one is faced with the broader problem : How does such an organization further the desirable aim of integrating the various fields within physics ? In effect this compartmentalization often provides the student with five (or six) "subcourses" in physics.

The textbook as a course outline

> The modern text retains much of the content of the text of one hundred years ago, for the importance of these fundamental concepts of mechanics, light, heat, sound, and electricity has only been emphasized by the discoveries in modern physics. In addition, the modern text presents the principles more recently discovered and included under the heading "modern physics."
>
> Inductive methods are prevalent in current texts. Starting with the familiar and commonplace, the pupil is led to the formulation of the basic laws of physics. Emphasis is placed on the unifying aspects of physics : as, for example, the manifestation and transformation of energy—the conventional units of mechanics, heat, etc.—are shown

to be interrelated and not "watertight" compartments. Stress is placed on "things to do" to encourage teacher demonstration and pupil experimentation.[7]

These texts are, however, far from perfect and have drawn criticism.[8]

While the present-day textbook in physics is markedly superior to that current only thirty years ago, the organization, the scope of the course, tends to negate these desirable features.

Rarely can the teacher of physics today cover the content of the entire text unless he goes back to the questionable methods of previous years where the pupil is expected to "learn" the material of the text in sequence for "quoting back" during the recitation. Where emphasis is placed on the development of ideas, on the consequences and social impact of these ideas, on the methods of experimental science and of the scientist, on learning through individual study and experimentation, less content will, in general, be covered but the pupil gains confidence in his ability for learning after formal education has ceased. The teacher *under these conditions* makes selections as to content to the studied intensively and provides appropriate interlinkage between the "blocks" of intensive study.[9]

The college-preparatory course

As we have seen, the organization of high school physics courses *today* is still cast largely in the "college-preparatory" or systematic mold. What was true in the case of chemistry is also true of physics : success in high school physics is an unreliable index of probable success in physics at college. The difference in breadth, depth, and intensity of college physics compared to the high school work is even greater than that between the courses in chemistry. A great many items in college work have not even been touched on or suggested on the secondary level. Angular momentum, rotational inertia, Kirchhoff's laws, and the like are often totally new experiences to the entering freshman. Far more significant and troublesome is the greater reliance on mathematics in the presentation of the college course ; many first-year courses involve introduction of the calculus.[10]

It is unfortunate, therefore, that so much of the high school physics clings to a format and a purpose for which it is no longer suited. Not all of our physics students will go on to college, and of those who do, only a small percentage will become specialists in physics.[11] Yet the "college-preparatory" course as it exists today is attempting to make every student a specialist in subject matter, even if only on the high school level, and it apparently is not doing even that very well.

We have already seen how the advances in physics have added more and more to the *content* so that even this cannot be covered adequately. If this be the case, how can such a course hope to achieve the "extra things" of science which provide for understanding by way of scientific attitudes and methods, and for emotional outcomes which will predispose the student favorably toward physics in particular and science in general at some future date ?

Table 11.2 shows, side by side, a high school college-preparatory physics syllabus and the table of contents of a standard college text. Do they show any value in terms of *general,* not special, education ? Suppose the student has learned the formula for centrifugal force, the method of determining the specific gravity of floating solids, Lenz's law, and so on ; what now ? What will he do with them in ten years ? How will they affect his future behavior ? What will they contribute to his future understanding, vocation, and so forth ? Will he even perform better in college physics, if he takes it ? *Will he take it* ?

Changes in college physics

For several years conferences and committees have been working to redefine more carefully the purposes of the introductory college course in physics. A major statement of results has been published :[12]

Table 11.2. College-preparatory and college courses

*High school**	*College†*
I. Mechanics	I. Mechanics
A. Forces in equilibrium	A. Nature of physics
B. Forces and motion	B. Liquids at rest
C. Work and energy	C. Air pressure
D. Machines	D. Vector quantities
E. Optional materials	E. Accelerated motion
1. Mechanics of fluids	F. Force and acceleration
2. Molecular forces	G. Force and counterforce
3. More on machines	H. Statics
	I. Work, energy, power
II. Heat	J. Rotation
A. Heat, a form of energy	K. Gravitation
B. Expansion	L. Elasticity
C. Measurement of heat	M. Fluids at rest and in motion
D. Change of state	
E. Heat and work	II. Heat
F. Optional materials	A. Temperature and expansion
1. Specific heat	B. Kinetic theory
2. Effects and application of evaporation	C. Quantity of heat
	D. Heat transfer
3 Meteorology	E. Change of state
4. More on heat and work	F. Heat engines
III. Transfer of energy by wave motion	III. Sound
	A. Vibrations
A. General characteristics of waves	B. Waves
	C. Sound waves
B. Sound	D. Hearing
C. Electromagnetic radiation	E. Other topics
D. Visible light	
E. Optional materials	
1. Additional general topics	
2. Sound and music	
3. Optical devices	
4 Further material on vision	

*Syllabus in physics from *Physics Handbook*. Bureau of Secondary Curriculum Development, New York State Education, Department, Albany, 1956,

†Frederick Saunders and Paul Kirkpatrick, *College Physics*, 4th ed., Holt, N. Y., 1953.

in physics

High school	*College*
IV. Electricity A. Static electricity B. The electric current C. Magnetism D. Induced electromagnetic force E. Optional materials 1. Chemical effects of an electric current 2. Terrestrial magnetism 3. Some applications of principles	IV. Electricity and magnetism A. Currents and charges B. Elementary electrostatics C. Electrostatic fields and generators D. Potential and capacitance E. Magnetism F. More on magnetism G. Conductors and circuits H. Conduction of electricity by liquids I. Chemical and thermal sources of electromotive force J. Heating effects of currents K. Induced current L. Generators and motors M. Alternating currents N. Electron properties O. Electric oscillations and waves
V. Alternating current and electronics A. Alternating current circuits B. Vacuum tubes C. Radio D. Television E. Optional materials 1. Other applications of electronics 2. Additional quantitative work on a c. 3. Vacuum tubes 4 Other applications of electronics	V. Light A. Some properties of light B. Reflection and refraction C. Lenses and curved reflectors D. Vision and its aids E. Dispersion and spectra F. Diffraction G. Colour and interference H. Polarization
VI. Nuclear energy A. Structure of the nucleus B. Radioactivity C. Fission D. Thermonuclear reactions E. Peacetime uses of nuclear energy F. Optional materials 1. Other particle accelerators 2. Further nuclear theory 3. Cosmic radiation	VI. Atomics A A survey of atoms B Relativity C. Waves and particles D. The outer atom E. Atomic nuclei F. Nuclear reactions

Conclusions

1. A thorough and rigorous coverage of a limited number of topics is more effective than an encyclopedic and showy introduction to a wide range of subject matter.

2. It is probable that no course of less than six semester hourse can present adequately the basic concepts of physics at the introductory level. A list of seven such concepts is given as the minimal set that should be covered.

3. Physics should be taught as a growing subject and the student should be given illustrations of problems on present frontiers.

4. Introductory physics courses should be available to freshmen. This may make it necessary for the instructor to introduce mathematical ideas, such as those of the calculus, in order that the subject be developed with the desired intellectual rigor. (Later, the observation is made that "introduction to the *concepts* of calculus does not imply mastery of its *techniques*.")

5. Senior and experienced staff members should engage in the teaching of introductory physics courses, in the training of teaching assistants, and in experimentation directed at the improved teching of physics.

Resolutions of the Conference

1. We hold that the goals outlined......are applicable not only to pre-engineering courses, but also to all physics courses, whether for physicists and other scientists or for nonscientists, including those taking integrated courses or general education science courses.

2. We recommend that the AAPT actively encourage experimentation with nonconventional courses...

Let us uncover physics, not cover it.

It was the opinion of the conference that a satisfactory introductory physics course could be constructed around the following seven basic principles and concepts and the material leading up to them:

1. Conservation of momentum.
2. Conservation of mass and energy.
3. Conservation of charge.
4. Waves.
5. Fields.
6. The molecular structure of matter.
7. The structure of the atom.

Furthermore, these seven principles and concepts outline the minimum content which *any* introductory course must encompass in order to provide a satisfactory treatment of present-day physics...

Whatever the content selected, it should:

1. Consist of sufficiently few topics so that each can be treated with thoroughness and intellectual rigor.

2. Present both classical and modern physics as growing subjects, having present-day frontiers in all areas.

3. Contribute to an understanding and appreciation of the unity of physics.

Three additional papers illustrate courses believed to meet these criteria in different types of institutions.[13]

Changes "to come" in high school physics

As this text is being written, the work of the Physical Science Study Committee, sponsored by the National Science Foundation is going on. At present, tha Committee's thinking is mainly concerned with the teaching of physics. Clearly, the course which is being developed will cause a reappraisal of the contents of the physics course, as well as of ways of teaching it. The purposes of the Committee are best expressed in the words of the following tentative statement prepared by the Committee; this course is undergoing "experimental" teaching in seven schools in the school year 1957-58.

> During the last few years there has been an increasing awareness of the inadequacies of present day teaching of the physical sciences in secondary schools. The dissatisfaction is general, and efforts to improve the situation have generated various views concerning the fundamental purposes of science teaching, the material to be taught, and

the teaching methods. Numerous groups representing these views are now at work on these problems.

In November, 1956, the National Science Foundation made a grant to the Massachusetts Institute of Technology, in support of an effort to improve the teaching of physics in secondary schools. The Physical Science Study Committee, established under this grant, consists of scientists from various universities, colleges, and industrial laboratories and of high school teachers and educators. (The list of participants is attached.)[14]

The group considers itself to be engaged in an experiment, of five or more years' duration, which will be a joint effort of science and eduction. Its point of view is expressed in three fundamental and interrelated aims : (1) to plan a course of study in which the major developments of physics, up to the present time, are presented as a logical and an integrated whole ; (2) to present physics as an intellectual and cultural pursuit which is part of present day human activity and achievement, and (3) to assist existing physics teachers, by means of various teaching aids, to carry out the proposed program.

The realization of these aims will require considerable effort over a considerable period. The Committee has studied various approaches and believes it is now in a position to prepare a realistic, effective program. The subject matter will be presented to teachers and students through several media concurrently textbooks, manuals, films and filmstrips, classroom demonstrations, laboratory work, and work that the student can do on his own, under the teacher's guidance.

Physics and chemistry are closely related, and their teaching in high school may eventually be integrated, possibly in a two-year course including both disciplines. As a first step the Committee will prepare a physics course for high school juniors or seniors, including fundamental chemistry that enters naturally.

The Committee realizes that this revised program of physical science is only a partial approach to the vast problem of producing high quality scientists in adequate number and of giving a better understanding of science to the educated nonscientist. The total solution of the problem could not be undertaken by a single group. The Committee feels that its own competence lies in the teaching of the physical sciences and that its best chance of reaching future generations of responsible citizens is in the last two years of high school, when children have their first, and often last, opportunity to learn physics and chemistry.

In the following pages some of the specific considerations guiding principles and aims of the Committee are illustrated.

Science in our day. Physical science holds a peculiar position in our culture. On the one hand, through the applications of technology and industry it has deeply affected our everyday life. Since the last world war and the opening of the atomic age, its impact on society has increased enormously. It has become a vital element of national defense, politics, and international relations.

On the other hand, science is not as widely appreciated and sought out as other cultural elements—like art, music, history, literature—despite the undeniable interest that it arouses in nonscientists. All are familiar with the artistic and literary visions of nature. Few realize that there is also a scientific vision, a special way of feeling and interpreting nature.

The scientific interpretation of nature is not private property of science and scientists : it is part of the intellectual wealth of mankind. To partake of it and to derive full pleasure from it, some effort is necessary, as it is for the enjoyment of art, poetry, and music. Many who are not going to be poets, painters, or musicians spend time to train their ears and eyes, to learn terms, to understand techniques and methods. Few make an equivalent effort to gain appreciation of science.

To the responsible citizen a sound scientific background would also be of practical value. An increasing number of issues are affected by science. The responsible citizen of our days must be able to judge technological and scientific questions as he judges political questions, by broad lines, even though he does not understand the details. To do this he must have a background, a frame of reference in which to fit what he hears and learns.

The scientific language. Perhaps the most important single bar to easy understanding between scientists and nonscientists is the fact that science has developed its own language, and some of this language has not yet been assimilated into common usage. All human activities have developed special terminologies to simplify the description of facts, methods, and processes. Even the art of cooking has created a terminology, for the interpretation of which many cookbooks have special glossaries. Navigation has created a richer terminology than cooking, and special nautical dictionaries were compiled. Parts of these terminologies slowly enter common usage and jointly form our common language ; others remain confined in the special fields.

Science has not only created a terminology to describe its observations but has also developed a language corresponding to a way of thinking. The scientific language is usually more precise and rigorous than common language : it uses abstractions with which most people are not familiar : it borrows formulas and notations from mathematics. It is molded on a special attitude of the mind, and therefore, it does not easily lend itself to precise translation. Thus, popularizations of science are useful to arouse interest and to illustrate achievements, but they usually fail to convey the spirit of science : in the process of translation science becomes adulterated. For the full enjoyment of science at least some of the scientific language must be learned, and the most appropriate place in which to learn it is high school.

Science and high schools. The situation of science in high schools has been recently the subject of many discussions both among the public and among educators, and is widely known. For a brief review of it, attention may be focussed on three main factors : the student population, the teachers, the curriculum.

The basic pattern of our high schools was set over eighty years ago when only a few children went past the elementary school. A much larger proportion of children is now attending high school and the total population of childern is rapidly increasing. Forecasts for the sixties, when the "baby boom" of the late forties will reach high school age, indicate some nine million students at the beginning of that decade and some twelve million by the middle of it, as against about seven million in 1954-1955.

The number of qualified high school teachers has not been increasing in the same proportion. The demand for teachers is already greater than the supply and is growing fast. This shortage is particularly acute in the case of science teachers : industries and government projects recruit more and more scientists so that fewer are left for less remunerative jobs. A paradoxical situation has ensued : as the impact of science on society is being more and more felt, and the demand for scientists is growing, the supply of teachers to prepare them is diminishing.

The third factor of the science situation in high schools is the syllabus. Several surveys were recently taken by educational groups all over the country. A special survey of physics textbooks was carried out by the American Institute of Physics, the American Association of Physics Teachers, and the National Science Teachers Association. Many of the texts were also examined by the Physical Science Study Committee. *All surveys reached the conclusion that high school physics courses present too much material, and choose that material unwisely.*[15]

The amount of accumulated physical knowledge has grown rapidly, but the time available for teaching it in high school has remained the same. The attempt to continue to survey the entire field of physics in a one-year course has resulted in a loss of depth and coherence. Since the course cannot illustrate the development of ideas for shortage of time, it is filled only with results of physics and laws to be learned by rote or through mathematical formulas. It becomes hard to understand and of limited interest. To enliven it, technological applications are often *added* and thus the bulk of material to be learned is further increased. The tendency to dress up science with the applications of its developments may stress its practical value, but further dims its cultural aspect. It fails to show science as a human activity, as the product of human thought. All the results surveyed in physics were obtained through the mental process of human beings : all the laws expressed by dry words and mathematical symbols were arrived at by men who possessed in high degree such human attributes as vivid imagination, power of abstraction and synthesis, perseverance, and patience. All this is now lost in a high school course.

Individual teachers who might like to improve the physics course are usually prevented from doing so by the existing conditions. Science teachers are usually overloaded with work : they must not only teach, but also plan, set up, and dismantle classroom demonstrations ; take care of laboratory equipment ; counsel students : talk with parents ; attend many kinds of meetings ; and often sponsor science clubs and special science activities such as fairs, exhibits, etc. If they wish to keep up with science and further their own studies, they must do so in the summer, renouncing summer employment, which they usually need to supplement inadequate salaries. Great load, low salary, and poor status in the community all contribute to general dissatisfaction. If, despite these conditions, teachers find time and energy to plan new teaching procedures, they usually meet with administrators' resistance to innovations and with lack of funds for purchasing the necessary materials. At the same time, textbooks are generally based on the traditional pattern of a physics course, and books deviating from this pattern are not likely to be accepted by either publishers or school systems. Thus the traditional pattern becomes more and more firmly established.

Nature of the Program

The Committee proposes to prepare a program showing physics as an intellectual activity. The new physics course will not be aimed specifically at preparing students for college physics, nor does the Committee expect that all high school students will take it. *At present about one-quarter of them take physical science and the new course will address itself to the same fraction.*[16] From this group come most of our lawyers, businessmen, statesmen, and other professionals who will not take science in college. The Committee hopes that the new course will build a sound scientific background in this section of the population ; that the resulting greater interest in science and better teaching methods will encourage more children to take science in high school and more young people with scientific aptitudes to elect science as their career.

The Committee gave careful consideration to the possible ways of striking a balance between two needs : the need of restricting the material taught in the course to allow time for illustrating the scientific method and the role of science in our culture ; and the need of giving to a student a sufficiently unified, comprehensive, and wide view of the whole field of physics, to satisfy his broader interest. To obtain this balance, the Committee will prepare a course and supplement it with a series of monographs.

The course will present a reduced amount of material, and will not treat it all in the same way. Some scientific developments especially lend themselves to illustrate the evolution of ideas, the interrelation of various fields of human activities, the scope of physical science. These will be explored deeply, slowly, and thoroughly. The field of optics and waves and that of mechanics have been chosen for this kind of treatment. Other parts will require broader coverage : thus the role of atoms in the physical world will be illustrated in many examples throughout the course. Other parts will be only surveyed. In order to stress the unity of physics and the coherence of physical ideas, the course will be focussed toward a unified picture of nature, the atomic picture. Thus the student will learn not only the physics of the past, but also the physics which is being evolved by men of our generation ; which is affecting his present and his future ; which is still an open field whose many paths leading to the unknown he may elect to follow.

The monographs will supplement and extent the course in awakening and satisfying the students' interest in physics and related subjects. Certain material that is traditionally taught is omitted from the textbook or offered in reduced depth or detail ; the monographs will make it available to those students who seek it. Beyond this, they will cover historical and biographical material, certain advanced topics that may appeal to the brighter student, technological applications, "how-to-do-it" subjects, and accounts of especially stimulating periods in the history of science. Each will be written by a qualified person, in his own style and according to his own views ; the student can thus become acquainted with a wide range of view-points and approaches. Altogether, the monographs will constitute a sizable library of low-cost, paper-bound books from which a student may borrow, or volumes of which he may buy for himself.

Tools of the program. In the preparation of the tools to implement the course, the committee is guided by two sets of considerations :

1. The most effective way of teaching physics is to use several methods and media concurrently. Some parts of physics, like historical evolution of ideas, mathematical deductions, etc., can best be learned if *read* over and over. The significance of physical phenomena, on the other hand, will best be understood if the phenomena are *seen* over and over again. And the experimental method can be mastered both by seeing how demonstrations are prepared and carried out on film and in the classroom, and by actual experimentation in the laboratory.

2. Students must learn physics not only through the formal teaching, but also by doing *physics*. Teachers must encourage and lead students to work independently, to make their own observations, and to push forward the frontiers of their knowledge. Students must *listen* and *see* in the classroom. *do* and *advance* in the laboratory and at home. Teachers and

students must col-laborate. In order to obtain the best results from this collaboration, there must be a carefully planned division and correlation of work between teacher and student. Experiments to be done by students must stimulate their interest and challenge their ingenuity. Thus experiments must not be too specialized, not so hard as to discourage students, and yet not so easy as to become routine work.

Among the materials which the Committee is preparing for both teachers and students are a detailed syllabus and a text-book, films and filmstrips, manuals for teachers and for students : suggestions and equipment for classroom demonstrations and laboratory work ; kits for students ; questions for tests and exams, for use both in the course and for college entrance examinations ; placards. etc. All this material will aim at the same goal : to show physics as a product of human minds in the pursuit of truth, an activity which has evolved through the centuries and is still evolving and which has created a philosophical structure and a particular way of thinking.

There is no need to explain these materials in detail, and a few words will be said about a few of them only.

The films. Approximately one-fifth of classroom time will be given over to films. These films will be an essential part of the teaching learning process. They are not intended to provide entertainment, or to make physics more "palatable." They will serve as follows :

1. To call attention to phenomena of common occurrence, but usually not seen because they are not obviously related to known causes. An example of such a phenomenon is the interference colour in an oil film on water.

2. To show unusual natural phenomena : an eclipse cannot be shown at will, but the movie can be made readily available.

3. To present demonstrations which require special apparatus and techniques and cannot be performed in high school laboratories, or which require more time for setting up than the teacher has available.

4. To show details of experiments through close-ups and slow motion.

5. To make it possible to show these phenomena and experiments over and over again.

6. To supplement graphs and illustrations through the use of animation.

The manuals. The radical change in the philosophy and methods of teaching physics in high school will place a burden on teachers. They must acquaint themselves with a new point of view and master new techniques and materials. To this end, the Committee will prepare a manual which will illustrate the aims of the new course in detail and explain the reasons for the pedagogic choices ; point out ways in which the aims of the course may be achieved ; offer suggestions for further examples and work not included in the text ; give technical instructions on the use of certain teaching aids like films and demonstration materials. The new approach to teaching will give rise to a number of questions from students for which teachers may not be prepared ; the manuals will therefore provide a list of likely questions and ways to answer them.

The manual for students will include basic questions meant to lead them to constructive thinking ; supplements to the films, which will integrate the subject of each film in the course ; workbooks and test books.

Kits for Students. It is hoped that many students will want to work on their own and experiment in various fields of physics. The Committee will make available a certain number of kits at low cost, containing materials and instructions for building simple instruments and guidance for their use. There will be for example, an optical kit with lenses, prisms, tubes, supports, colour charts, etc. ; the student will be able to build telescopes, cameras, etc., and use them to make his observations.

Exams. Any change in a high school course must be reflected in the exams that the student will be asked to take, and especially in the college entrance examination. The Committee is taking steps, and making good progress, to achieve complete coordination between college entrance tests and the new program of high school physics.

Procedures. In the working out of this program, the active collaboration of the educational profession is being used. Educators and high school teachers are heavily represented on the Committee, and science teachers in limited numbers have been recruited for full-time work. Some preliminary material is now being circulated among working teachers for comment, and procedures have been established for continued development of the concepts of the Committee inside the classroom. A preliminary edition of the textbook is being used in a limited number of classrooms during the academic year 1957-1958 ; an increasing amount of new laboratory material is being prepared and will be available.

The Committee feels that the widest possible dissemination of its work is necessary if it is to profit from the experience and the skills of the teaching profession, and the scientific community. Consequently, it intends to make available, upon request, details of its activities in the various phases of its program. Progress reports on the program as a whole will be published at regular intervals, and will provoke, it is hoped, comments and suggestions.

Specific Objectives of the Program

In teaching the physical sciences certain objectives must be kept in mind, and the subject matter must be organized so as to bring them into evidence. They are :

1. *The unity of physical science.* Physical science aims at interpreting the world around us. It cannot be divided into many independent fields because the phenomena it covers are interrelated. This can be seen by the fact that certain laws, like the conservation of energy, apply to a very large range of phenomena.

2. *Coverage.* A course which does not give a fairly wide picture of the role of atoms in the physical world is essentially incomplete. Broad coverage on atoms and their use in examples is therefore desired throughout the course.

In order to show the coherence and power of physical ideas, certain narrower fields must be explored deeply, slowly, and thoroughly. The two fields of optics and waves, and of mechanics are chosen for this kind of intensive treatment.

3. *Regularities.* The observation of regularities in physical phenomena is necessary before laws covering the phenomena or models underlying them can be established.

4. *Many independent arguments for one law.* In establishing physical laws many independent arguments should be used to help show the solidity with which the laws are founded.

5. *Models.* Models are often useful to put a possible explanatory background behind observed phenomena. They often suggest relations between phenomena which can then be investigated.

6. *Deduction of phenomena from laws.* From laws established to correlate one set of phenomena or more, we can deduce many other physical conclusions. We should make many deductions from the laws to show their power and scope. Even the simplest physical law, such as the law of refraction, can be extended from a few cases to many more complex cases.

7. *Limitations of laws* Over the range of phenomena and within the range of accuracy for which they are established, our physical laws are not subject to future modification. The range of validity of a law may indeed extend beyond the phenomena on which it was originally based, but the applicability of laws is usually limited.

8. *New models include the old.* New models and more refined laws are occasionally established to extend the range of applicability to include new phenomena. An old model may thus be superseded by a more refined one, but we wish to stress that the new model includes the old.

9. *Controversy.* Controversy played an important role in the evolution of science. Examples of famous controversies and their significance in relation to their times will make it possible to tie science with history. In this respect one may point out that ideas and interpretations that have been discarded are

still considered "scientific." The Ptolemaic model of the universe had its role and its use in the development of the Copernican model.

Tentative Outline of the Course

The first day of the meeting various groups presented outlines, parts of outlines, or views on preparing outlines. Their approaches proved to be different more in appearance than in essence. The morning of the third day an outline was worked out at the meeting and fully accepted by it.

It was agreed that physics would be more meaningful to the student and its unity would be stressed if the presentation of the subject matter were focussed toward one goal and that this goal ought to be the atomic picture of the universe. This does not preclude specific goals for single parts : the Newtonian picture of the universe can still be taken as the goal of mechanics. The atomic picture will show physics as an open field of knowledge, where much has still to be done, rather than as a closed discipline.[17]

I. *The universe and other things*
- Sizes and numbers
- Structure of universe
- Atomic structure of matter
- Molecular interpretation of chemistry
- Size and numbers of atoms

II. *Light waves*
- Rectilinear propagation
- Reflection
- Refraction
- Corpuscular and wave models
- Mechanical waves
- Interference
- Measurement of wave length

III. *Mechanics*
- Inertia
- $ft = m\Delta v$
- Mass ; force ; kinetic energy ; conservation laws
- Gravitation from planetary motion
- Kinetic theory of gases
- Coulomb's law ;
- $F = eE$; $F = ev \times B$
- Induction on moving conductors

IV. *Atoms*
- Discreteness
- Electron charge
- Nuclear model of atoms
- Size, charge, mass of nucleus

Table 11.3 An applied physics course*

I. Electricity : Much of the work of everyday life is performed by electricity
   - A. Familiar uses of electricity
   - B. Safety procedures and devices
   - C. Home appliances
   - D. Circuits used in home wiring
   - E. Generation and supply of electric current

II. The automobile ; An application of physics that has vastly increased man's mobility.
   - A. Parts of gas automobile
   - B. The engine
   - C. The fuel system
   - D Ignition
   - E. Valves
   - F. Cooling system
   - G. Power flow
   - H. Control devices
   - I. Safe driving
   - J. Care of the car

III. Engines : With which man does his heavy work, and which make rapid transportation possible, make use of the princip es of applied physics.
   - A. Types of engines
   - B. The gasoline engine
   - C. Diesel engine
   - D. Jet engines
   - E. The rocket
   - F. The steam turbine
   - G The steam engine
   - H. Advantages and disadvantages

IV. Hobbies : Science gives us greater understanding and enjoyment of the hobbies with which we occupy out leisure time.
   - A. How music is produced
   - B. The phonograph
   - C. Tape, wire, and film recording
   - D. The Camera
   - E. Darkroom techniques
   - F. Home movies
   - G. Model making and operation
   - H. Amateur science

V. Energy : Living has been made easier by harnessing the world's energy supply to do our work.
   - A. How work is done
   - B. Power-driven machines
   - C. Types of energy
   - D. Availability of energy and the standard of living
   - E. Development and use of the world's energy supply

VI. Atomic energy : Science has succeeded in releasing the energy of the atom with its tremendous possibilities for peace and for war.
   - A. Origin of atomic energy
   - B. The atomic nucleus
   - C. Production of nuclear energy
   - D. The chain reaction
   - E. Peacetime uses of nuclear energy
   - F. Problems of international control

*New York City syllabus in applied physics.

VII. The airplane ; Applied physics has opened up the air as a highway of commerce.
- A. Parts of the airplane
- B. How the wing provides lift
- C. How thrust is obtained
- D. Supersonic airplanes
- E Controls
- F. Safety in the air and at the airport

VIII. Electronics : Discoveries in the field of electronics have given us radio, television, and other communication devices.
- A. Essentials of the radio receiver
- B. Tuning
- C. The vacuum tube as amplifier
- D. The speaker
- E. AM and FM
- F The television set
- G. The picture tube
- H. Rader

IX. Temperature : Applied physics has given us devices for controlling temperature in the home and in industry
- A. Refrigeration
- B. Cooking and heating processes
- C. Thermometry
- D. Industrial temperatures
- E. The electric refrigerator
- F. The electric furnace
- G. Welding
- H. Fuels
- I. Air conditioning

X. Health : Science has given the physician tools with which to diagnose and fight disease and to improve health.
- A. Doctor's diagnostic tools
- B. Clinical thermometer
- C. Stethoscope
- D. Electrocardiograph
- E. Sphygmomanometer
- F. X-ray
- G. Microscope
- H Radiation therapy
- I. Eyeglasses

XI. Hearing : Science has enabled man to apply the principles of sound to improve his range of hearing.
- A. Factors affecting hearing
- B. Improvement of hearing
- C. Improvement of audibility
- D. Acoustics
- E. Sound-recording
- F. High fidelity
- G. Ultrasonics and its applications

XII. Visions : Physical devices widen the range of information and enjoyment that we receive through our vision.
- A. Factors affecting sight
- B. Operation of the eye
- C. Types of eyeglasses
- D. The camera
- E. Projectors
- F. Motion pictures
- G. Stroboscope
- H. Telescope
- I. Colour and the spectrum

In this order the emphasis moves naturally from the kinematic toward the dynamic description of phenomena.

The applied physics course

For the nonacademically minded (the science shy), or for those whose high school education is terminal, or for those going on to college but with no further interest in science, physics certainly has value in its major development as general education. Yet the regimen of the typical college-preparatory course has not made physics "palatable" for such students.

An effort to provide for such students has come in the introduction of courses in applied physics. Here, the emphasis is placed, not on the theory or concepts behind various phenomena, but on their applications. Mathematics is minimized. One need not be able to state Pascal's principle in order to appreciate the operation of the hydraulic press or brake; neither is an understanding of the mathematical statement of the principle essential to the student. One need not know how to calculate efficiency in order to observe the benefits of a pulley. To know the mathematics of image formation in a plane mirror is not required in order to appreciate the properties of that image. The course in physics abounds in topics whose "teeth can be drawn" so that the student can learn to appreciate the values of the subject matter and to see why others might desire and use mathematical formulations for more precise predictions.

One danger exists in the construction of such courses. If they are made by taking a college preparatory syllabus and selecting the topics *we teachers* believe will be of value to the student, we are very likely to construct a syllabus which is a fair replica of the original (replete with technical vocabulary) *which will defeat the purpose of the course.*[18] A course in applied physics should instead be built from the ground up, with the student as the focus, and it should be coupled with a view to the needs and interests of the students. What might be a suitable set of problems in a big city might be quite unrealistic in a farming or mining community; what might be suitable for a seacoast town might be unsuited to an inland community.

The outline of one course in applied physics allows us to examine the subtopics ; these give the flavor of the word "applied" in the course. Compare this with the college preparatory course in Table 11.3.

Summary

We can illustrate at least five kinds of biology courses and innumerable courses in general science and several courses in chemistry, although the majority are similar to the so-called college-preparatory courses. Yet we can find few variants from the so-called college-preparatory course in physics. Changes are, however, in the wind, *viz.*, the work of the Physical Science Study Committee.

Frames for developing a course in physics

As we have indicated, there are as many ways of designing a course as there are of skinning the proverbial cat ; although we probably use our ingenuity in skinning a cat at least as often as we use it in solving this problem of education. That pattern followed by the teacher in his student days is not necessarily the best experience, and it certainly is not the final experience. There are, as in the other courses we have discussed, various frames of reference which help in designing one's own course.

Conceptual schemes as a frame of reference

Physics has a flavor which arises out of the concepts and principles which are peculiar to it alone. Thus :

A body immersed in a fluid suffers an apparent loss in weight equal to the weight of the fluid displaced.

Pressure applied to an enclosed fluid is transmitted unchanged in all directions.

At constant temperature, the volume of a gas varies inversely with its pressure.

For every force there is a "reaction" force, equal in magnitude and opposite in direction.

Heat may be (partially) converted into useful work by properly designed machines.

When a magnetic field is cut by a wire, an electromotive force is induced in the wire.

An electric current in a wire consists of motion of electrons.

The sum total of matter and energy in the universe is constant.

Light, x-rays, ultraviolet, radio waves, etc., can be considered to be electromagnetic radiations which travel in transverse waves and do not require a medium of transmission.

But all these may be summarized briefly. If biology places emphasis on life processes and the conceptual scheme of continuous organic change, while chemistry highlights the structure and changes of substances, then the keynote of physics is energy. It is therefore possible to subjugate all of the foregoing (and many other) statements into one broad conceptual scheme : "Within the universe the total quantity of matter and of energy is constant : under extreme conditions matter and energy can be observed as interchangeable." This would of course be subdivided into other concepts and principles (which would in turn be subdivided). Thus :

1. The physical properties of matter, e.g., inertia, gravitation, etc.
2. Atomic structure
3. The concept of energy
   (*a*) The forms of energy
   (*b*) Translating energy into work
   (*c*) Matter as froz enenergy—$E=mc^2$

Such a scheme provides a common denominator for any and all aspects studied. Rather than a study of light, heat, and sound as separate and distinct topics, we have an organization which studies them together, thus emphasizing both their similarities and their differences. The claim will be made that this is also done in the traditional course of study where these are studied separately and their features then brought together, generally in the form of a table : but, in this treatment usually the "tail wags the dog." It often amounts to nothing more than a compilation of facts with the unifying concept never seen or comprehended.

Boyle's law would not now be a particular manifestation of gases : rather, it would bear relation to the kinetic energy of molecules. Friction in a machine and resistance in a wire would now be comprehensible in terms of degradation of energy. These conceptual schemes enable the teacher to cut across the relatively rigid structure of physics and treat it as a whole.[19]

Topics as a frame of reference

Select a syllabus (or text book) in physics at random. Unlike general science or biology, more like chemistry, its organization is highly predictable. There will be five topics or "blocks," one each on mechanics, heat, light, sound, and electricity. To these has often been added in recent years a sixth, on nuclear energy. These will be subdivided further into *logical* sections, the "logic" is of the formal, after-the-discovery type. Thus, the broad field of mechanics will start with an introductory portion on the properties of matter of interest in physics, and will be followed by material on the metric system, laws of motion, mechanics of gases and liquids, work, energy, power, and machines. That of electricity will be divided into magnetism and static electricity in one part, and "current electricity" in the other. Later treatments have amplified the treatment of alternating currents as applied in radio and television.

Such an arrangement may be detrimental to the teaching of physics, in three ways. First, it divides the subject in such a way that the student is often unaware of the unity of the science. Second, it starts the course with material hardly calculated to arouse great interest – the properties of matter and the metric system.[20] And third, it plunges the student shortly thereafter into mechanics, a troublesome subject for the beginner, particularly because of the emphasis on mathematics. The initial (and alas, often lasting) impression is that the subject is difficult. Two current textbooks have broken away from this routine by starting with units on sound and light, which can be treated in a more descriptive way, with less emphasis on mathematical treatment.

Different topics in physics are not of equal difficulty, and some require ample time for "digestion," But a topical approach requires that each section be completed as a whole, as a subcourse. Hence, the student is carried through the sequence of work while the initial ideas may still be more or less undigested. The result is often difficulty with, and failure in, the later stages of work.

Further, a topic such as the metric system, which should *pervade* the course, is taught all at once, after which the student is expected to know it perfectly. Some teachers have adopted a "spiral" approach in handling such topics. For example, the idea of specific gravity is obiviously simple (to the teacher), but it turns out to be a great hurdle for many students. In the spiral plan, the teacher completes the work on Archimedes' principle and delays consideration of specific gravity until some later time. Then the "digestive process" is well along; time has been allowed for incubation, and the student approaches a more difficult aspect of a familiar problem with vigor and confidence. Applied broadly, the plan spiral divides, or organizes, topics so that the easy and difficult parts appear some weeks or months apart.

What readiness does the student have for a new topic? That is, what does he already know about it? Since physics is generally taught in the twelfth year of schooling, students have accumulated considerable knowledge about parts of physics from their general science classes, chemistry, and just living. While physics teachers customarily complain that they do not have time for all they wish to do, rarely do they seem to inquire what the students already know, and start from there. Discussion based on a simple demonstration will reveal much of what is operational and what is confused or unknown. Simple "situational" paper-and-pencil tests, asking "What would you do now?" will also be useful. Inevitably some incorrect and some incomplete ideas will appear. This is the line of demarcation for the new instruction which will remedy, in part, the confusions. Students will also have opportunity to appraise what they know, and take part in such planning as is necessary.

While the topical approach is commonly used in planning physics courses, it has severe limitations. A topical plan does not indicate the intent of the instruction. Neither does it indicate in detail the content. A topic such as "heat" or ' levers" does not specifically inform another teacher what ideas will be included, what context will be employed, how detailed the treatment will be, or where and how this topic will touch the lives of the students. The fact that most physics teachers will get a fairly clear idea of what is implied by topics like "levers" and "heat" is evidence of the standardization of the course that is taught irrespective of the audience.

Problems as a frame of reference

Whatever means we use to teach physics will necessarily result in the accumulation of a store of facts and principles, But what they will mean to the student, how will they will be understood, what values they will have later will depend not on a recall of the facts or principles as such, but on the way in which the student has been led to them and the variety of contexts in which he recognizes them as applicable. Consider the following cases.

A student is called to the demonstration table to use a claw hammer in removing a four-inch nail which has been driven deeply into a block of wood. He soon discovers that the removal becomes more difficult as the nail is withdrawn. He himself is aware of two questions. Why does this happen ? What can be done to make removal of the nail easier ?

Or a small model of a fish is placed at the bottom of an aquarium tank filled with water, and the student, in imitation of a spearfisher, is asked to push a slender glass rod through the water to strike the fish, working from a number of angles. He misses repeatedly, except from straight overhead.

Or a 20 ampere fuse has just "blown" and you have only 15-ampere fuses for replacement. Can they be used :

These situations will bring into play a host of the facts and principles that are the domain of physics. But they will have arisen out of a *problem* ; they will have original not in artificial questions propounded to initiate the study of a predetermined topic, but in an honest-to-goodness situation which may have confronted, or will confront, the student in his life Now we involve the interest of the student and increase his effort to understand. And to answer these questions, he must utilize known facts and principles or discover them by further questions and experiments. The inductive method comes into play, and with it, understanding, appreciations, and attitudes. Emphasis on dealing with real problems helps in concept attaining, even if it is just "problem doing" Problems can be used in many ways :

1. Problems can be used to develop interest in a topic. There is the problem of the spearfisher stabbing for "fish." Snell's law applies, bul the students discover it for themselves, or see its meaning.

2. Problems may serve to apply facts and principles. If students who have previously, possibly in general science, learned the facts and principles of the lever are confronted by the hammer and nail experiment, the teacher (and the students) will then know whether they have understood the principles or simply memorized the "facts." Where there is understanding, there is appreciation of the practical significance of the knowledge and where it is applicable.

3. Problems may serve to test understanding. A beaker two-thirds full of water and a 200 gm metal weight are counterpoised on a scale. If the weight is placed in the beaker so that it is fully submerged, will the weight increase, decrease, or remain the same ? Or copper and tungsten wires of the same dimensions are connected, first in series and then in parallel. If 110 volts is now applied to each combination, which wire will be heated to melting first ?

4. Problems may be used to stimulate individual study and research. Many new problems appear as the student shows curiosity regarding the history of scientific developments. How was the size of a molecule first determined ? How can the wave

length of visible light be measured ? Does Boyle's law have any practical value ? The problem situation then has value in terms of needs and interests.

5. Problems may be used to develop a point of view. Whose point of view ? The student's of course ; and in helping the student develop a position, the teacher may change his. For instance, some topics cannot be demonstrated. But a film may be used to raise the tremendously pertinent question of the use of the physicist's great contribution ; atomic energy. By allowing full but informed discussion, the teacher helps the student build a point of view.[21]

Needs and interests as a frame of reference

> That material which will be of greatest interest and value to students will (1) help the student the better to understand his own behaviour ; (2) help to explain, through reference to larger underlying principles, the common phenomena and devices of his own environment. Material that does not meet these criteria becomes of suspect value and may be considered for deletion.[22]

Apply these criteria to such topics as the laws of capillarity, images in a concave mirror. Lenz's law, the formula for centrifugal force, and the relation among image distance, object distance, and focal length in a lens (as usually presented), and these topics are found wanting.

On the other hand, a course built around the automobile will introduce the elements of hydraulics, mechanics, and electricity in a manner that arouses interest and satisfies needs. This idea has often been suggested in the *statements* of a syllabus, but the matter has rested there. Occasional reference is made to the automobile (or other theme of interest), after which the work reduces to the usual treatment of the areas mentioned. To be effective the central theme must remain central ; all of the areas must be integrated around it.

College teachers have often introduced novel and interest-holding central themes. For example, at Brooklyn College,

Peach[23] designed an introductory course around a model railroad, which ran on the table at varying speeds, pulled loads, turned corners, puffed smoke into a "wind," etc.

No two courses based on needs and interests should be alike, because this type of course should be fitted to the group being taught. It should be capable of change "at a moment's notice." A course of this type based on the needs and interests of students in a rural community is presented in the "Excursion" at the end of the chapter.

What are some of the typical studies in physics that may be stimulated by needs and interests ? Is there a photographer in the class ? Challenge him to take an actual photograph with a pinhole camera. His results will reap a wealth of information regarding optics applied to the camera, but he will have accumulated this out of genuine interest. Are there musicians in the class, or a school band or orchestra ? Have students sound as A on the violin, clarinet, trumpet, etc. ; the meaning of the quality of sound will become clear. But there also arises a stimulus toward finding out why the qualities differ. Is there a radio "ham" in the class ? Put him to work demonstrating the action of various stages of a set, etc. While these activities may arise initially out of the needs or interests of a single (or a few) student(s), they accrue to the benefit of the class as a whole. Latent interests appear, for the adolescent is interested to the undertakings of other adolescents. What they report or demonstrate will receive more earnest attention than the same material presented by the teacher. Questions from the class will reveal the limits of clear knowledge and stimulate further study.

Historical approach as a frame of reference

Some teachers prefer the historical approach. Even here the student can be stimulated to think reflectively. For instance, note how Galileo's discoveries may be used as a resource.

Ask a student what he can say about an object dropped from a height. He knows (from experience) that the longer it falls, the faster it will fall. Now ask him how he would measure the changing speed, but here, *take him back to 1600.* There is no high-speed photography, no electrical timing device, etc. Now, how would he do it ? And so the student is confronted with the same problem that faced Galileo. A wealth of appreciation results when the student learns how Galileo employed an inclined plane to study the phenomenon in "slow motion," as well as the realization of a subtle point ; the fact that an object decending on an inclined plane is also a falling body.

Or consider the pendulum. Very definitely, the formula represents cold, hard fact, but *how* was it discovered ? Start with Galileo, kneeling in a cathedral, attracted by the slow swing of a chandelier overhead. How long does it take for one swing ? How is he to measure it ? Here the student gets an appreciation of scientific ingenuity as he too times the swing of a pendulum with his pulse beat. After the experiment has been refined with a stop watch, what other aspects might be studied ? And here the *student* suggests the weight of the bob, the length of the pendulum, the nature of its materials, etc. It is not long before the relevant facts in the motion of a pendulum are *discovered* by the students ; a study of the data is assigned for homework with a view to ascertaining any regularity (law) involved. This approach has made the student the center of attention by *identifying* him with Galileo, whose intellectual footsteps he has been led to retrace. There will be not just a recall of facts and principles stated in a book or by the teacher, but a deeper understanding, augmented by appreciations, attitudes, realization of method.[24]

Special Considerations in Teaching Physics

The flavour of the course

By virtue of its accent on energy, physics has one point of similarity with chemistry. None of the properties which fall into its domain can be ascertained until something is done to, or with, an object. Physics and chemistry are based on active verbs. The property of inertia is not evident until we start (or stop) a car ; expansion and contraction are meaningless until the temperature changes ; the refractive index of a piece of glass is not apparent until light passes through it ; the rectifying properties of selenium or cuprous oxide cannot be realized until an alternating current is applied to it.

But there is an additional feature of physics on which all students will agree—its ideas are *subtle*. We expect the heavy object to fall faster than the light ; but it doesn't. We learn that light is transmitted by a wave motion ; but if it can pass through a vacuum, what is it that "waves" ? We learn that a body submerged in water apparently loses weight, and we expect it to lose more weight on being submerged further ; but it doesn't. We pull on the window pole or push on the lawn mower with a *single* force ; yet this can now be divided into *two* forces. Ice water ought to cool tea and coffee as fast as ice does (it has the same temperature) ; yet it doesn't. And so on, *ad infinitum*. It is this subtlety in the facts, concepts and principles of physics that may account for the impression on the part of many students (and unfortunately some teachers) that physics is a "hard" subject. But the answer should be positive, not negative. The methodology of physics teaching should be challenged to make this feature an asset, not an obstacle in the work. Problems which the children state will be attacked with enthusiasm by the "classroom detectives."

Projects that flavour the physics course differ from those in other sciences :

The use of oil films in determining the size of molecules.
Experiments with Newton's rings.
Construction of wind tunnels and air-stream speed indicators.
Construction and use of a stroboscope to study motion.
Crystal, tube, and transistor radios.
Photocell experiments and solar batteries.
Construction and calibration of thermocouples.
Resonance among coupled pendulums.
Construction of a device to show a free fall of 4 feet in $\frac{1}{2}$ second.
A homemade Prony brake for horsepower measurements.

Perpetual motion machine models.
Center of gravity experiments.

The place of laboratory work in physics

The kinship between chemistry and physics also extends to their problems; for everything that presents a problem to the teacher of chemistry also poses a problem to the teacher of physics. Thus, we have to choose our own blend of individual laboratory work and demonstration to help in concept attainment.[25]

Without going through the argument again, it is abundantly clear that both the laboratory experiment and the classroom demonstration have a central place in the high school science program. They present firsthand evidence. A considerable body of research has failed to reveal that either teaching technique is so inferior to the other as to justify abandoning it. Each has its utility, but for different purposes. In cases where the laboratory lesson appeared fruitless, one might suspect that laboratory ineffectiveness is not due to inherent weakness in this form of pedagogy, but to unimaginative, uninspired, and generally unsound patterns of laboratory procedures which should be re-examined and reconstructed in terms of the changing character of secondary school science education.[26]

Apparently no sizable study of the effectiveness of laboratory work in secondary school physics (like that of Horton in chemistry) has been made. College teachers have, however, been seriously concerned about the "payoff" on laboratory work in physics, which requires much instructional time, space, and money. Kruglak with others has carried through a series of investigations attempting to isolate, through both performance tests and paper-and-pencil tests some evidence of what is learned in laboratory work.[27] Thus far the study has not answered the question well. For example, "performance tests measure instructional outcomes other than those measured by conventional achievement tests"; also, "paper-and-pencil laboratory tests designed to evaluate *specific* laboratory outcomes have few elements in common with laboratory *performance* tests consisting of more comprehensive tasks." The tests used by Kruglak dealt mostly with specific skills and specific experiments. They did not involve the larger concepts about the role of experimental evidence and the attitudes of the students toward such experimental evidence.

Many colleges have devised interesting variations on the routine laboratory procedures. At Smith College a special laboratory section was designed for premedical students in the introductory course. This laboratory cleverly involved basic physical concepts and equipment in the study of physiological and anatomical problems. The students gathered most of the data from observations on their own bodies. Among the problems investigated were : the compression exerted on the 5th intervertebral disk when the student bent over ; the variations in personal temperature (3 observations per day for 3 weeks) : metabolism test and the heat of combustion ; conductivity of nerves (using a Wheatstone bridge, "lie detectors," and brain waves) ; and tests of visual acuity, sensitivity, and colour vision.[28]

At the Massachusetts Institute of Technology, Brown investigated the results of high school laboratory work on entering freshmen.[29] On tests of the recognition and purpose of laboratory equipment used in the schools, determined by a study of manuals used and particular experiments done by these students, the high school laboratory time showed very little residual retention. This posed some sobering questions about both the prior school laboratory work and that in the college course for which similar retention was no greater.

Recently the introductory laboratory work at M.I.T has been completely altered.[30] This grew out of a dissatisfaction with the previous laboratory program, aggravated by large enrollments (about 1400), space needs, and expense. The first decision was to abandon any attempt to develop manipulative skills in a comprehensive manner. Second, no attempt was made to have the laboratory "cover the subject" or to be in step with the lectures. But now the laboratory has a purpose of its own : to practice "sciencing" in physics. Each student has laboratory only every third week, or five times a semester.

He knows the problem in advance and is expected to plan carefully the use of the equipment to provide useful information. The important point is this. The laboratory is to provide data which can solve a problem when developed through a chain of theoretical arguments in connection with other known data. This laboratory work is an exciting challenge to the students, not just confirmation of a result they already know. That it is successful and interesting is evident : a surprising number choose to do a sixth experiment, even though it cannot be counted toward their grade and comes at the inconvenient time when semester examinations are being held.

Such science laboratory work stimulates a high order of learning by doing, consistent with modern educational psychology. But there is another problem which flavors the teaching of physics, even more than it does chemistry. This is the abundance of mathematics.

The place of mathematics in physics

Mathematics, like laboratory experimentation, also offers difficulty in physics, but not for reasons of expenditure or administrative schedules. The mathematical side of physics is often a stumbling block even to intelligent students.

> It might be supposed...that the values of science instruction which are our primary concern in general education might be conveyed more successfully without these elements [direct observation, experiment, and mathematical reasoning]. What this notion fails to appreciate, however, is that direct observation and precision are among the most important values and basic ideas that science should contribute to general education.
>
> What might be conveyed without them is not only not science, but in a very real sense antiscientific. It comes perilously close in spirit to the scholasticism with which modern science broke at its very inception. It possesses the typical scholastic reliance upon verbal authority—in this case the authority of the writer of scientific tests—it has the same

> predominantly deductive logical structure, and the same preoccupation with words rather than with the objects and processes which they only imperfectly symbolize. The thought that an understanding of science might be conveyed as well or better without direct observation, experiment, and mathematical reasoning involves a fundamental misapprehension of the nature of science.[31]

"Very well," one might say, "but the fact remains that students in physics cannot handle the necessary mathematics or in some cases are afraid of it. What shall we do then ?"

> Many science teachers complain that their pupils have not been adequately prepared by the mathematics teachers. In the opinion of numerous educators, the mathematics teachers have just as much reason to say that the science teachers have not prepared their pupils properly...The transfer of the mathematical concepts taught on a symbolic basis in the mathematics classroom, to the social and scientific applications is left to the pupil. Unless a definite effort is made to assist him in applying mathematics to science, he will continue to fail to solve equations and formulas which arise in the science classroom even when he has had little trouble in solving the same basic problems in the regular mathematics classroom.[32]

What is the teacher of physics to do about this situation ? Mathematics remains a language ; we speak in numbers and equations as well as words. What has been forgotten by those who use mathematics as a tool is that a "foreign" language must be *translated*. Certainly the competent teacher of mathematics teaches his pupils the applications of their work in other fields, but he too is subject to the same rigors of a syllabus and schedule which are the lot of the physics teachers. Regardless of his efforts, the pupil coming to physics meets the mathematics *in a new context*. The teacher of physics will find it useless to claim that the students have been poorly prepared ; they are captive in his class. He may, of course, fail these students, but this is hardly an answer. It remains instead his opportunity, even his *obligation*, to teach those mathematical concepts which are fundamental to success in physics. For example : From teacher demonstration, the class has gathered data for Boyle's law. What do they show ? A graph of the data will reveal a possible relation between pressure and volume. When this is checked further, the familiar relation will be discovered. In our experience, students have often found this to be the first time when actual data obtained from experiment has been graphed. The graph comes alive. Students will often indicate that this is the first time they have understood a graph and understood the meaning of "inversely proportional." The student does not come "ready made." We must assist him in *all* phases of our particular course, whether it be mathematics, English, or habits in general. The behavioral objectives of education remain with us.

For a mathematical description of the world to have any significance to the student, the critical aspect is the *search for meaning*. The course must be taught with some questions always foremost. What goes on here ? What pattern can I find ? What can I predict and how well ? In more elegant terms, the student must be searching for a *function*, a clean, concise description of a relationship among the aspects of the problem selected as probably important. Initially this will always be a *qualitative* description. As the pressure rises, a gas gets squashed or compressed. Then follows the nicer question : By how much ? This second question stimulates a desire for quantitative information and perhaps a mathematical relationship, or "going-togetherness. Such a numerical or algebraic description is needed to permit predictions of "how much." Not all children will wish to go that far with each question, but they should see how the mathematical descriptions are desired and evolved, and why they are so useful.

From this analysis several conclusions appear. First, the student must be interested in the phenomenon ; he must want to know something about it, qualitatively or quantitatively. Therefore, the initial context in which the problem arises must be significant to the pupil. Secondly, the qualitative analysis of "what sort of relationship do we have ?" must always precede the quantitative. If no pattern seems present among observations of temperature, pressure, and volume of a gas, there will seem to be no point to looking for a quantitative result. This point is often overlooked by hurried teachers. Thirdly, with interest, a qualitative relationship in mind, and data, *time* must be allowed for the student to uncover a mathematical description and to test it. Time will also be needed for the comparison of various results, for not all students will achieve the same answer. Which is better? What are the criteria of "betterness"? Does it satisfy more closely the existing data? Does it predict more exactly conditions later confirmed by experiments?

To many teachers a procedure such as this seems painfully slow. Since the answer (law, etc.) is known, why not tell it to them and get on to something else? Such a process, all too commonly used, leaves the student out of the creative activity. He may remember for a time, but he has not identified with the study; it is not his. Often he does not care or really understand; forgetting is rapid. The approach we have outlined is at first very slow; the student is beginning a whole new art in scientific work. But as he practices this approach, he sees his own pattern of learning and can apply it with increasing quickness to later problems. He is "learning how to learn."

By a search for functions, we mean the type of insight and logic which Faraday used in his monumental investigations. Lacking in formal education, Faraday used little or no algebra in describing his results. Yet he searched for the essential attributes (qualities) within the phenomena and found those which went together and in what kinds of patterns. James Clerk Maxwell, who applied mathematics to many of Faraday's results, said:

> As I proceeded with the study of Faraday. I perceived that his method of conceiving phenomena was also a mathematical one, though not exhibited in the conventional form of mathematical symbols.[33]

This provides the physics teacher, in fact all science teachers, with a critical distinction. Students can be encouraged to think functionally, even mathematically, without necessarily involving mathematical symbols. Many will push on to that more abstract formulation, but others can have the "feel" of how a scientist works without the algebra.[34]

An excursion, lengthier than usual, in developing one's own course in physics

11.1. In a workshop we encountered a teacher of physics who determined to try the device described for chemistry. He tried it for two years, and it worked.

He found he could deal with the mathematical portions of physics in class ; his students could read the descriptive portions. In class, therefore, he dealt mainly with topics such as optics, nuclear physics, mechanics, wave theory, and electricity. Students read by themselves, mainly about simple machines, measurement, heat, applications of physics (toasters to pulleys), He added this modification : he reviewed briefly all materials read before developing any principle with mathematical background.

He found he had time to teach in the leisurely fashion which good teaching demanded. He could go into the highways and byways ; he could deal with the methods of scientists ; the class had the time to develop major concepts and conceptual schemes ; the class had time to develop its needs and interests.

11.2. Another teacher of physics tried a device which we have seen operating in three Midwestern schools.

This teacher gave his class a standard workbook. He suggested this method of study each student in the class could do each "exercise" at his own speed. The class would use several textbooks (school and college) for reference. A schedule was decided upon ; each student could either go ahead at his own speed and do the exercises one after the other, or if he were ahead of schedule, he could stop after a certain block (say, machines) and do a project of his choice.

Students would take examinations on text and lab work at scheduled times.

The class was given the opportunity to discuss the advantages or disadvantages of this method. It was adopted. Is it surprising that this class did as well in its examinations as did other classes that selected the conventional method ?

11.3. At the end of the spring term, 1957, Professor Harvey White of the University of California completed 162 TV lessons of a whole course in physics. Professor White taught the lessons in a TV-teaching "experiment" in the Pittsburgh schools ; his lessons were also filmed in colour and in black and white. Now we are not suggesting that this course replace you, the teacher (although some have seriously suggested that these films be used where there is no teacher of physics). We suggest that this provides one of the few times that teachers have the opportunity to observe another teacher at work. If the funds are available, it would be worth while purchasing or renting the films.[35] They would furnish excellent material in a critical seminar on objectives, philosophy, and teaching method in physics. Also excellent demonstrations are presented.

11.4. There are further deviations from the standard course. The following suggestion[36] is applied to a "course" suitable for rural schools. Note, however, that the generalizations have the same drift as in a "standard" course. It is in the *devices used to illustrate* the principles that the course differs.

> Here a farm lighting plant might be selected as a familiar and useful application of principles of physics worthy of study. It would be treated as a complicated device for the conversion of stored energy into forms useful in daily life. The gasoline engine would be treated as a device for converting the stored energy of the gasoline into heat, and the heat into mechanical energy for turning the electric generator. The generator would be treated as a device for converting the mechanical energy into electrical energy. The storage cells would be treated as devices for converting electrical energy into chemical energy and

chemical energy into electrical energy. Various household and farm machines would be treated as machines for converting the electrical energy taken from the power plant or the storage cells into useful forms of energy. The electric lamp would be considered as a means of converting electricity into heat and light, two other forms of energy; the electric iron as a means of converting electrical energy into heat. Friction in the machines, necessity for lubrication, and the heat developed in moving parts of machines could be used as a means of building up the notion that energy is not lost or destroyed, but merely changed into other forms, some of which are not directly useful for the human purpose for which the machine was built. It would be possible to trace the energy stored in the gasoline back to the crude oil, the crude oil to prehistoric primitive organisms, and the stored chemical energy of these organisms to the radiant energy of the sun. Pupils might eventually see that radiant energy given off from the electric lamp in the living room on a particular winter evening came from radiant energy released from the sun ages ago. Through such study pupils might be enabled to enlarge their understandings of such generalizations as the following.

1. The sun is the chief source of energy for the earth.
2. Energy may be derived from matter.
3. Energy may be stored in chemical substances.
4. Energy is not destroyed.
5. Machines serve the purpose of changing energy into its different forms.
6. All matter is probably electrical in nature.
7. Chemical changes are accompanied by energy changes.
8. The "loss" of energy in machines is only apparent. These losses may be accounted for by energy transformations which are not parts of the useful output of the machines.
9. Electricity, heat, and light are forms of energy.
10. Complicated machines may be reduced to a relatively few simple types of machines.

In urban situations a similar treatment might be made of the local electric power supply. Certain extensions of the foregoing generalizations would be possible with power supplied from coal and steam plants or water power and through the increased ramifications of power supplies to modern transportation and industry.

11.5. And as we might expect in the light of the history of development of courses, there should be and there is an attempt to develop a course in physical science. This attempt is in the tradition of the development of biological science from botany and zoology.

11.6. You may find it illuminating to compare the contents and organization of several current physics textbooks. How similar are they ?

11.7. In several physics textbooks, compare chapters on the same subject for the concepts included. Examine the technical vocabulary used in these books. How many of the words are clearly defined ? How many are necessary ?

11.8. For two units in the syllabus on applied physics list the major concepts that might be developed. To what extent would mathematical (algebraic) results be necessary ?

11.9. What are the lesser concepts contributing to one of the concepts from the list ? What different experimental problems (or demonstrations) could be used to work toward these concepts ?

References

1. By definition of the I.Q. scale, just over 25 per cent of the population can score above 110.
2. Although, of course, the total *number* of students taking physics has increased considerably, and so has the *percentage* of the high school *age group*.
3. Smith and E. H. Hall. *Teaching of Chemistry and Physics.* Longmans, Green N.Y. ISSI. p. 269.
4. For a list of these 10 experiments, most of which are still commonly performed, see S. Rosen, "A History of the Physics Laboratory in the American High School (In 1910)."

American Journal of Physics, 22, 194, 1954. Many of the historical sidelights are drawn from this paper.

5. S. Rosen, *op. cit.*, p. 203.
6. Ralph W. Lefler, "Trends in High School Physics." *National Association of Secondary School Principals Bulletin*, Jan. 1953, p. 74.
7. R. W. Letter, *op. cit.*, p. 79.
8. G.A. Compton. "The Secondary School Textbook," *Amercian Journal of Physics*, 21, 537, 1953 : see also W. C. Michels. "High School Physics—A Report of the Joint Committee on High School Teaching Mate ials," *Physics Today*, *10*, 20, 1957.
9. R. W. Letter, *op. cit.*, p. 79 : see also Eric Rogers. "The Block and Gap Scheme for Physics Courses." *American Journal of Physics*, *17*, 532, 1949.

   A J. Hatch and D.F. Cope. "Flashback Teaching Technique Applied to a Block-and-Gap Physics Course," *American Journal of Physics*, *19*, 137-45, 1951.
10. See page 291, under section heading, "Changes in College Physics."
11. In a study of physics in 370 California high schools, McRary found that 70% of those enrolled in physics intended to enter college, while 17% anticipated a career in physics. W.L. McRary. "Physics Instruction in California High Schools," *Physics Today 10*, 25, 1957.
12. R.R. Palmer (Chm.), "Improving the Quality and Effectiveness of Introductors Physics Courses," Report of a Conference Sponsored by the American Association of Physics Teachers, Carleton College, Sept. 1956, *American Journal of Physics*, *25*, 417, 1957.
13. Gerald Holton. "Syllabus for the One-Year College Course in Physical Science" (Harvard), *American Journal of Physics*, *25*, 425, 1957.

    Walter C. Michels, "One-Year Introductory Course in a Liberal Arts College" (Bryn Mawr), *American Journal of Physics*, *25*, 430, 1957.

    R. M. Whaley, "Three-Semester Introductory Course for Engineers and Science Majors" (Product, *American, Journal of Physics*, *25*, 432, 1957.
14. Further information may be obtained from the Physical Science Study Commitee, 94 Massachusetts AVC, Cambridge, Mass.
15. These italics are added.
16. These italics are added.
17. The extreme tentativeness of this outline is to be stressed. It is being revised daily.
18. We are reminded of a teacher in such a course who said he taught "applied physics" where the principal came to visit, but otherwise he taught "physics."

19. See the recommendations of the Physical Science Study Committee; pp. 297-98 as a guide.

20 Measurement, as a topic, seems particularly sterile (that is unless one goes deep into the philosophical and semantic problems involved in measurement, which is most unlikely in high school physics). It contains few, if any, major ideas about the world. Rather, it represents a tool (technique, scales, etc.) for describing the world, *when such a description is desired.* Like any classification system, it was devised and later refined when people had something they wished to describe more closely. In the physics course, measurements should appear when they are needed to provide accurate data which relate to some interesting idea. No one measures just for the fun of measuring : one measures to get needed data.

21. A list of films is available in the accompanying volume. *Teaching High School Science : A Sourcebook for the Physical Sciences.*

22. NSSE, *Forty-Sixth Yearbook,* op. cit., p. 210.

23. H. Peach, "Complete Physics Course Through Model Trains," *American Journal of Physics, 20,* 314, 1952.

24. A good example of how this approach can be applied to physics (and any other science) will be found in an unusual testbook on the college level. L W. Taylor. *Physics, the Pioneer Science,* Houghton Mifflin, Boston, 1942.

25. Five articles on laboratory work in general appear in the *National Association of Secondary School Principals Bulletin, 37,* 191, Jan. 1953, beginning on p. 96.

26. For an interesting account of how one thoughtful physics teacher gradually changed his approach to laboratory work, see R.W. Lefler. "The Teaching on Laboratory Work in High School Physics." *School Science and Mathematics,* 47, 531, 1947.

27. H. Kruglak and others have written a number of articles summing up the indications of the results of these investigations. This series on evaluation of laboratory work appeared, over a period of five years, In the *American Journal of Physics,* as follows : 19, 223 and 546, 1951 : 20, 136, 1952 : 21, 14, 1952 : 22, 442 and 452, 1954, 23. 82 and 257, 1955. See also H. Kruglak. "Some Behavior Objectives for Laboratory instruction," *American Journal of Physics,* 14, 223, 1951.

28. N. Mohler, L , Lorentz and . Bunce, "Elementary Laboratory for Premedical Students. *American Journal of Physics, 19,* 170, 1951.

29 S.C. Brown, unpublished results.

30. S.C. Brown, "Elementary Physics Laboratory Instruction at the Massachusetts Institute of Technology." *American Journal of Physics, 25,* 446, 1957.

A similar analysis was made by Leo Nedelsky, "Introductory Physics Laboratory." *American Journal of Physics, 26*, 51, 1958.

31. *General Education in a Free Society*, Harvard U. Press. Cambridge, 1946, p. 153.

32. A.J. Hall, "Relations Between Science and Mathematics in the Secondary School." *National Association of Secondary School Principals Bulletin*, Jan. 1953, pp. 93. 94.

33. James Clerk Maxwell, *Electricity and Magnetism*, 3rd ed. 2 vols. Dover Publications, N. Y. 1954.

34. For examplary material, you might wish to peruse M. Faraday, *Researches in Electricity*, Everouette's Library, No. 576, N. Y. 1914; and I. Newton, *Optics*. Dover Publications, N.Y. 1952, Laboratory of B. Franklin on electricity are also similar.

35. Available from Encyclopaedia Britannica Films.

36. R.K. Watkins (Comm. Chm.). *A Program for Science Teaching*, Part I *Thirty-First Yearbook*, NSSF. U. of Chicago Press, Chicago, 1932, p. 255.

12

The Demonstration Method

There are time when nothing but the demonstration will do, for example, when the teacher wishes :

To begin a lesson and demonstrate a phenomenon at variance with ordinary experience (*e.g.*, a balloon sticking to the chalk-board, by electrostatic attraction).

To end a lesson leading to an extension of work at home (*e.g.* just a few minutes before the bell is to ring ending the lesson, he begins testing foods with litmus-oranges, lemons, etc.—the bell rings and he wonders aloud who would finish this at home and report to the class).

To develop a point during the lesson (*e.g.*, students are discussing the difference between a single animal cell and a single-celled animal ; at a suitable point the teacher switches on a bioscope or microprojector or film to show a paramecium and a check cell).

To highlight safety procedures in the laboratory (*e.g.*, the first time students work with glass, the instructor needs to demonstrate how to insert glass tubing into a rubber stopper, how to bend glass, etc).

To demonstrate processes generally too dangerous or too complex for students to handle (*e.g.*, the Thermit process, the reduction of CuO, the dissection of an embryo pig, the first experience with circuitry in an oscillator).

To demonstrate additional aspects of laboratory work (*e.g.*, it may not be desireable to have students do all types of preparations of, say, oxygen ; one or more procedures might be demonstrated).

For whatever purpose the demonstration is used, its major function is to present evidence for a concept by doing, seeing, testing.

Who does the demonstration ? The class ; every student participates, in one way or another. The demonstration is part of the lesson ; as such, it would be wasteful to lecture as it is being done. For instance, one teacher presented the routine preparation of oxygen in a general science class as follows :

1. Students set up the apparatus (they had read beforehand).
2. The teacher asked these questions :
   - (*a*) What substances are we to use ? (The student who replied added the materials.)
   - (*b*) What is the equation for the reaction ? (A student wrote it on the board.)
   - (*c*) How shall we proceed ? (The students told the teacher, who added appropriate cautions on safety procedures.)
   - (*d*) How shall we collect the gas ?

In the interim between these questions students watched and took notes. The next day they went to the laboratory, and prepared oxygen according to the procedure they had watched. They then spent the rest of the double-labperiod testing the properties of oxygen by procedures they had read about in their text and in a supplementary chemistry text.

A demonstration, in short, may be considered a *group experiment* in which selected members actually do the experiment, while all observe carefully and suggest procedures, devices, controls, are safeguards. All students take notes ; all are expected to use, in future work, the knowledge gained.

The demonstration is not, of course, a substitute for the laboratory ; it is but an additional tool of the teacher.

The following references offer useful suggestions for demonstrations.

Selected Books

Crouse, W.H., *Understanding Science*, N.Y. : Whittlesey House 1948.

Freeman, M., and I, Freeman, *Invitation to Experiment*, N. Y., : Dutton, 1940.

Joseph, A. F. Morholt, and P. F. Brandwein, *Teaching High School Science : A Source book for the Physical Sciences*, N. Y. : Harcourt, Brace, 1959.

Lord, Engene H., *Experimenting at Home with Wonders of Science*, N. Y. : D. Appleton Century, 1942.

Lunt. J.R: *Eleclricity for Everyone*, N. Y., Macmillan, 1943.

Lyñde, C. J., *Science Experiences with Home Equipment : Science Experiences with Inexpensive Equipment : Science Experiences with Ten cent Store Equipment*, Scranton, Pa : International Textbook Co., 1937, 1939, 1941.

Miller, David F , and Glenn W. Blaydes, *Methods and Materials for Teaching Biological Sciences*, N. Y. : McGraw-Hill, 1938.

Morgan, A.P. *Things a Boy Can Do with Chemistry*, N.Y. ; D. Appleton Century, 1940.

Morholt, E., P.F. Brandwein, and A. Joseph, *Teaching High School Science : A Source-book for the Biological Sciences*, N.Y. Harcourt, Brace, 1958.

Richardson, J.S., and G.P. Cahoon, *Methods and Materials for Teaching General and Physical Science*, N. Y : McGraw Hill, 1951.

Schneider, H., and N. Schneider, *Now Try This*, N.Y. : William R. Scott. 1948.

Simmons, M. P. *The Young Scientist*, N. Y. Exposition Press, 1951.

Sutton, R., *Demonstration Experiments in Physics*, N. Y. : Mc Graw-Hill, 1938.

Swezey, Kenneth M. *After dinner Science*, N. Y : Whittlesey House, 1948.

Selected Pamphlets

Association for Childhood Education, *Uses for Waste Materials*, Washington, D.C., 1951.

Blough, Glevin O., and P. E., Blackwood *Teaching Elementary Science*, Washington, D.C., U. S. Government Printing Office. 1948.

———*Science Teaching in Rural and Small Town Schools.*

Washington, D. C. : U.S. Government Printing Office 1949.

Bruce, Guy V. ; *Experiments with Water And Fuels* : *Heat Magnetism and Electricity* ; *Sound* ; *Light* : 7 vols. Washington D.C. National Science Teachers Association, n.d.

Davis Hubert J., *Some Handy Recipes for Science Work*, Mississippe State College, Department of Adult Education, 1952.

Instructor Series of Illustrated Units Dansville N. Y. : F. V. Owen Publishing Co.

THE CHALK-BOARD

The somewhat derogatory word "chalk-talk" has its purposes ; unfortunately, it casts aspersions on chalk, which is one of the most useful "tools" of the teacher. Its unfortunate connotation, in science at least, arises from the fact that very often the chalk-board is used only as an aid to the lecture and as a substitute for the experiment or the demonstration, as a substitute for seeing or doing.

Naturally, the teacher who has adapted the lecture to his own personality will use the chalk-board as skillfully as he uses his personality and his language. When he has finished his lecture, students will clearly see on the board the evidence, argument, and conclusion of the lesson. But use of the chalk board is not restricted to the lecturer. Teacher and students, no matter what the pattern of the lesson is, can make good use of the chalk-board.

As an aid in demonstration : Six students breathed on the board through their mouths ; the class saw six spots of moisture appear and then evaporate. (Other similar devices are to be found in the accompanying volumes. *A Sourcebook for the Biological Sciences* and *A Sourcebook for the Physical Sciences*).

As an aid in illustration : One teacher draw diagrams of many different protozoa as an aid to identification for the first microscope lesson.

As directions in aiding an experiment : One teacher drew wiring diagrams in colour to assist his students in their *first* attempt to develop circuits.

As an aid to discussion : As points are made, students write their conclusions on the board for all to see and evaluate. Written statements are more easily analyzed than ones made orally.

As an aid to a report : As a student made a report he listed his major points, and the most difficult (technical) words he used.

As an aid to projections : One teacher we know projects his slides directly on the chalk-board. He then outlines in chalk the object projected, emphasizing major points or structures. When the projection is switched off, there, on the board, appears whatever the teacher wished to emphasize.

As a reminder : One teacher had a permanent sector of the board titled "A Reminder." There, schedules of visiting lecturers, field trips, demonstrations in the assembly, schedules of tests, or required reading were posted. No student could say he didn't know about them.

To emphasize and reinforce : And, of course, the skillful teacher uses the chalk-board to emphasize a point made by a student or the teacher himself.

THE FILM, WITH DIRECTORY OF DISTRIBUTORS

We assume that you have the catalogues of educational film producers, most of whom are listed. Certainly your school library has the comprehensive *Educational Film Guide*, with regular supplements[1].

Even a most casual examination of the catalogues or the compendium shows a rich variety of films, both sound and silent. But it is the *use* of these films with which we are concerned. (Analysis of kinds of equipment we leave to texts on the subject and to the teacher, who knows his needs. In purchasing equipment as follow two simple rules: (1) we examine the equipment and use, as a base for comparison, demonstrations by salesmen who explain the merits of their product : (2) we use the resources of the Department of Audio-Visual Aids of the National Education Association, or other expert.

What are the uses of films ? Again we repair to classroom observations.

As introduction to a topic : For instance, one effective way to introduce and capture interest in the topic of classification is to show a film of a variety of interesting plants and animals. Or in stimulating interest in metallurgy, show an industrial film, possibly on the winning of a metal. There are many such films available.

We think it a mistake, however, to use the film constantly to introduce a topic : in teaching, as in life, variety of approach retains interest. For instance, we should not use a film to introduce a topic in which there is already great interest, such as satellites.

As a review of a topic : For instance, there are many films on light and sound which may serve as a review of the topic.

As a vicarious field trip : One cannot always go on a field trip to a farm or a laboratory or an industry, one can use a film instead. For instance, the class can visit a beehive (unless you want to keep one) via one of the many films available. So a class by means of a film can go on a field trip to see a farm harvest, an operation in a hospital, a cancer laboratory, erosion and its prevention, a Bessemer furnace, the manufacture of plastics, the mining of sulfur, a cyclotron– almost any kind of field trip you would want to devise.

Of course, a film does not take a place of a field trip. It is a vicarious experience, like the filmstrip, model, or chart, a next best way of getting experience and evidence.

As an accessory experiment : Not all schools are fully equipped ; not all classrooms have gas, electricity, and water for every student ; not all experiments can be done with facility by everyone. For instance, to show that light exerts pressure requires complex equipment : to demonstrate that bacteria do divide under special conditions is difficult. At that time a film may serve But if it is to be a substitute experiment, then it might as well be treated as one :

1. Before the film is shown, the experiment is planned by the class ; that is, an experimental design is devised. This heightens interest as the class compares its own design with the films'; it also forms a base for criticism.

2 Only that part of the film which is concerned with the experiment is shown. For instance, part of one film on hormones[2] ; is given over to an experiment on the effect of parathyroid harmone ; the rest of the film is not shown at this time. The selected portion may be shown again and again until the class has milked it dry of meaning.

As an accessory microscope or microprojector : There are some things which cannot be readily shown at the appropriate time through ordinary microscopes or microprojectors (bacteria or other cells dividing, sperm entering egg. etc.) There are films which record these processes.

Again, the technique is as in the accessary experiment—to use only that part of the film and to observe it again and again (by running it again and again). After all, the portions of the film concerned with the observation desired take up only two or three minutes. And these portions need to be studied much as the same sort ; of things would need to be studied using the microscope or microprojector.[3]

As a test : One teacher we knew told the class at the beginning of the term that he would use a film at the end of the term as a test to their knowledge. When the time came, he showed a sound film but cut off the sound track. The students were required to reconstruct the findings in the film. This technique is useful for films dealing with a specific experiment.

And, of course, as a full-period lesson : The film can be used successfully as a full lesson, but unfortunately the use of the film is often less than creative :

1. The film is put on, and the class watches. Discussion, if any, is carried on after the film. No notes are taken.

2. Too often the narration is above (or below) the level of certain students, or even of the whole class. The narration can be cut off and the teacher can substitute his own.

3. Too often the film "teaches," even preaches, conclusions not justified by the evidence presented in it. We consider the film as a means of presenting evidence ; the conclusions should be reached by the students through discussion and argument. Again, the teacher can turn off the sound and the music.

We have found that it is a most useful procedure to develop the topic in which the film is used as we have described for the filmstrip (a "tool" section immediately following this one). Except that the film is used where motion lends meaning to what is being studied, the technique of its use is similar to that of other visualization.

The film can be controlled ; it can be stopped during its showing at suitable points for discussion or for a class demonstration or experiment. It does not substitute for the teacher because the teacher uses the film as part of his design, as part of his plan for producing changes in behaviour, for improving the skills, knowledges, and attitudes of the students in his care.

Films, like TV, can be used by the teacher ; but since teahing is not to be equated with telling and showing, the teacher in the film is not the same as the teacher in the classroom. The film is but one more tool in the arsenal of the competent teacher.

THE FILMSTRIP, WITH DIRECTORY OF DISTRIBUTORS

We should begin by noting that there is probably available a filmstrip useful for every unit (or large organized field of learning) in your courses of study. We urge you to develop a library of catalogues, which usually have brief descriptions of the filmstrips, as part of your resource file.

Generally speaking, the purpose of the filmstrip is to develop a sequential series of visualized ideas aimed at the building of concepts, although it may sometimes be used merely to furnish a tour (*e.g.*, of an industry).

We have before us several filmstrips—one aimed at the concept of electromagnetism, another at the concept of scientific method, another at the concept of photosynthesis. All of them lend themselves to an approach which we have seen fine teachers use, and which results in widespread participation. This is but one way, of course, of using a filmstrip :

1. The preceding day the lesson is decided upon ; it may be planned with students, or be a sequence the teacher has in mind, or be part of an assigned report a student will make or be chosen for some other reason.

In any event, overnight the students read in the general area of the subject of the filmstrip. The teacher examines either the filmstrip or its guide. Most guides have a fully illustrated sequence of the strip, with all the captions.

2. Next day, the teacher (or a student on the laboratory squad) puts the title frame on the screen (before the class period so that class time is not wasted). As soon as the lesson begins, the teacher (or student) snaps on the machine, and the title (*e.g.*, "How Green Plants Make Food") is flashed on.

3. The teacher asks, "What do you expect to find in this filmstrip ?" In the very brief discussion which follows, the attention of the class is focused and the mental activity of students stimulated. Even those who "know" how green plants make food have their expectancy stimulated.

4. As each frame is on the screen, the teacher discusses it with the class. Questions are asked by the teacher ; students draw upon their experience ; notes are taken ; all the devices of good teaching are exercised.

5. At any appropriate point, the teacher (or a committee, or a student, if it is so planned) does a demonstration, for two reasons. First, the tempo of attention is altered ; but second, and more important, not everything can be learned from the filmstrip—some things are learned better in other ways.

6. As each "eureka" develops, it is placed on the board.

7. When the filmstrip has been shown, each student is asked to write a brief summary. He may refer to his notes, to the board, and to his recall of past experience and reading.

8. Selected summaries are read in class and rated by the class (that is, after a summary is read the teacher will say, "John, what mark would you give this out of 10 ?" If John says "8," the teacher asks "Why ?" The class can quickly decide on the grade). The teacher gives the student two grades —the one given by the class, and the teacher's own.

One teacher we know reviews in this way : After showing the filmstrip and discussing it as above, he flashes on a frame, with the caption masked with a card. He then asks the students to describe the frame.

In any event, whatever approach is used, effective teaching practice indicates that the filmstrip be *used in* a lesson, and *not substituted for* a lesson. A filmstrip properly used is a lesson using visualization to help the teacher alter the behaviour of his students in a desirable way.

Using a filmstrip properly in an art, and, with the increase in the quality as well as the number of filmstrips, it is becoming an excellent one in the arsenal of teaching tools.

Directory of filmstrip distributors

Academy Films, Box 3088, Hollywood, Cal.

Encyclopaedia Britannica Films, Inc., may be obtained at the following offices :

101 Marietta St., Atlanta 3, Ga.
3745 Crabtree Road, Birmingham, Mich.
161 Massachusetts Ave., Boston 16, Mass.
1860 E. 85 St., Cleveland 6, Ohio.
1414 Dragon St., Dallas 2, Tex.
5625 Hollywood Blvd., Hollywood, Cal.
7421 Park Ave., Minneapolis 23, Minn.
202 E. 44 St., New York 17, N. Y.
2129 N.E. Broadway, Portland 5, Ore.
1150 Wilmette Ave., Wilmette, Ill.

Filmstrip House, 25 Broad St., New York 4, N. Y.

Jam Handy Organization, 2821 East Grand Blvd., Detroit 11, Mich.

Life Magazine, Inc., Filmstrip Division, 9 Rockefeller Plaza, New York 20, N.Y.

New York *Times*, Office of Educational Activities, 229 W, 43 St., New York 36.

Photo Lab. Inc., 3825 Georgia Ave., N.W., Washington 11, D.C.

Popular Science Publishing Co., Audio-Visual Division, 353 Fourth Ave., New York 10, N.Y.

Society for Visual Education, Inc., 1345 W. Diversey Parkway, Chicago 14, Ill.

Sugar Information, Inc., 52 Wall St., New York 5, N.Y.

Universal Colour Studies, P.O. Box 216, Grade Square Station, New York 28, N.Y.

Visual Education Consultants Inc., 2066 Heiena St., Madison 4, Was.

Young America Films, Inc., 18 E, 41 St., New York 17, N.Y.

THE LIBRARY LESSON

It cannot be taken for granted that students know how to use the library, especially in science. It is valuable to devise lessons which require the use of the library during class time. Naturally, these lessons are planned with the librarian, who then becomes the teacher.

For instance, the topic "Plant and Animal Breeding" might be developed into a library lesson in this manner :

1. The topic might be stated "How have we improved plants and animals ?"

2. The class, under its chairman, divides itself into groups concerned with various aspects, *e.g.*, "For Food," "For Work," "For Beauty," and so forth. Some may search out specific aspects, for instance, "Dogs," "Horses," "Apples", "Blucherries," "Honey bees".

3. The class goes to the library, and if this is the first lesson, gets from the librarian a demonstration of the cataloging and storing devices used in the library, as they apply to science.

4. The class begins work during that period and each individual student completes his assignment after class.

5. Students then report to the class on what they have learned.

A library lesson is particularly useful in general science. If it is given once every month or every two months, whenever an appropriate topic is available, the students learn a valuable technique. Some topics we have found useful for a library lesson are :

Plant and Animal Breeding
The Lives of Scientists
The History of Atomic Energy
Science in Industry
Industrial Processes (steel-making, soap-making, paper manufacture, etc.)
The History of the Earth.

THE LABORATORY LESSON, WITH A NOTE ON WORKBOOKS

The word "laboratory" has been endowed with a mystical connotation : it is as if it were a church where one went in supplication and came out always with the desired answer—the solution to the problem. Discussions of the place of the laboratory by teachers of science sometimes border on unreality :

If only students could use the laboratory to solve problems, the ways of the scientist would be taught.

If only the "cookbook" experiment were eliminated, if only we did not use "workbooks," we should truely teach science.

Yet reflection will show that the laboratory experiment is only *one* way of the scientist ; before he enters it and during his work there, he spends much time in *thinking*, *reading*, and *consulting*. Furthermore, much of his work in the laboratory is routine ; the design of an experiment is perhaps more a matter of thinking than of working with one's hands.

It would seem to us that a full laboratory experience in high school should include the following.

Opportunity to learn to plan sequential work. First there is a period of *acclimation.* Students begin with directed laboratory work. These directions may be developed in the teacher's own work sheets, or may be found in good workbooks ; the purpose of this work is to give students the feel of the laboratory, to find out where equipment is, and the like. Most important, its purpose is to permit the instructor to note ways of work and to note particularly those students whose habits of work may result in accidents.

After this initial period of acclimation, students are given the topic of an experiment and the necessary equipment, and asked (as an assignment) to plan their own experiments ; these are checked and approved. The students then proceed on their own. For instance, after the first week's work on simple machines in the physics laboratory students may plan their own experiment on the inclined plane.

After a few such experiences students are ready to try a longer experiment. For instance, in chemistry students may work on an "unknown" requiring many periods of work. In biology students may classify an "unknown" animal under the microscope, dissect an unusual speciman, or go so far as to determine the gēnetic make-up of a special stock of *Drosophila.*

Opportunity to learn skills. Students learn to use burners, balances, microscopes, first in relation to work directed by laboratory sheets, then in relation to an experiment they plan. They are given "practical examinations" (such as those described) in use of the tools and in identification of microorganisms, rocks, and so forth.

Opportunity to repeat some of the classic experiments in science. This has been called "looking over the shoulder of the scientist". For example, in dealing with Lavoisier's classic experiment in heating mercuric oxide, the class begins with an assignment on Lavoisier, his life and times ; reports are given. Then the experiment may be done as a demonstration by a group of students or by the teacher, according to Lavoisier's description.[4] This may be followed by individual or group work with HgO in the laboratory, studying its properties, percentage composition, etc. Then the class extends this work by continuing with Lavoisier's experiments in burning.

(Students might, as a project, prepare such an investigation into the history of science a month in advance of its "trial" in class—Priestley's experiments, Winogradsky's experiments, for example.)

Opportunity to vary standard experiments along "original" lines. Students are constantly asking questions after doing the standard experiments. For instance, after testing the reaction of *Paramecium* to salt, they may ask, "May we try ink ?" The reaction of *Paramecium* in shooting out trichocysts in reaction to ink is most edifying and may lead to further work. Standard experiments may be varied ad infinitum.

Opportunity to do an "original" experiment or project in the laboratory. This can be sustained over a semester, or over several years. We discuss the project. There is, of course, the matter of room for these experiments. Facilities for experimentation of this kind are at best limited. But many of these projects can be, and have been, carried out in the preparation room ; in a corner of the laboratory ; in the ordinary classroom (a table set up in one corner, perhaps) ; at home, in a college or university laboratory ; in a museum.

A note on workbooks

Rarely does a meeting of teachers go by without someone's attacking the workbook. The controversy between users of workbooks and laboratory manuals is likely to continue for some time. Neal[5] has summarized what to us are salient points in the "workbooks, yes : workbooks, no" controversy. He writes :

Workbooks for use in connection with secondary school science textbooks have recently been discussed at greater length than space permits here. Those who argue for the present type of workbook usually hold that it should be possible to do better workbooks—publications which would offer inspirational thinking exercises on a variety of levels for pupils of differing abilities. These same proponents also say that cost and time limitations usually prevent the publication and use of the type of workbooks which it is claimed would be desirable. Arguments in favour of the usual read-the-book, fill in the blanks type of workbook are[6] :

1. It saves teacher time spent in writing exercises and other workbook materials on the blackboard for pupils to copy and use.

2. The preparation of workbooks—objective exercises, suggested activities, review questions—requires greater skill and more time than most teachers have for this phase of their work.

3. Workbooks assure study guidance for all pupils.

4. Workbooks assure some pupil time spent on daily homework.

5. Workbooks give practice in following printed instructions, an activity that is common in adult life.

6. Workbooks usually contain illustrations accompanied by sufficient exercises and questions to give the pupil real experience in interpreting illustrations or diagrams.

7. Workbooks provide practice in reading for information rather than merely for pleasure, a skill which young people need to develop.

Those who argue[7] that present type workbooks are worse than none label them as hodgepodges of poorly selected, poorly organized, pedagogically unsound teaching devices. They observe that workbooks are often constructed in the cheapest possible manner with poor typography, low quality paper, cramped writing space, and are inconveniently sized. It is further argued that time devoted to routine workbook exercises, questions, and tests could be better devoted to simple experiments, field trips, observations, and activities that are more stimulating and satisfying. A publisher might answer that publication of the best possible workbooks would be as costly in time, editorial effort, and money as textbooks, and that the product would necessarily be priced outside any existing market for workbooks.

We find similar arguments applied to laboratory manuals for secondary school science. There are some who oppose published manuals because they tend to standardize pupil activity in the laboratory and discourage learning through individual experimentation. The critics often refer to even the best published laboratory manuals as "cookbooks." They argue that the only good laboratory manual is one made by the teacher on the job each year after he is acquainted with the interests and abilities of individual pupils. The *pro* arguments are to the effect that there would be much less laboratory work without printed manuals : that pupils with special abilities can design their own individual experiments : that the great majority need proved and printed procedures in order to achieve any results ; that teacher time is saved · that expensive laboratory materials and equipment are conserved ; that the printed laboratory manual need not be a "cookbook" in the hands of a skillful teacher.[8]

Preparing one's own workbook. We have seen teachers prepare their own mimeographed workbooks to meet particular situations, e.g. :

1. A teacher of chemistry wished to introduce his laboratory work based on semi-micro techniques. (By the way, the evidence is by no means conclusive that skills in chemistry are learned better by semi-micro techniques, although they are an interesting variation.) There are now several workbooks which use these techniques.

2. One teacher developed "case studies" in biology ; these led to laboratory work.

3. One teacher modified certain college physics laboratory work for his high school class.

4. One teacher (dealing with science-shy students—in this case slow learners) developed a full set of laboratory sheets in applied chemistry.

A deviation in the use of workbooks. One of the most interesting and fruitful interpretations of the workbook we observed was this : A teacher gave his class a "standard" workbook in chemistry and explained that this was their guide to the course. They would meet in the laboratory daily and each student could work as fast as he wished, but a deadline was set for all. He would need to supplement his work with reading in various texts ; the examinations tested the subject matter of chemistry.

The teacher was in the laboratory for consultation : when he saw a general difficulty, or upon request, he would caution, ask questions carry on a discussion, or do a demonstration. Apparently, a workbook can be used creatively.

1. The class finished the standard work in eight months, two months were left for doing "original work."

2. The gain in skills over a "regular" class was obvious even to the casual observer. The students were workmanlike and adult in their approach to the laboratory work ; they had learned to plan.

3. On standard examinations this class scored higher than "standard" classes of similar pupils. For instance, in the state examination the mean score for this class was eight points above the others.

The quest for originality. In a heterogeneous group, there will be some students who will not be able to do even carefully directed workbook exercises. Some will manage well enough. And some will want to do more and learn more ; a way of giving scope to such gifts in the laboratory may be indicated in this approach :

A student on the laboratory squad is assigned to each class. Students who have finished an exercise, or who, because of their skill or knowledge, have the teacher's permission to do so, may get equipment from this student laboratory assistant and proceed to "original" work (the plan is checked by the teacher, if only to avoid accident and possible injury).

Thus, any given laboratory may find students varying in the kind of work they do, from repetition to true originality.

Work in the laboratory, like work in the classroom is an invention of the teacher and the students. But the teacher is responsible for the climate and the opportunities.

THE FIELD TRIP

Throughout this book we have mentioned various kinds of field trips ; we assumed in doing this that the field trip is a necessary part of teaching science. The basic reason for trips is clear : to provide additional evidence and experience that cannot be had within the classroom.[9] Even apart from the main purpose of the trip, biological, astronomical, etc., there are many concomitants :

1. Students get to know their community, or its surrroundings, better.

2. They get insight into vocational opportunities (e.g., a trip to a dam or bridge may inspire an engineer ; a trip to a pond, a conservationist or biologist ; a trip to a weather bureau, a meteorologist).

3. They collect materials : animals (frogs, harmless reptiles, small invertebrates) : plants (ferns, mosses, fungi, seeds) ; rocks and minerals ; building materials (insulating materials, stone, brick) ; and so on.

4. They may develop hobbies : photography, astronomy, hiking, making and displaying collections.

5. They have fun, and develop better relationships with the teacher and with each other.

6. They may develop a sense of beauty.

Probably any teacher could add to this list of desirable concomitants to a field trip. It must be remembered that these things do not automatically occur ; they must be planned for just as carefully as the subject-matter purpose of the trip is prepared for. The students can do much of this preplanning, and we feel, should take on responsibility for finding appropriate solutions to questions which must be answered when a field trip is being considered—where, when, why, what, who, and how ? If the trip is to be significant to them, they should share in the responsibility. This will relieve the teacher of soms details and also will help keep the group under control and give purpose to the effort.

Although a field trip can yield so much if it is well conducted and prepared for, it is a difficult thing to carry out. A field trip takes more time than a class period ; it disrupts administrative procedures ; there is danger of accidents ; and, above all, the field trip takes careful, even arduous, preparation.

A file of possible field trips with specific instructions about persons to contact for permission (address, telephone number), route to follow, transportation, fees, hours possible, meals available, housing (for overnight trips), rest rooms, etc., is exceedingly valuable. One such file for the school, or even the school system, is better than a separate file for each teacher ; by pooling our knowledge and experience, we can eliminate much of the drudgery.

Preparation for the field trip. Almost any kind of field trip requires preparation like the following (plus careful planning of the subject of the trip) :

1. Obtaining permissions : principal or superintendent, parents, landowner or director of museum, industry, etc.

2. Note to parents : purpose of trip, time of leaving and return, place, cost (if any), equipment and clothing recommended, kind of transportation.

3. Planning with assistant leaders : guides, managers, parents, student helpers, briefed as to age and interest level of group, goals of teacher.

4. Safety : first-aid kit checked (assorted bandages, roll of gauze, adhesive tape, scissors, antiseptic, naphtha soap, other items depending on nature of trip), rules understood by students, forethought given to danger points.

5. Equipment : notebooks and pencils, other equipment depending on nature of trip : if collecting trip, containers, newspaper, trowels, vasculums, knives, nets, guides and keys,

field glasses, cameras, etc. ; classroom set up in advance to accommodate whatever may be brought back.

6. Transportation arranged and permission obtained.

7. Lunch : individual or group ; preparing and clean up committees.

8. Alternate program in case of rain or other cause of cancellation.

9. Follow up : reports, discussion, conclusions, new activities.

One approach to a field trip to study plant life. There are many ways to study plants in the field : the teacher may conduct a guided tour : students may be taught the use of the key in the lesson before, and taken out to practice what they have learned ; students may simply collect specimens on a field trip, and bring them back to the classroom to identify them. Or perhaps the following approach may be useful.

On a field trip to a pond area students began to ask, perhaps idly, "What kind of tree is that?" The teacher suggested that they identify it as follows :

1. Give each type of tree a number instead of a name.

2. Note the characteristics of each type of tree, particularly those which set it off from the others. (For instance, the lobed leaves, opposite branching, and winged fruits of the sugar maple were listed as identifying. "Tree No. 1.")

3. Take a "practical examination" (this required them to associate the numbers with the sets of characteristics).

Students thus learned the characteristics of the different trees by numbers ; they did not have the obstacle of learning scientific names at the beginning.

While the students were eating lunch after this activity, the teacher placed labels on the numbered trees, giving their common and scientific names. Some-how this procedure excited the students, so that they spent special effort in associating the name with the characteristics they had previously learned.

One approach to a field trip in astronomy. Two major types of astronomy field trips come to mind ; one for field observations, the other to an observatory or planetarium. Let us explore a trip for observations.

When : probably best taken in the autumn when the evenings are still warm but the sun sets early. A moonless night, perhaps about seven p.m., when the sky is nearly as dark as it will be, would be the best time to arrive.

Where : any convenient place, relatively away from street lights and auto lights, with a fairly clear horizon (the local football field or a hilltop farm), as near at hand as practical ; long drives take time and may result in "lost cars." Arrange in advance for permission to use the property chosen.

Transportation : on foot if possible. Possibly by school bus, otherwise by automobile. In any case, get signed permission slips from parents. Check drivers for liability insurance, as well as driving skill. Provide each driver with written instructions of route, including a map. Proceed in a convoy if possible.

Who : preferably all students in the class plus others who may be interested ; parents, both as drivers, and because they may be interested (good "public relations") ; amateurs who may bring telescopes and otherwise help with the group.

Why : to obtain firsthand answers to questions important to the students.

Special equipment : flashlights, star maps, warm clothes, telescopes (if available by loan or with owner), binoculars, one or two cameras for pictures of constellations and star trails (loaded with the "fastest" film, like Tri-X).

Possible observations : A special trip such as that indicated is not necessary for observation (projected) of the bright sun or the moon, which can be observed during the day from the school grounds. Possible observations :

1. Any bright planets : Venus, Mars, Jupiter, Saturn, Uranus. The last is greenish in colour, but not readily found ; it shows a disk only under quite high magnification. Take note

of the colour, angular diameter, surface markings, phase, crescent (if any), annual motion across sky, satellites.

2. Stars : Star patterns (omit the faint, inconspicuous ones), stability of patterns with time (zodiacal constellations named some 5,000 years ago). Rising and setting of star groups, circumpolar motion of Big Dipper and Cassiopeia. Set one camera with wide-open lens pointing toward polar zone and take one-hour time exposure. Also take short exposures of one minute of polar region and of other interesting star groups (Northern Cross in Cygnus, Lyra, Cassiopeia). Star colours (relation to surface temperature). Star brightnesses. Location of naked-eye variable stars (Algol, Mira, Delta Cephei). Note the band of the Milky Way. In October, the "summer Milky Way," including Cygnus, will be visible ; note great split or rift in Milky Way and faintness of western side (due to interstellar dust and gas). With binoculars or telescope, observe faint stars not individually visible to the naked eye (mention Galileo's discovery of fainter stars). With the aid of a star map or list of interesting objects, locate and observe a double star, a star cluster, a gaseous pebula, and possibly a galaxy.

3. Possibly meteors (shooting stars) and auroral activity.

4. Questions and comments for further investigation in the classroom.

THE TEXTBOOK

Too much has been said about the shortcomings of textbooks. The most violent criticisms usually come from those who look on the text as a substitute for the teacher or a crutch for the poor teacher. We think that most teachers recognize the text as an aid to their teaching, although no text is *exactly* what they would like for a particular class.

The teacher does have some choice of text. Despite the greate variation in legal, restrictions upon the books considered —ranging from completely free choice of every teacher in some of the northeastern states, to a three- or four-book state-approved list in many states, to the rate state where the book is prescribed state-wide—teachers generally have some voice in the texts they use, even if they have to wait for the previous ones to wear out.

Authors and publishers of texts, who invest many long hours and a great deal of money, develop their texts to meet the demands of the purchasers, the teachers ; for it goes without saying that the book is designed to sell. With many alternate texts available, the competition is severe, and the demand, evidenced through sales, shapes the future supply.

There are some teachers who prefer the organization provided by a text and follow it assiduously. At the other extreme are teachers who disdain the use of a text as a guide and leave their teaching to the planning of students. And there is a whole range in between. Since we have stressed that teaching is a personal invention, we can only observe that it would be a poor inventor who neglected the work of other inventors. We would expect the teacher to turn the text to his own purposes, his own teaching invention.

How is a teacher to select a text ? Among many ways of appraising texts is the use of scorecards like those reproduced by Cronbach.[10] Often these scorecards deal with mechanical attributes, important but perhaps not critical. In any case, the format of these cards may be useful. We suggest that the teacher examine sample texts and select the one most appropriate to his intentions. The way in which the text is to be used is also a guide to selection.

Some uses of science texts

Teaching how to read in science. We described teaching students how to read a text by searching for the major thoughts in each paragraph, summarizing these thoughts in writing, and using the table of contents and index. We found that teaching reading of science this way reduced the time students needed to do their homework, and raised reading scores on an objective test. The method we described was particularly useful with the science shy, but also improved the reading of the science prone.

We have found it useful to give a lesson in which students use their texts in class every week or so. The occasion for this may be a lesson planned by the class (again we note that "the class" includes the teacher), or planned by the teacher who recognizes that students are not using the text fruitfully. Topics which seem suitable for this type of lesson are :

A first lesson on the periodic table.

A lesson on classification.

Plant and animal breeding.

Industrial applications of chemistry (metallurgy of iron, Haber process, uses of nitrogen compounds, uses of nonmetals, etc.).

The solar system.

Predicting weather (including weather maps).

In using the text in class we have observed several devices particularly useful for discovering the poor reader. If the teacher goes from desk to desk (assuming, of course, a permissive, nonthreatening atmosphere), students will admit their difficulties, which are often easily remedied. Perhaps a student doesn't realize that he can make use of the glossary or a dictionary ; perhaps he doesn't realize that he should take notes of the major thoughts as he reads : perhaps he sticks at certain words and worries about them, instead of going on and looking them up later. By using the text in this way, of course, the teacher helps the students acquire more efficient study habits.

Toward the end of the lesson, time may be taken to have students read aloud their summaries, which may then be criticized.

In addition, if students have been taught to use the text properly, they can very easily review for a test ; their summaries should be saved for this purpose.

To read ahead. By means of the test described, students are stimulated to read ahead, If they do advance reading, even in order to raise their grades, at least they have done the reading. It is to be hoped, of course, that the teacher will make the work of the class so interesting that the students will want to read ahead even without the bonus of extra points.

The text in the laboratory. When a laboratory session is scheduled some teachers wheel in a library cart with some reference texts, some college texts, some industrial applications, and others such as *How To Do an Experiment.*[11] Better yet, have such books continuously at hand, and mention those of special pertinence to the laboratory work.

Supplementing the text

It is impossible to find or write one text which fits the entire range of ability in a class. In reading ability alone, tests of more than 4,000 ninth-grade students showed scores of 4.5 (fourth grade) to college level. Even homogeneous classes will be heterogeneous for some ability which has bearing on the text they use. To help all student's in the class learn as much as possible, diversified reading materials are essential. The following procedures have been helpful in overcoming the problem of varying ability :

1. All students are provided with one basic text chosen for general coverage, ability to interest students, and accuracy.

2. All students are provided with a second text appropriate to their abilities : the science prone with a college text perhaps, the science shy with an easier text, or pamphlets, or texts for slow readers.[12] The purpose in providing dual texts is obvious : to improve reading level, the student should have not only a text on his present reading level, but also at least one above it. If funds are not available to provide each child with a second text, a few copies may be made available and the students encouraged to use them.

3. Of course, a good library is needed to amplify any text. For useful suggestions for beginning a library, see the volumes accompanying this text, as well as part of The Professional Library. Without a library a basic text can hardly be expected to meet the varied needs and interests of children.

One way of pointing students to the library is to have them do, as an assignment, the suggested activities at the end of the chapter of the text : these often indicate additional reading and can also lead to project work.

4. In addition to books in the library, encourage students to buy their own. A good number of excellent paperbacks are within the price range of most students ; some of these are listed in The Professional Library.

5. In addition to supplementing the text with additional material, the teacher will find it necessary to supplement it with recent news. One of the excitements of science is the new developments and ideas, which can be emphasized to the students by attention to news reports. Have you tried a bulletin board titled "The Current Text" ? On it students could post information about recent discoveries or articles from *Scientific American*, *Science News Letter*, and other magazines and newspapers. Or the teacher or students can write summaries of recent advances and mimeograph them.

We hope that the teacher will have at hand diversified text materials appropriate for his own use. Fortunately, the variety of texts available in the United States is immense. But the text, no matter how readable or thorough, is only one of the instruments used by the teacher to attain his purposes.

THE ASSIGNMENT

Let us consider three assignments on the topic, "Metallurgy of Aluminium" :

1. Answer questions 1 through 6 on page 371 of your text.

2. Give (*a*) one commercial preparation and (*b*) five uses of aluminium.

3. Choose one of the following (*a*, *b*, or *c*) : (*a*) A five-minute report on the life of Charles Hall : (*b*) A five-minute report on "Aluminium and the Conservation of Iron" ; (*c*) How has aluminium helped you live a better life ? Give specific examples.

Entire class : prepare for an examination to be given next Thursday. At least one question will be taken from those listed on page 371 of your text.

Note the topic in the list of term projects : "A model of the electrochemical production of aluminium."

Which of these assignments is most interesting? Which meets the variety of abilities in a heterogeneous group, and still requires a knowledge of content? Which takes most trouble to prepare?

If an assignment is worth giving, it is worth making interesting and significant. It is also worth checking to see whether it is understood. To make an assignment significant is to make it more interesting. But it must also be attainable; that is, it should not be overburdensome. After all, the students do take courses besides yours in science.

Here are several ways in which we have seen assignments used:

1. The assignments are not merely busywork. They do not repeat the work, but extend it. Thus if the structure of the cell has been studied, the assignment is not "Identify the parts of the cell and define their functions." It might be "What is the difference between a single-celled animal and a single animal cell?"

2. The assignments are varied in any-single day; they meet the needs of the slow, the moderate, and the rapid learner. For instance, in studying weather instruments the assignment may vary from studying a rain gauge, to studying a psychrometer, to a fairly complete understanding of a weather map.

3. The assignments are varied in the kinds of skills and knowledges they call upon: a report on a TV program or a movie; a book review or biography, an experiment at home (testing acidity of foods); reviewing an examination; analyzing reading materials; reporting on a special topic (satellites, a visit to a laboratory); doing the end-of-chapter materials in the text.

One final note: While the assignment cannot always be made interesting, it can always be made useful.

THE REPORT

Essentially, the report is a short lecture given by a student; if the reporter is not skillful, the report can be boring and confusing. If it is not carefully prepared in advance, it is not only boring, but also a waste of time. Hence it is important for the teacher to teach the technique of *student reporting*. The English teacher will probably be delighted to cooperate.

A few students are skillful in communicating information, but most are not. Yet all students need to learn the skill of oral communication of information ; and communicating scientific information requires especial clarity.

One teacher we know used the following techniques in teaching reporting :

First, he discussed with the class the problems of reporting skillfully. The students generally agreed that to give a report the reporter had to plan his report and give it in an interesting fashion. Of course, the classmates of the reporter would take notes because they were responsible for information in the report. The teacher discussed with the class the nature of lesson planning. A report was planned under the following heads : (1) The beginning ; (2) The middle ; (3) The end.

The *beginning* was intended to gain the interest of the audience ; the title of the report was woven into the brief beginning. The *middle* was the body of the report ; here the information was given with illustrations (slides, film-strips, demonstrations, models, charts). The *end* was a summary. All reports were open to questions by classmates, who were responsible for the information communicated, and the teacher, who could often help make a point clear.

The practice this teacher followed was that of giving the first report himself. He tried to demonstrate :

Reference to notes (without reading them).

Brevity (he limited himself to a stated time—five minutes at the most).

Simple illustration (he used the chalk-board for simple drawings, demonstrating, by the simplicity of his illustration, what most students could do).

Loudness and clarity of speech.

At the end of his report, the teacher again discussed with the class the features of the reporting technique.

During the term every student had an opportunity to give a report, and in that way gained confidence and skill. And every now and then the teacher again reported to the class to afford students an opportunity to discuss the reporting technique, and, in reappraising it, to improve their own method.

THE PROJECT METHOD

The project is meant to individualize instruction. It is clearly an effort to equalize opportunities (once again, equal opportunity does not mean identical exposure) so that those who have special abilities have the opportunities to fulfill themselves. Every youngster is an individual and the best instruction is for the individual need ; the project, whether individual or group, helps us do this.

The project approach was discussed in part. But here we want to deal with it as a tool for the special care of the individual, gifted or not. In our experience, this is one of the best ways not only to stimulate interest in science, but to help young people grow and gain status.

Sponsors for project work. Project work takes the time of interested people. Who sponsors it ?

1. Interested teachers who are willing to give time to students before, during, or after school hours.

2. Interested parents with special training—engineers, doctors, or technicians of all sorts.

3. Scientists in the local industries.

4. Scientists in the local university.

5. Scientists, or teachers, who advise students by correspondence. (One of our students corresponded with a scientist on the West Coast, and completed a project in a field in which we had little skill or information.)

6. Any responsible person, with time and ability.

In one city, three schools banded their facilities and sponsors.

Sources of project work. Since the project should have a bit of originality about it, many teachers feel they should not attempt the work unless they have special training . Of course, as one does project work, one develops skill in aiding youngsters break through the thin walls of their tiny sphere of the unknown—their project. There are many ways to get suggestions for projects, some of them are :

1. Your colleagues.

2. Readings in the *Scientific American, Science News Letter, The Science Teacher, The American Biology Teacher, The Quarterly Review of Biology, The Journal of Chemical Education, Physics Today, Science World, Popular Science,* and many others. Does your library get these journals?

3. In chemical, biological, physics abstracts are regular reports—abstracts of papers—by scientists. When students leaf through these they get ideas for projects. They may correspond with the scientist who is the author of the "project" report, the abstract of his research. We have found scientists in industry and in the university generally gracious in corresponding with students who ask reasonable questions.[13] In many instances this has helped a student decide for a career in science.

4. Future Scientists of America, Science Service (Westinghouse National Science Talent Search),[14] and other organizations have helpful publications, as listed.

Space for project work. Often projects are not done for lack of space. A corner in the laboratory, the demonstration table in the preparation room or in the classroom, a cellar in the house of one of the students, a table in a garage—anywhere where the facilities needed are present will do. In onc community, the Parents' Club donated the funds for the equipment : in another community, the students worked in the fire house ; in another, they worked in one of the town garages. In still another community, the high school had excellent facilities, but the local college furnished additional facilities.

How does the teacher help a student do a project ? Originally we had written a rather lengthy section, How To Do a Project. This was before Philip Goldstein's book, *How To Do an Experiment*,[15] became available. This book is so complete, so useful that we recommend it without reservation. A student who refers to it can begin a project, and with the aid (over the rough spots, such as purchasing equipment) and blessing of his teacher and other sponsors, complete his project or experiment.

SCIENCE CLUBS AND SCIENCE FAIRS

The science club

A science club is not a new idea. The Royal Society of England was an early "club" for purposes of scholarship. In a very small way, our science clubs are "royal societies" of their own ; those who join these clubs are on the royal road to learning--doing more work, learning more, and willing to spend time to do so. A science club consists of a group of students so interested in science that they group themselves (to serve their interest, perhaps) beyond the regular class time ; usually a teacher is the focus, even the reason, why the students have the interest they do.

In our experience, and from our talks with principals and departmental chairmen, clubs seem to center around an inspiring teacher ; poor teachers do not have clubs. Since participation in a science club is a free choice, students must have considerable freedom to operate their own club. A dominating or restricting sponsor will attract few club members. The clubs varied their activities from the general, such as "The Science Club" to the special, such as "The Geneticists." One school had fourteen science clubs. Another had one, with twelve divisions from the "Camera Group" to the "Fossil Hunters."

How is a club organized ? What does a club activity involve ?

Fortunately, a good deal of help is available ; one of the best sources is the *Science Club Sponsor's Handbook.*[16]

The science fair

Science clubs often lead to science fairs, where students exhibit their work. Some schools have their own fairs ; other schools group to have city fairs ; cities and towns group to have county fairs ; county fairs group to have state fairs ; state fairs group to have national science fairs.

How does one organize a science fair ? How does one gain entry into existing fairs ? What are the standards of a good exhibit ? Here, again, a good deal of help is available. Information may be obtained from Science Service, from *A Manual for Science Fairs,*[17] and from the organizations listed and described in The Resource File.

STUDENT LABORATORY SQUADS

All teachers of science have a heavy schedule ; not only do they teach a normal number of classes (as do their colleagues in English), but also they need to prepare and repair equipment, and prepare for demonstrations and laboratories. Many of the routine chores necessary in preparing the next day's lesson can be accomplished through student assistance ; that is, by organizing a student laboratory squad.

Some of the tasks a laboratory squad can take upon itself are offered below as examples :

1. Show films and filmstrips (where teachers call for such help).
2. Clean equipment (microscopes, balances).
3. Maintain animals (rats, frogs, fruit flies).
4. Prepare, catalogue, and store charts.
5. Check inventories of chemicals.
6. Collect materials necessary for study (frog's eggs, cocoons, seeds, rocks, discarded radio parts).
7. Build equipment of various kinds (germinating boxes, pinhole cameras).

Although no one plan can be tailored for all schools—for each school is more or less unique, with varying specializations and divisions of labour—the following flexible plan may serve as a pattern. The procedures suggested here apply to the larger schools where there may be several classrooms and one or more laboratory rooms for science, and so not all the suggestions will apply to the smaller schools. Yet every teacher will find some that can be adapted to his own situation.

An individual teacher may send out a call for volunteers. In a large department, a more cohesive organization can be evolved if all the teachers in it work together. Since students must work under a teacher's supervision, "working time" for students and teachers may be before school, after school, or better, during students' free periods throughout the day. The method used will depend on which blocks of time can be coordinated with the teacher's time allowance.

Filling orders

Under the guidance of a single teacher or a laboratory assistant.[18] Students can be trained to prepare the materials teachers have requested for the day. One plan which works successfully in large schools is to have teachers list all the specific materials they want twenty-four hours in advance,

Teacher	Day
Class	Period
10 large test tubes	rubber bands
test tube rack	10 corks to fit
from thymol blue	test tubes
3 sprigs of elodea	beaker
carbon paper	straws

perhaps on an order blank like the one shown above, and deposit the lists in a box reserved for them. Two students might be given the responsibility to read through these order slips and inform teachers of conflicts (two teachers want the same teaching materials) so that the teachers involved may either share materials or resolve their needs in some other fashion. Thus, where necessary, the teacher is given time to plan for other activities in advance of class.

Delivering supplies

Student laboratory assistants are trained to find the materials in the laboratory. This presupposes an orderly arrangement of the laboratory, with drawers, shelves, and cabinets clearly labeled to identify their contents. Small orders may be stacked on a tray large orders involving glassware, chemicals, microscopes, and the like, may be stacked on a cart which can be wheeled to classrooms. Materials should be distributed to the classrooms and returned to the laboratory by students when there is no traffic in the corridors. *This is an imperative safety regulation.* (Other safety regulations are the same as those for all students in the laboratory ;[19] in addition, dangerous chemicals, such as bottles of acids, and stacked Petri dishes, should be placed within a larger battery jar or box to avoid spilling or smashing in transit.)

Cleaning up

When materials are ready for return to the laboratory, they should be replaced immediately in their storage locations. Some teachers find it convenient to store materials in boxes organized by unit or problem area. However, this often immobilizes pieces of equipment. Part of the laboratory squad should wash up glassware used the previous period, while other students on the squad distribute the materials to the classrooms for that period.

In smaller schools, the student assistants may be responsible for getting, from the storeroom, materials teachers list as required, so that they are immediately available either at each student's work table or in an assigned place in the room. They can also be given responsibility for cleaning up after the laboratory period or at a time convenient to both teacher and student.

In addition

Some students on the laboratory squad work well with their hands. Those with manipulative skills may be stimulated to devise wall racks for magazines or for glassware and storage racks for charts, among other laboratory needs. Students with artistic talent can prepare charts drawn on window shades or muslin sheeting, or drawings on glass slides for projection. Models can be made in clay or papier-mache.[20]

During lulls in the laboratory work (dependent on the size of the squad), there may be time for those youngsters with deep interest in science to make explorations, to try out demonstrations, to perfect skill in the use of the microscope and other tools, and to read widely.

A typist in the group can be given responsibility for sending requests for free materials, ordering films for the next term's use in the classrooms, and making neat labels for exhibits.

Although students vary in their abilities and are thereby assigned appropriate and specific responsibilities in the laboratory, it is important that there be mutual cooperation. Everyone should "pitch in" when needed. There should be a rotation in the routine chores, if only to maintain esprit de corps.

Continuity of the squad

Since time and training accompany the molding of a responsible squad so that it becomes a cooperatively functioning unit, there arises the problem of replacements. There is always some turnover from year to year. However, many students dc continue to work on a laboratory squad until they are ready to graduate from high school. One solution to the problem is that an experienced laboratory worker, during his last term on the squad, may be able to assume responsibility for training a novice from a lower term, possibly a freshman. By this method a laboratory squad always has some experienced students in its ranks and thus, in a sense, is self-maintaining in membership.

In return

The prestige and camaraderie afforded by membership on a laboratory squad which has high standards of work, will draw youngsters of many talents and many motivations. Some youngsters may be interested mainly in the sociability developed ; this, too, is healthy and a necessary aspect of adolescent life. A wise teacher can be firm yet kind in demanding fulfillment of responsibilities.

Those few youngsters who seem to lack any special talent or those who seem to "forget" responsibilities quickly, but who say they are interested in science (it may be no more than the fascination of sparkling glassware), can be assigned more mundane chores, such as dusting, straightening up, washing glassware, or assisting in taking inventory. They have expressed a desire to work on the squad ; let them satisfy that desire. High grades in science should not be the criterion for selecting students for work on a squad. Furthermore, such assistance should not be counted towards grades, although the experience will show on tests and reports.

In many instances, the work on the laboratory squad gives young people an opportunity to develop interests which lead to a future vocation or avocation. Or they may develop friendships. Or they may develop a sense of service, of citizenship, of giving, if you will. This last, some teachers think, is the most important contribution of the laboratory squad to its members, and of its members to the school.

THE BULLETIN BOARD AND THE EXHIBIT CASE

The bulletin board

Throughout the country, school bulletin boards are used as follows :

For notices. Notices of new books, articles in magazines and journals, scholarship examinations, fairs and exhibits, club meetings, and so forth.

Current events. A recent bulletin board exhibit had newspaper accounts of the latest earth satellite with photographs. In addition, students had developed their own short history of the development of rockets and satellites. There was also a section entitled "For Further Developments."

Problem of the week. Once a week a committee of students posted a problem in physics, in chemistry, in biology. Students were free to answer it. At the end of the week, the answer was posted for comparison.

Special bulletin boards. In one school, one wall in the laboratory was given over to a series of small bulletin boards, each designed for one club. Notices of meetings, topics for discussion, lists of members, and notices of visiting speakers were posted. In another school, with a weather station, one bulletin board called "The Weather Vane" was a popular stopping place for students, who compared forecasts of student weathermen with professional ones.

These are but a few examples of the use of bulletin boards as teaching tools. Frequent changes in the materials posted and attractive arrangements are essential. Interesting bulletin boards will attract attention, and extend science into the life of the school.

The exhibit case

The floor plans show exhibit cases. These cases are exceedingly useful for, among other things :

Exhibits of materials related to the topic at hand : examples of invertebrates (study of classification), minerals and rocks (study of geology), etc.

Exhibits of projects : individual or group.

Exhibits of books and printed materials : by librarian or teachers.

Exhibits of laboratory set-up for the day (if it is to be complex).

We have found that students like to set up exhibits. They introduce novelty and frequent change to attract attention. Learning is thus stimulated outside the classroom, and is reflected in work in the classroom as well.

References

1. H.W. Wilson Company 950 University Ave., New-York 52, N, Y.
2. Note that we do not mention specific films : we believe that mention of a film or text in a book of this sort might be interpreted as a recommendation. Selection of films, texts facilities, etc , remains, like teaching methods a personal choice.
3. In the accompanying volume. *A sourcebook for the Biological Sciences*, a description of a homemade microprojector, effective for most materials used in the high school, is given.
4. See the Ha vard Case Studies, described in this book.
5. Natilan A. Neal Textbooks, Workbook, and laboratory Manuals in Science." *National Association of Secondary School Principals Bulletin.* Jan 1953, pp. 129-37.

6. Jack Hudspeth, "Workbooks ? Yes" *The Science Teacher, 18*, 74 Marh 1951.
7. Herbert S. Zim, "Workbooks ? No" *The Science Teacher, 18*, 75, March 1951.
8. Greta Oppe. "Workbooks—Worktests—Laboratory Manuals." *Metropolitan Detroit Science Review*, Vol. 2. No. 4. 1. 1952.
9. See F.G. Watson, *Using Museums for General Science Classes*, Bulletin 6. Wesley an University Press, Education Center, Columbus, Ohio free.
10 J. Cronbach *et. al.*, *Text Materials in Modern Education.* U. of Illinois Press, Urbana, 1955.
11. P. Goldstein, Harcourt, Brace. N. Y. 1957.
12 Such books are now available in general science and biology. In ninth-grade general science a book with a seventh-grade reading level is used in addition to the regular text. Also, some general science texts contain sections appropriate for slow readers. Pamphlets even the General Electric "comic books") can be used as starters for the very slow readers.
13. In the name of good public relations, make clear to your students that they should not write asking for "*all* the information about, turties, comets, cyclotrons, etc." Such letters cannot be answered either effectively or politely. Specific questions based on thought and reading will produce helpful replies.
14. Have you seen the publication of Science Clubs of America Science Service, *Thousands of Science Projects* ?
15. Harcourt, Brace, N. Y., 1957.
16. Science Service, 1719 N. St., N.W., Washington 6. D.C.
17. Prepared by Educational Section. American Museum of Atomic Energy, P.O. Box 117, Oak Ridge. Tenn.
18. Some large cities in New Jersey and New York employ trained Laboratory assistants. These are people carefully trained in science who prepare the laboratories, maintain equipment, and help students carry on projects. They are extremely valuable.
19. For one set of safety instructions, see the companion volume. *A Sourcebook for the Biological Sciences.*
20. See the accompanying volume. *A Sourcebook for the Biological Sciences.*

Index